MACKENZIE KING OF CANADA

Mackenzie King of Canada

A Biography

by

H. REGINALD HARDY

GREENWOOD PRESS, PUBLISHERS
WESTPORT, CONNECTICUT

TO MY WIFE

FOREWORD

I WOULD NEVER have attempted the writing of this book had it not been for the encouragement, co-operation and assistance of my colleagues in the Parliamentary Press Gallery, many of whom placed at my disposal not only their written files but the secret treasury of their memories. In addition, scores of other friends and acquaintances who, over the years, have come into close, personal contact with W. L. Mackenzie King contributed their share by journeying back into the past, to return laden down with a dusty freight of dim but persistent recollection. Thus, to a degree, the book is the product of many minds.

While Mr. King, himself, took no part in the preparation of this volume, he was kind enough to read over the series of newspaper articles published under the title of "Mr. Canada" upon which the book is based, for the purpose of verifying dates, names and other data of a factual nature. For this assistance I should like to express my deepest thanks.

I should also like to thank the Southam Company, Limited, for permission to make use of some of the subject matter contained in the series of articles which appeared under my name in the Southam Newspapers during the summer of 1948. In this connection I should like to point out that this book is not merely a collection of those articles. The volume runs probably five times the length of the newspaper series and contains a great deal of new material, while every word of the series has been re-worked and revised in an effort to give a complete chronological story of the life of W. L. Mackenzie King.

FOREWORD

I hesitate to mention the names of all those to whom I am particularly indebted, lest by some mischance I overlook the most helpful of them. In any event, most of them, I am sure, would prefer to remain anonymous. I should like, however, to extend a special word of thanks to H. L. Staebler and A. L. Breithaupt, both of Kitchener, for their great kindness in furnishing me with much valuable information touching upon Mr. King's youth.

The book is not offered as a studied and detailed critique of a particular political era. It is intended essentially as the life story of a great Canadian, of one who has played a unique 'role, as civil servant, politician and statesman, in the development of the Dominion. The story must of necessity be presented against the background of an unusually vital and important period in the country's political history. If that background has been sketched in but roughly, nevertheless a sincere attempt has been made to preserve its main outlines in all their essential details.

It would seem superfluous to add that I am one of Mr. King's sincere admirers. For this reason I have made a genuine effort to present both sides of the story. Perhaps, in my desire to attain complete objectivity, I have, at times, tended to over-accentuate the less-imposing side of the medal.

Finally, the reason which prompted the writing of the book is a very simple one. Here was a truly great story waiting to be told!

H.R.H.

The Parliamentary Press Gallery,
House of Commons,
Ottawa.
July, 1949.

CONTENTS

CONTENTS

ILLUSTRATIONS

xi

ILLUSTRATIONS

MACKENZIE KING OF CANADA

I

ON THE WINGS OF THE STORM

A COLD, BLUSTERY December night, in the little Western Ontario town of Berlin. The year, 1874.

All day it had stormed, and now the town lay bedded down beneath a thick and sometimes wind-rumpled blanket of snow. There were few people abroad, and those who were pressed their mittened hands against their frost-pinched faces and hurried about their affairs as quickly as they could.

For the most part the streets were in darkness, but here and there a light showed through a snow-curtained window and cast a pale yellow patch upon the snow. Once in a while the sputtering oil-lamps on the corners beckoned like tired will-o'-the-wisps, as the driving storm alternately obscured and made visible their flickering and uncertain beams.

Anyone passing along Benton Street, however, would have remarked at the unusual display of illumination that came from one small house which stood somewhat back from the street, a little two-storey frame-and-stucco dwelling that snuggled down among the snow-covered tangle of shivering elms and maples. Strangers plodding through the drifting snow wondered who could be entertaining on such a miserable night. A few residents who lived close by, however, smiled understandingly as they passed and cast a quick, appreciative glance at the upstairs windows.

The Kings were a fine young couple and this would be their second child!

3

As Isabel King nestled her newly-born child in the crook of her arm, tears of happiness filled her eyes; because at last she had a son, a son who would bear the name of her beloved father. Even now she whispered the words over and over to herself: "William Lyon Mackenzie King! . . . William Lyon Mackenzie King!" The name had a fine ring to it, and a familiar one; for had she not decided upon it months before when first she had known she was to have another child? Now she and John would have a real little family and William (they would call him by his first name) would grow up along with little Isabel Christina, their first child, born the year before.

She hoped that her husband would soon return so that she could share her happiness with him right from the beginning. Then she smiled. After all, was it not she who had urged him to go to his political meeting and deliver his speech, assuring him that the moment she would want him by her side was still some time distant? Was it not she who was always encouraging him to take a leading part in the political and social affairs of the community?

As the nurse moved quietly about in the half shadows of the room, the young mother's thoughts turned again to the child at her side. She wondered what the future held in store for him. Would he be a lawyer, like his father, or would he, perhaps, some day become a great public figure, a member of parliament, a statesman like his grandfather?

The wind moaned suddenly, driving the slanting snow against the frost-patterned window-panes, and its voice rose and fell, and rose again, as it curled around the little frame house. Isabel King closed her eyes and sleep came creeping closer.

Downstairs, there was the sudden sound of a door being flung open, the stamping of snow-sodden feet, the wonderful sound of John King's deep, resonant voice. In a moment she was wide awake again. She looked towards the door of the room and counted the seconds.

Billy King was not born with a silver spoon in his mouth, but he was the recipient of something of much greater value: a healthy body and a sound mind. He inherited the intense political inclinations of both his parents; and the grim, uncompromising and militant figure of his maternal grandfather was held up to him as a model from his earliest youth.

Throughout childhood he was exposed to the political and intellectual atmosphere of the King home. He was weaned on his father's active Liberalism and rocked to sleep with his mother's tales of her rebel father's exploits.

Even as a lad in the lower grades of public school young King talked to his chums of the day when he would be a great statesman like his grandfather. This ambition never deserted him, but became deeper and more demanding as the years went by.

When other children of his own age were reading *Robin Hood* and *Huckleberry Finn,* young King was mulling over the political writings of William Lyon Mackenzie and was being instructed by his parents in political history.

"Any idea I may have had as a boy of entering public life," he was to say towards the closing years of his career, "was certainly inspired by the interest which my parents took in political affairs. The story of my grandfather's struggles in the early history of Ontario fired my imagination, and I must admit that from time to time I had dreams of representing North York some day."

Certainly, from his earliest years, King was accustomed to the battle of ideas, for his home was the meeting place of people who held very definite opinions on the current problems of the day.

Man finds immortality in "mind made better by their presence" and in this respect the deeds and thoughts of King's grandparents had left their imprints on the minds of his father and mother and were, in turn, to become definite directing factors in his own life.

The better known of his two grandfathers was, of course, William Lyon Mackenzie. Born in Scotland in 1795, he had come to Canada in his early twenties, had engaged in various commercial pursuits and, in 1824, had founded at Queenston, *The Colonial Advocate,* which at that time was the most westerly journal in Canada.

Later he moved to Toronto where he continued his journalistic career and engaged in various other commercial enterprises So successful were these ventures that he was soon financially independent. He owned the largest printing establishment in Upper Canada, and soon had acquired a great deal of real estate.

In 1828, at the age of 32, Mackenzie ran for parliament in the County of York, and was elected. Thus began an active political career which, while it won him the support of thousands of Canadians in Upper Canada, resulted in his election as first mayor of the newly-incorporated City of Toronto, and brought him to the forefront as one of the country's great public leaders, was to have its darker pages. The militant part he played in the Rebellion of 1837 was to win him a place in the history books of Canada, but it was also to result in the confiscation of all his personal property, his exile to the United States, and a long period of poverty and hardship from which he never fully recovered.

Perhaps Mackenzie was wrong in that he attempted to gain by force what he should have continued to press for by peaceful means. He sought only true responsible government, the right of Canadians to enjoy in Canada the same rights as were enjoyed by the King's subjects in Britain itself. Years later, his grandson was to say: "It was the assertion of British rights, and their denial by those in authority, and nothing more, which occasioned the Rebellion."

At any rate, Mackenzie's armed revolt was an abortive affair. An attack on York was a failure and, later, at Montgomery's Tavern, he and his supporters were routed. Mackenzie, with a price of 1,000 pounds on his head, escaped with some difficulty. Travelling around the head of Lake Ontario to the Niagara frontier, he crossed the Niagara River and found asylum in the United States. The trip was a hazardous one; he travelled by night, hiding in caves and hayricks by day. Near Hamilton there is still pointed out a cave where Mackenzie hid for some time. Occasionally he was befriended by those who believed in his integrity and in the justice of the cause for which he was fighting.

But after Mackenzie reached the States his native caution deserted him once more and the part he played in instigating the attempted invasion of Navy Island was a violation of neutrality laws which was to result in his imprisonment in the United States for over a year.

He was destined not to see Canada again until 1849 when, following the passage of the Rebellion Losses Bill, he was pardoned and allowed to return to the Dominion. His friends and supporters rallied to his side and bought him a house in Toronto. Here he lived until his death in 1861.

Vindication of the position he had taken was forthcoming in the first election contest which followed his return. He was elected a member of parliament for Haldimand.

Throughout his long fight for those principles which he considered right, Mackenzie's gift for bitter and colourful invective found full and free expression. In biting, blistering terms he attacked the enemy from all sides, and at every opportunity. There was a white-hot fury and a desperate recklessness in his assaults that bordered on mania.

"Not to gain the wealth of the Indies," he shouted, "would I now cringe to the funguses I have beheld in this country, more numerous and pestilential in the Town of York than the marshes and quagmires with which it is environed!"

Again, in an open letter to Attorney General John Beverley Robinson, he declared: "You have been alternatively the football and pincushion of power. You have retained the fawning, cringing manner which is, to the acute discerner, the surest sign of political dependence and degredation."

At times his vilifications and defamatory utterances reached a crescendo of thunderous proportions. Samuel Jarvis was a "murderer" for he had shot a man to death in a duel; Egerton Ryerson was a "hypocritical priest"; their friends and their relatives were all rogues and rascals. Mackenzie's writings and his public utterances bristled with such hysterical and venomous personalities.

But even some of those whom he had maligned and scorned were to make allowances for Mackenzie's bitter words and give the devil his due. Ryerson, with considerable magnanimity for one who himself had been singled out for Mackenzie's attentions, was to write: "With a Scotsman's idea of justice and freedom, Mackenzie felt a longing desire to right the wrongs he saw everywhere around him. This constituted, as he believed, his mission as a public man in Canada, and it furnishes the key to his life and character. Every evil which he discerned was in his estimation truly an evil and all evils were about of equal magnitude."

King's paternal grandfather was John King. He was a native of Aberdeenshire who had received a military education at the Royal Military Academy at Woolwich. Not much is known about him, but he was, in his own way, a man of parts. He was the author of a work on gunnery and military engineering. He came to Canada with the Royal Horse Artillery and during the Rebellion of 1837 he served with Her Majesty's forces and actually took part in suppressing the revolt. King was a man of scholarly as well as soldierly bearing and he was to bequeath to his only son, if not a great deal of this world's goods, an inheritance of high principles and right-thinking.

King died in Quebec in 1843 and was buried there. One hundred years later, his grandson, W. L. Mackenzie King, meeting in the Citadel of that storied city with the President of the United States and the Prime Minister of Great Britain, was to take a few moments off from affairs of state to visit the Cathedral and scan the record of John King's death and burial. The record itself was all that remained. Some years before, the church authorities had moved many of the graves, including that of John King, to another part of the cemetery. Here, in a common plot, the dust of the military men who had been buried in the cemetery had now intermingled.

One can only indulge in romantic speculation as to the early conversations which took place between young Isabel Mackenzie, the daughter of the rebel, and young John King, the son of the rebel-hunter, when the two first met in Toronto.

9

One can imagine her warmly defending her father's actions, during her early meetings with John King, and, later, relating to him that she had been born while her father was an exile in the United States, and telling him something of the privations the family had endured during those bitter years of poverty and expatriation.

Apparently, however, the young couple found little difficulty in resolving the problem posed by the fact that their parents had been on different sides. This was a real love affair. In the bright, flower-bedecked glory of an Ontario spring the trials and tribulations of another generation seemed somehow unreal and unimportant.

When Billy King was about eight years of age the family moved from their modest home on Benton Street to "Woodside", a fine ten-roomed house on Spring Street, just on the outskirts of the town. The house was surrounded by wide, sweeping lawns and set in the heart of a big wood. English ivy scrambled over its gray brick walls and framed the long French windows on the ground floor. Lilac and honeysuckle snuggled up to the doorways, and a spring-fed stream chattered its way through the tangled masses of ferns and lily-of-the-valley at the rear of the estate.

It was approached from the public highway by a narrow lane which curled through the soft gloom of the wood to open, at last, upon a vista of sunlit lawns and formal flower beds in the midst of which nestled the ivy-covered house. The place had an atmosphere of gentility and permanence which was to have a profound effect upon King's childhood.

"It provided one," he recalled in later years, "with a certain background that remained with one throughout one's lifetime."

By the time the Kings moved to "Woodside" the family had grown. There were now four children: Isabel (Bella) who was now nine, and who was King's senior by a little more than a year; Janet (Jennie) who was six; and Mac-dougall, a chubby youngster of four.

They were a happy and carefree little family. Mrs. King was kept busy with the multitudinous cares of the household, not the least of which was keeping an eye on her four young charges all of whom indulged in the usual pranks of childhood. There were times when they would escape her watchful eye and wander far afield and get lost in the deep wood. Or they would tumble into the brook, or let the chickens out of the chicken-coop, or get their clean print dresses soiled and torn.

As the elder girl in the family often does, Isabel found herself in the position of having to share with her mother much of the responsibility of taking care of the younger children. Because Billy was only a year younger than Isabel he, too, was often called upon to share this responsibility. Quite often the care of the two younger children was, by parental command, equally divided. Isabel was entrusted with the specific duty of watching her sister Janet, and Billy was told to keep an eye on his brother Macdougall.

John King had been building up a fairly substantial law business over the years which, if it was not to make him wealthy, was to enable him to provide comfortably for his family. Labour was cheap in those days and soon Mrs. King had a couple of girls to help her with the housekeeping, and a man to look after the garden and to see to the other heavy chores about the house.

As a boy Billy had no reason to suffer from an inferiority

complex. His father held a prominent place in the social and professional life of the community. His parents, and their parents before them, had been important people. The Kings kept their own horse, and, on occasion, permission having been granted, Billy would harness it up and drive into town. Life moved along smoothly and pleasantly at "Woodside" and apart from the usual minor maladies of childhood, such as an occasional experience with mumps or measles or chickenpox, there was no serious illness in the family, or other untoward event to detract from the tranquillity and content of the household.

In the long summer evenings the children were allowed to sit out on the big low verandah that opened off the living room and remain with their parents until the twilight had deepened and it was time for bed. As often as not there were callers or guests, and usually the conversation ran along intellectual lines. Young Billy loved to hear his mother talk about her father's years in the States. Her memories of that period must have been indistinct, for she was only six when the family returned to Canada, but no doubt they were enhanced and given meaning by the stories she had heard her parents tell.

Doubtless she told her children how her father had left prison without a cent to his name, how he had borrowed $50 to go to New York, how he had secured work as an actuary, then as a clerk in the New York Customs House at $700 a year, and then, finally, how he had obtained a position writing for Horace Greeley's *New York Tribune*. That had been in 1846, just three years after Isabel Mackenzie was born.

At the time of Isabel's birth the fortunes of the Mackenzie family were at their lowest ebb. She was the fifth of the five children to be born in the United States—

three boys and two girls—and at that time the prospect of another mouth to feed constituted a practical problem of major proportions.

In fact the poverty-stricken couple frankly wondered if it was worth-while to attempt to raise this fragile infant. Somehow the child survived, though she was to see her brothers and sisters die, one after another.

The stories of these years of hardship were to make a lasting impression on young Billy King. He was to ponder over them many years afterwards when he found himself in the fortunate position of being able to extend financial assistance to his parents, his brother, and his brother's family.

King liked, too, to listen to his father expressing himself on political and social questions. Like his mother, his father could also tell exciting tales of the days when Her Majesty's troops were fighting the rebels. Young Billy had difficulty sometimes in understanding what the Rebellion had been all about, and sometimes he wondered who had been right and who had been wrong, and whose side he was supposed to take. Because, while his mother's father had led the Rebellion, his father's father had been an officer with the Royal Horse Artillery and had, on one occasion, actually ordered his men to train their guns on an old mill in which Mackenzie was believed to be hiding. As it so happened, however, Mackenzie was not in the raiding party, but safe in New York.

To his demands for an explanation of the whole affair his parents used to reply, with an understanding smile, that it was all far away and long ago and that it really did not matter now.

But Billy liked to hear his father talk, no matter what he

talked about. For his father had a fine resonant voice and his choice of language was quite different from that used by the fathers of many of Billy's friends. He could soar away on fine flights of oratory and these rhetorical accomplishments always made a deep impression on his son. Billy longed for the day when he, too, would be able to express his thoughts in such fine-sounding words and phrases.

John King had a distinct literary bent. At college he had distinguished himself for his literary style and for his outstanding ability as an orator, being a first prizeman as English essayist and public speaker. In a thesis entitled *Our English Shakespeare* he won the last university prize awarded for the best thesis by candidates for the degree of M.A. Upon graduation from the University of Toronto in 1864, and before he set up a law practice, he edited, for some time, the *Berlin Telegraph*. In later years, when he was practising his profession, he was a continuous contributor to newspapers, professional journals, and other periodicals, on a wide range of subjects.

To add to these accomplishments John King had served at the front during the Fenian troubles in 1866 with the University Rifle Corps. Throughout his life he took a keen interest in politics and the Liberal Party, and on more than one occasion was asked to stand as the Liberal candidate in North Waterloo, an honour which he persistently refused.

The winter evenings were times of particular intimacy in the King home. Then, after dinner, the family gathered in the big, comfortable living room, the children busy at their lessons, Mr. and Mrs. King sitting before the open fireplace chatting over the events of the day.

Often the children looked up from their books and paused for a moment or two to listen to the discussions which their parents loved to engage in—rambling talks on history, theology, politics, social conditions. Most of what was said passed over their young heads but nevertheless, as the years rolled by, they began to understand a great deal of what they heard and their own ideas began to take shape and expand.

Sometimes, when Mr. King had closeted himself in his book-lined library, Billy or Macdougall would seek him out for advice and assistance in their own studies. He was always ready to discuss their problems with them, always took their questions seriously, and as the boys grew older they came to him regularly with the practical problems posed by their particular preoccupations and tasks. Thus John King became as much a friend and companion to his sons as a father, a fact which had an important effect on many of the decisions they reached in later years.

As to Mrs. King, she was a sweet and lovable person and the affection which her children bore her was an unusually close and unquestioning one. They all knew that she had suffered privations as a young girl, and that these hardships had affected her health. The girls were always at her side, and her two boys worshipped her. Perhaps the moments they loved best of all was when their mother gathered them around her chair and read aloud to them. One of her favourite volumes was the Bible, and in later years, Billy King, moving towards the close of his distinguished career as Canada's Prime Minister, recalled that he had never forgotten the lessons he had learned from his mother.

The story of her childhood made a profound impression on young King's mind and was probably an important factor in the tender and worshipful attachment which he preserved for her throughout her lifetime. The influence of his mother definitely constituted one of the most important ruling factors in his life. He never forgot her great Christian qualities of patience, understanding, charitableness. Between mother and son existed an exceptionally powerful intellectual, emotional and spiritual bond.

One of the stories that Billy's father was fond of relating within the bosom of the family circle was how his name nearly came to be changed from King to LaFontaine. Following the death of John King's father in Quebec, the widow moved to Toronto with her young son. In those days parliament met alternately at Toronto and Quebec, and when Louis LaFontaine came to Toronto to attend the session he happened to put up at the same house which sheltered Mrs. King and her son. Young John King and LaFontaine became great friends. Lafontaine bought the boy his first pair of skates, and the lad used to accompany him to the Parliament Buildings and carry his brief case. LaFontaine became so attached to young King that he offered to adopt him, defray the cost of his education and bring him up as his son.

But Mrs. King, despite the fact that she was a widow of limited means, and no doubt appreciated the advantages and opportunities which might come her son's way as a result of such an arrangement, could not find it in her heart to part with him.

It is interesting to speculate as to what might have happened had Billy King's surname been LaFontaine. It is more than likely that the possession of a French name would have had a most interesting influence upon his political career.

But the intellectual atmosphere of the King home was not a smothering one. There were gay, carefree times, too. There were plenty of parties at "Woodside" when the family was growing up and the four children (there was a difference of only six years between the youngest and the eldest) used to bring their friends home with them. Birthdays, holidays, and other special occasions were usually celebrated, and celebrated well. Sometimes Billy would be permitted to have one of his friends to stay overnight. Invariably there would be youthful horseplay, with pillow fights always a special feature.

Those who played with the King children recall Mrs. King as a wonderful mother and a fine hostess. She invariably entered into the spirit of the children's gatherings as if she were a young girl herself, playing their games, joining in their laughter, romping about with them. Mr. King, on the other hand, while always kindly and hospitable, was inclined to be dignified and reserved. He may not have possessed his wife's ability to throw adult dignity and decorum to the four winds on such occasions, but in his own quiet way he took part in the festivities and enjoyed them to the full.

When Billy was old enough to carry a school-bag and find his way home without getting lost, he was packed off to the Central School on Frederick Street.

He was an average student with the average boy's well-developed faculty for getting into mischief. Such extramural activities as ringing door-bells, playing hookey to go swimming in the Grand River, and stealing apples and plums from local orchards were all a part of the day's routine.

He did display one particularly outstanding characteristic even at this early age, however. For a youngster he was more than ordinarily pugnacious. He didn't always come out top man, but he never went out of his way to avoid a fight. One of King's contemporaries, recalling an early memory of the Central School playground, remembers arriving at school one morning to find a large group of boys gathered at the far end of the playground where a noisy fight was in progress. The situation was explained by a bystander's casual comment: "Billy King's fighting again."

But, as has been noted, Billy was not always the victor and one Kitchener resident has a distinct recollection of having ambushed him on the way home from school on one occasion and exacting satisfaction on account of some school-boy disagreement.

Billy always tried to be the leader of the gang when escapades were being planned, and he often succeeded. He wasn't a quarrelsome youth and there was nothing of the bully in his make-up, but he was brimful of energy and animal spirits.

Even in church and Sunday school he sometimes had difficulty keeping his mischievous tendencies in check. Services in old St. Andrew's Presbyterian Church were often intolerably long and tedious in those days and generally before service was half through Billy and his two young sisters were doing their share of fidgeting. And sometimes, despite the watchful eye of his father, Billy would lean over to his sisters and send them into fits of suppressed giggling over some detail of the sermon or other occurrence which had tickled his sense of humour. Then Billy would sit back with an innocent look on his face while the girls received a reproving glance from their mother.

Again, Billy's sense of humour found practical expression in the work of busy little fingers. For instance, there was the case of the missing bustle. In those days the bustle was in its hey-day and ladies vied with each other in flaunting new and unusual styles in these startling posterior protruberances. Many of them were "detachables" and were tied, buttoned, or otherwise attached to the rear of the dress. Thus, when Billy found himself in Sunday school one afternoon, directly behind a teacher who was wearing an unusually jaunty bustle, he was offered the tempting proposition of untying it and then anchoring it firmly to the rungs of the teacher's chair. When, eventually, the young lady rose the Sunday school was treated to the unusual spectacle of seeing dress and bustle part company as if by magic.

But Billy got something more out of Sunday school and church than an opportunity to exercise his sense of humour. He enjoyed the long afternoon classes and as a small boy he vied with his chums in memorizing the texts that were handed out each Sunday on brightly coloured little cards. As he grew older the social and community life of the church became increasingly important to him.

When in his declining years, he returned to Kitchener to receive an official welcome from the town, he recalled the vital experiences of those early years. "The more I see of life," he declared, "the more thankful I am that I had a good Sunday school training and a good home upbringing. As I visit 'Woodside' I know that many happy memories will be revived. I know that I shall experience anew feelings that, more than half a century ago, lay deepest in my nature. I know that I shall think again many thoughts that were mine in those formative years of my life. I thank God that while, with the passing of the years, much has changed and gone, the power of the influences by which I was then surrounded have never wholly left me. The responsibilities, the strain and stress of six years of war let me see how strong may be the sustaining power of the influences which surround one in childhood and youth.

"Of the influences of early years, those of home are,

generally, the strongest and most enduring. For most of us, fortunately, it would be difficult to think of home apart from school and church and their associations."

Again, when broadcasting a message to the people of Britain during the blackest hours of the war, King dwelt upon this same theme: "If I were called upon to sacrifice, out of my life, all save one of the influences of the past, or of my present possessions," he said, "the one thing I would wish to retain is the influence of the Christian training of my childhood days."

By the time King reached high school he had begun to fill out. He had never had a day's serious illness and now he began to develop the sound, rugged physique which was to serve him so well throughout his lifetime. He radiated good health, and this in turn made for a happy, good-natured disposition. He was stocky and solid. He had a bland, open countenance which was enlivened by a pair of light blue eyes which twinkled when he talked, and a wide mouth that spread itself in a big, slow infectious grin when he was happy or amused. Billy King was not handsome by matinée idol standards, but he exuded health and vitality and good spirits, and he was popular with his companions.

Contrary to some of the legends that have grown up around King, he was not, during his secondary school period, an exceptionally brilliant scholar, and his teachers saw no promise of his future brilliant career at the University of Toronto. He did, however, excel in English and History, and he was beginning to win a name for himself as a speaker and debater. In the high school literary society debates he distinguished himself by his precocious platform manner and his fine command of language, both of which placed him head and shoulders above his classmates. King's

"WOODSIDE"

"It provided a certain background that
remained throughout one's lifetime."

ability in this direction was secretly envied by all his fellow students, and, possibly as an antidote to their feeling of inferiority in this respect, they dubbed him "The Rebel." This was all in a spirit of friendly rivalry, however, and doubtless young King enjoyed the reference to his famous grandfather.

The old Kitchener High School boasted a staff of three teachers, all colourful personalities in their way. The Principal was J. W. Connor, a profound English grammarian and classical master, and co-editor of the High School Grammar. David Forsyth, who pioneered the game of soccer in Canada, taught mathematics and science; and Adolph Mueller, a Swiss-born scholar, taught French and German.

They were all strict disciplinarians and possessed personal eccentricities of a distinguishing character. As might be expected the three masters had their work cut out managing a school full of husky, active-minded young men. One of the favourite diversions indulged in by the students was imitating the mannerisms of their teachers, and King took a leading part in these efforts. Occasionally unexpected interruptions on the part of one or the other of the teachers would result in a variety of disciplinary measures. Mr. Connor's favourite reprisal was the exaction of one hundred or more apposite phrases to be taken from the school reader and to be placed in his desk before the culprit left for home. This task was frequently performed in a rather perfunctory manner in the hope that the check-up would be made in a similarly slip-shod fashion. Sometimes King and his school-mates managed to deceive Connor, but as often as not their attempts at evasion resulted in additional periods of detention.

As an indication of Billy King's inability to master some

of his high school subjects as readily as he did others, one might recall a class-room incident which occurred during his last year in high school. It happened during the German period while Adolph Meuller was returning marked examination papers to the students. When he came to King's paper he looked over the top of his glasses and caught Billy King's eye. "King," he asked, "how is it that you are always at the bottom of the class?"

For a moment Billy was at a loss for a suitable reply. Then, suddenly, he brightened. "Well, sir," he declared with incontrovertible logic, "*somebody* has to be at the bottom!"

King never excelled at sports. At high school he played football, and he had a bent for cricket, a game which was also the principal's hobby.

As a result of David Forsyth's great interest in soccer, Berlin had become, in the eighties, almost the focal point of that sport for the entire continent. Many soccer stars of later years were athletes who were trained by Forsyth. While King never shone at the game he did succeed on one occasion in being a member of the high school team which competed with Galt for the inter-school trophy.

Actually, King never developed any great degree of enthusiasm over competitive sports. His heart was not in them, and as a result they never became a drain on his store of physical energy. He was not as quick on his feet as his brother Macdougall who was later to win distinction as a football player at the University of Toronto. Billy's mind always moved much faster than his body.

During the summer holidays King and his friends sometimes had difficulty putting in the time. Occasionally they organized camping trips, and his friends recall one particular outing which was successful in more ways than one. On this occasion King, two of the Seagram brothers, David

Bowman, H. L. Staebler and a number of other Berlin boys pitched their camp at the forks of the Grand and Conestogo rivers, close to the village of Conestogo.

Camp life, despite its many attractions, was not without its periods of boredom, and the time came when the boys decided to visit the village in quest of excitement. Their arrival was greeted with some misgiving by the lads of the town who noticed that their village sweethearts displayed a rather too-obvious interest in the newcomers. Their appre-hensions were fully justified when the members of the camping party began to monopolize the attentions of the best-looking girls. In retaliation the Conestogo boys chal-lenged the interlopers to a baseball game. The village boys with their superior brawn and muscle gave a better account of themselves in this assault-at-arms than they had in defending their laurels as men-about-town. But it was not until the boys from Berlin had broken camp and had vanished out of sight down the river that the village belles returned to their former swains.

Berlin possessed its fair share of attractive girls in those days and Billy King was popular with the majority of those who moved in his particular circle. If he was no football hero, his glowing vitality and good-natured disposition won him many admirers. He was an excellent dancer and always shone in the company of young women of his own age. But during those high school years he failed to make any lasting attachment. He regularly squired girls to dances, box socials, and other similar functions, but he never singled out any particular one as the sole object of his attentions. Certainly he didn't fall in love with any of the girls he knew in Berlin; or if he did he kept it a secret. He appeared to be quite content to play the field. Girls had their place in his life, but it was not a vital one.

King has never forgotten the time when he and half a

dozen of his friends who belonged to a little riding club nearly spent the night in the town jail. One Saturday afternoon they went for a canter and rode as far as Preston. On the way back, as they neared the outskirts of Berlin, they decided to have a race. They were tearing along at a fine clip when they reached the town limits, but when they tried to rein in they found themselves unable to manage their horses. So they galloped wildly down the main street (reckless driving would be the charge today) while the good townsfolk scattered in all directions.

The noise and confusion occasioned by their wild ride through town unfortunately attracted the attention of the town constable who, as a rule, was usually to be found inside one of the local hotels. He can out into the middle of the street and called upon them to stop.

But his warning shouts and gestures only encouraged the horses to still greater efforts, and the little posse swept by in a flurry of dust. When at last the boys managed to pull up on the other side of the town they were at a loss as to what to do. They were afraid that the constable had recognized them and that he would soon be calling around at their homes. They worried about it for a week or more, but apparently the constable was less concerned than they were, for they heard no more about the incident.

In the summer of 1891 Billy King wrote his matriculation examinations with satisfactory results. In the fall of the year he enrolled at the University of Toronto. He had his eye set on a career before the bar, and he was eager to get on to college and meet the greater challenges which university life offered.

II
COLLEGE YEARS

IF THE YEARS at "Woodside" were happy ones for King his college days at the University of Toronto proved no less memorable. During his freshman year he roomed with two other Berlin boys, A. L. Breithaupt and Shannon Bowlby. This arrangement was made by Mrs. Bowlby who apparently believed that young Breithaupt and her own son would be in good company if they were with Billy King. By now Billy had achieved the reputation of being a good, steady boy. He didn't smoke, didn't drink and was a hard worker. The arrangement worked out very satisfactorily for all concerned because while King never interfered with the extramural activities of his room-mates he certainly set them a splendid example as a student.

He was methodical to a fault and seldom overlooked an opportunity to put his time to good advantage. Every night, when he was through with his books, he jotted down a synopsis of the work he had covered on a narrow strip of paper. This he attached to the head of his bed, and then, while he undressed, he paced up and down going over his lessons.

It was the same next morning. As he dressed he ran over the synopsis again. If something puzzled him he snatched up his book and sought the answer. Then, as all three strolled over to their classes, King gave a final polishing up to his work, reciting his lessons, usually without a mistake. In this way he trained his memory. It was a great help to his class-mates, too, for whenever they needed help

King was ready with the answer. He was always ready to help out a friend. He was patient and painstaking and interested in seeing his class-mates do well.

Friends of his college years recall him as a moderate young man. None remember having seen him in a temper. He always seemed to have perfect control of his emotions and of his mind. If he had no minor vices, he was no prig, and he didn't attempt to set himself up as an example to others or question their actions. He was never a bookworm to the extent that he forgot everything else, but he did like to engage in debate whenever opportunity offered.

If King had shown only a casual interest in sports at high school he devoted even less time to them at college. The expenditure of physical energy seemed to become more and more distasteful to him.

On Saturday afternoons while his friends made preparations for a hike down the Don Valley, King was usually busy at his desk putting his work in shape for Monday. He would dismiss their warnings that all work and no play made Jack a dull boy with a wide grin and a quotation or two of his own which gave the lie to the old adage. Once in a while, however, when the day was a particularly fine one or his roommates seemed more than usually determined to have him along he would slam away his books with a sigh and yield to the tempting prospect of a free afternoon in the open. But, on these rare occasions, he went with a guilty conscience and the conviction that he had left undone those things which ought to have been done.

During that freshman year, every Sunday, King kept an engagement with clock-like regularity. Rain or shine, he set out for the Toronto Sick Children's Hospital where he spent part of the day telling stories to the children. After his first few visits his roommates began to display considerable curiosity. They wanted to know what kind of stories Billy told the children. Were they Bible stories, fairy tales or stories of adventure? King used to dismiss these interrogations with a smile and an airy wave of the hand. They were just stories. When his roommates suggested that they accompany him some Sunday and find out for themselves King told them flatly it was none of their affair and that he preferred to go alone.

In later years King was to confess that it was these Sunday pilgrimages to the Sick Children's Hospital that taught him how to think and speak on his feet. He used to talk to the entire ward and the stories he told were more in the nature of little fireside chats. Had he been to see *Faust* on Saturday night, then he would tell the children all about that opera. Had he been impressed with a sermon or a lecture, then he would attempt to reduce it to terms understandable to the children. Sometimes he would tell a simple story, a fairy tale or a tale of adventure. Many of the parents began to look forward to these chats and soon were attending them regularly.

King used to forget completely that there was such a thing as time, so absorbed would he become in his storytelling. On one occasion the three freshmen had been invited to Sunday dinner at the home of Hon. G. W. Ross, then Ontario Minister of Education. It was quite a feather in their caps to be honoured with an invitation to the home of the Minister of Education and they were all excited at the prospect.

But, of course, King had to go down to the hospital as usual, so Bowlby and Breithaupt warned him to get his story-telling over early and meet them at their room in plenty of time.

The hours passed by and no sign of King. His com-

panions waited as long as they dared, then decided to go on
without him.

The meal was half-way through when Billy finally
arrived. He was profuse in his apologies to Mrs. Ross and
obviously deeply embarrassed over the whole affair. But
he had become so absorbed in his task that he had completely forgotten his important dinner engagement.

Young King had always liked children and this liking
may have been one reason why he directed his mind
towards social work. The plight of under-privileged children affected him deeply. Thus, in addition to his work
among the sick children, he was, a little later, conducting a
newsboys' club. The paper-carriers met uptown once a week
and King presided. There were games and contests and
something special to eat. King used to give the boys little
inspirational talks and do what he could to assist them with
their personal problems.

In 1893 the King family gave up "Woodside" and moved
to Toronto. Despite the fact that Mr. King had an excellent
law practice in Berlin, was the solicitor for the county and
for one of the banks, and even operated an office in Galt, he
was deeply interested in the prospect of teaching law. He
was enamoured of the atmosphere of the law school, and
the whole family felt that they would be happier in Toronto
and more in the midst of things.

Thus, when Mr. King received the appointment of
lecturer in law at Osgoode Hall, the way was cleared for the
change. The post as law instructor provided him with a
competence which he was able to augment by his own
private practice.

Perhaps some of his struggling colleagues were not sorry
to see John King move to Toronto. For there was not too
much legal business in Berlin and what there was King

usually managed to corner. It was not unusual for him to have 15 out of 17 cases when an assize was held. There were too many lawyers in Berlin and the opportunities were limited. The little law-abiding community could not provide a competence for all.

There was a particular reason for this, too. The citizens of Berlin were largely of Pennsylvania Dutch origin. It is against their religion to go to law. They settle their differences in church through the medium of church committees. That was the case then and it is largely the case today. This circumstance was a definite limiting factor in the amount of legal business available in the town. When John King left for Toronto the other lawyers in Berlin breathed more easily.

The next few years were very happy ones. John King was doing the work he delighted in, the family was together, and Billy, known by now to all his friends as Rex, was deep in his studies.

The family had taken a house at 147 Beverley Street. Soon it was the gathering place for King's college friends. Mrs. King made everyone welcome, and Mr. King, deeply interested in the life of the university, and impressed by the eagerness and ability of the students, was usually on hand to talk with them and give them the benefit of his fatherly as well as his professional advice. Isabel, Janet and Macdougall each had their little coterie of friends. The King home was a busy place of an evening. Once in a while King would bring his newsboys home for supper and Mrs. King would go out of her way to make the occasion a memorable one.

It was a pleasant, congenial atmosphere and here King and his friends frequently studied together in the evenings. One of his closest friends at that time was Norman Duncan who later became famous as the author of *Dr. Luke of the Labrador*. Both were deeply interested in sociological subjects and they spent much time together doing university settlement work.

It was during his college years that King first met Henry Albert Harper, a young student from Barrie, Ont., who later became his associate in the Department of Labour and whose friendship was to have a lifelong influence on much of King's thinking.

Another friend of his college years was C. W. Cross, who was one day to become Attorney General of Alberta. Many a night young Cross and King studied together at the King home. Both were studying political economy and they would exchange notes and ideas.

Among his other contemporaries at Varsity were R. H. Coates, who was to become Dominion Statistician; Harvey J. O'Higgins, Bernard K. Sandwell, Arthur E. McFarland and Evelyn Durand, all of whom were destined to win literary fame; Arthur Meighen, who was to become leader of the Conservative Party and face King across the floor of the House of Commons; Thomas Hamar Greenwood, later to be known in British public life as Sir Hamar and then Lord Greenwood; and many others who were to distinguish themselves in their chosen fields of endeavour.

Reminiscing about his college years, King recalled the home on Beverley Street:

"It was not a very large house, and some time later we moved to No. 4 Grange Road. This was a larger house and it stood on the property adjoining The Grange which was the home of Goldwin Smith. My father and Goldwin Smith were great friends and I think that Goldwin Smith rented the house to my father to make sure that he had a congenial neighbour. My mother and father used to spend many evenings visiting at The Grange and altogether it was a very happy arrangement."

Like nearly every other young Canadian college student of the day King was an ardent disciple of the works of the "Sage of The Grange." It has been said of Goldwin Smith that most modern Canadians remember him very vaguely as "a bitter old man who had no faith in Canada and who advocated annexation to the United States." His writings are to be found today only in the larger libraries, and his pessimistic conclusions as to the possibility of Canadian unity, and in respect to Canada's relations with the United States and Great Britain, while somewhat out of line with subsequent events, were thought-provoking and stimulating to the extreme at the time they were put forward. He was a great stylist, a brilliant speaker and conversationalist, and much of what he foresaw in respect to U.S.-Canadian relations may yet come to pass.

Before Smith left England in 1868 to become professor of history at Cornell University he had written a book entitled *The Empire,* a discussion of the relationships between England and her colonies. He had much to say about Canada, which he considered the most important of the colonies, and he strongly advocated colonial emancipation. He saw Canada as the "second great democratic nation in North America" providing she could free herself from the influence of "English aristocracy and feudalism."

"But grant that Canada cannot stand as a nation by herself," he wrote, "it is with a nation in America, not with a nation in Europe that she must ultimately blend. . . . As a province she cannot form the independent character or assume the clear lineaments of a nation. There is but one way to make Canada impregnable, and that is to fence her round with the majesty of an independent nation."

How much young King was influenced by Goldwin Smith's theories it is hard to say. Certainly he held out for Canada's right to act as "an independent nation" within the greater framework of the Commonwealth of British Nations. Under King, Canada was not only to obtain greater freedom of action, but was to win for herself complete autonomy in all matters relating to foreign policy and international relations.

In those early, impressionable years at University King indulged in some uncertainties as to what particular profession he should prepare himself for. There was a period when he desired to teach, to surround himself with the warm, intellectual atmosphere of the campus and the lecture room. Such a life of cloistered study, affording as it would boundless opportunity for inward contemplation and the development of literary and philosophical inclinations, would have appealed to a well-developed side of his nature. Already his visions of a brilliant career before the bar had lost some of their lustre and more and more he found himself turning towards the teachings of the leading social reformers of the day. They talked of a bright new world and of how such a dream might come to pass. The apparent sincerity and enthusiasm with which they put forward their proposals intrigued King. Was this a field of endeavour in which he could usefully serve?

At this time he possessed all the quixotic romanticism and emotional instability of youth, a good deal of its sentimentality and sensitiveness, and much of its impracticability.

Thus we find him becoming quite excited and enthusiastic over the possibility of subsidizing poets and song-writers. When a friend suggested that a foundation should be set up to assist struggling writers and artists King thought the idea was a good one. Here was the romantic idealist at his best, with the cool, calculating, hard-headed, methodical King of later years pushed far back into some remote and inaccessible corner of the intellect.

He had a good deal of the poet in him at that time, and more than a trace of it persists today. He had many poet friends during his youth, men like Wilfred Campbell and Duncan Campbell Scott, both of whom he knew intimately.

He was always intrigued at the ability of such men to make a song out of simple words, to find beauty and music in the most unexpected places.

"The wild witchery of the winter woods!" once mused Campbell in King's presence, as he poured a bucket of slop into the feed-trough for his pigs.

King was amazed that anyone could wax lyrical while engaged in such a mundane task.

Although John King was making ends meet, the cost of raising a family of four was constantly increasing and every penny counted. It was only natural, then, that Billy should look about to see where he could earn a dollar. He decided that during the summer holidays he would try his hand at newspaper work. He had already given some thought to becoming a professor of the then novel subject of social science and it seemed to him that journalism might prove a stepping stone to that end. Off and on, he found employment as a reporter with the *Globe,* the *Mail and Empire* and the old Toronto *News*.

Although he has always been proud to call himself a former newspaper man he never regarded himself as a star reporter. As a matter of fact he used to become so engrossed in the social welfare aspects of police court cases which he was sent to cover that he would often forget that the city editor was waiting for copy and would fail to return to the office in time to get his stories into the paper.

III

A CALL TO OTTAWA

THE WINTER OF 1896-97 found King at the Graduate School of the University of Chicago whither he had gone on a fellowship in political economy. Apparently all thoughts of following in his father's footsteps had been abandoned. His studies in political economy had opened up a field of thought and action which seemed to have practically limitless horizons. King read everything he could lay his hands on; but, in addition, not satisfied with merely an academic approach to the subject, he went out of his way to study social conditions at close range.

He put up at Hull House Social Settlement and moved about amongst the hordes of immigrants who were pouring into the United States at that time from a dozen European countries. Thousands of these immigrants were being cruelly exploited by callous individuals and corporations who capitalized on this endless supply of labour to force down wages and institute conditions of employment which in many cases were little short of inhuman.

King came to know the famous social worker, Jane Addams, and to work alongside her and her assistants. He saw at close quarters the criminal results of sweating, substandard housing, the lack of proper medical and hospital facilities: all the unspeakable conditions which were to be disclosed by Upton Sinclair when he wrote *The Jungle* which, while it was specifically directed at the Chicago meat packing industry, nevertheless disclosed conditions which were all too common to many other industries.

34

It was seven miles from Hull House to the University and King travelled this distance every morning partly on foot and partly by elevated railroad. This meant getting up at six o'clock in the morning.

"It was first-class exercise," he once recalled. "It gave me a vivid contrast between life as it is lived in Jackson Park and the existence which is eked out in the foreign slums of Chicago. I worked very hard in those days, but looking back upon my experiences I can truthfully say that they gave me much enjoyment."

Later, in *Industry and Humanity*, King was to write: "The Settlement and its surroundings and my studies brought me into touch with such concrete problems as those presented by the tendency of foreign populations in large cities to become grouped in 'colonies' representative of different nationalities; and by the tendency of home life to be transferred from single dwellings into overcrowded tenements, allied, too often, through opportunities of social intercourse, with some neighbouring saloon and its light, warmth, music and boon companions. The problem of the 'sweated trades' was another of the problems confronted."

As a result of his observations King concluded that much of the undermining processes commonly observed in slum areas was, in one form or another, but a manifestation of the "Law of Competing Standards."

It was only natural that what he saw and heard and learned during these months of intensive study and observation should make a profound impression on his mind. To a young man of twenty-one, who had been reared in a quiet little Ontario town where poverty and social distress was a rarity, the monstrous and criminal labour conditions to be found in a great metropolis like Chicago came as a startling revelation. King was no wide-eyed innocent. He had read much, and he had known that such disgraceful conditions of employment, housing, and general environment did, in truth, exist in many large cities, but to read about them was one thing. To see and touch them was quite another. It is true conditions had improved greatly over those which had existed a few decades before when the 15-hour day was not unusual and children of six or seven worked all day in sunless plants; but the need for reform was still great.

When King returned to Canada in the summer of 1897 the memory of what he had seen was still fresh in his mind. It occurred to him that such conditions conceivably might be paralleled, if not completely, then in part, in large Canadian cities.

As his home was in Toronto, and as the city was the centre of a large number of important and rapidly growing industries, he decided to use it as a test-tube for his investigation into labouring conditions in the Dominion. He made arrangements to write a series of articles for the *Mail and Empire* with the hope of showing to what extent conditions similar to those which he had found in Chicago's labouring communities had or had not developed in Canada.

The results were startling. Canadians who had been listening to Theodore Roosevelt thundering against the trusts, who had read Ida Tarbell's indictments of big industry in *McLure's,* and who had complacently assumed that these things could not happen in their own country, learned that the United States was not the only country in the New World where workers were being exploited by unscrupulous employers who were apparently only too eager to take advantage of the poverty and need of a certain section of the community.

36

KING'S MOTHER AND FATHER
"Sweet and lovable . . . a friend and companion."

King visited the homes of workers in the garment trade. He was amazed at some of the conditions which he found. Among other shocking discoveries was the fact that letter carriers' uniforms, being made up under contracts awarded by the Post Office Department, were being produced under the most unfair and distressing conditions.

"On questioning one of the workers as to the remuneration she was receiving for sewing-machine and handwork," King reported, "I found that it came to a very few cents an hour. I shall never forget the feeling of pained surprise and indignation I experienced as I learned of the extent of that woman's toil from early morning till late at night, and figured out the pittance she received. The circumstance that it was government work, and that the contracting firm was one of high repute in the city, did not lessen the resentment I felt. As I visited other homes and shops, I found the conditions in one province had been played off against the better standards in others. Within the separate provinces, the workshop standard had been played off against the factory standard, and the home standard against the workshop standard. Machines operated by power had been played off against machines operated by the worker without mechanical aid; machine-work had been played off against handwork; work by piece, against work by the day or week; and the work of women and girls, against the work of men.

"Even the unpaid work of 'learners" had been set over against the work of expert hands. More than that, the sub-contractors of one nationality had been placed in competition with those of another, and the bids of sub-contractors had been played off against each other. Pin-money earnings of one class of workers had been played off against the extreme necessities of other classes.

"With what result upon labour standards? In some instances, women and girls had been working excessive hours, under unwholesome sanitary conditions, and had been receiving for actual work performed payment at the rate of three and four cents an hour!

"Contractors, in one or two instances I learned of, had received profits, on the contracts the government had awarded, as high as one hundred per cent!

"The lowest standards came to prevail wherever economic conditions permitted its application. The mean man was enabled to profit because of his meanness. As inferior standards came into effective competition with superior standards, the efficient and faithful worker was reduced, little by little, to lower levels."

At the time King discovered the existence of these conditions Hon. William Mulock was Postmaster General. He had been a member of the Liberal administration formed by Sir Wilfrid Laurier following the general elections of 1896, a member of the "Cabinet of All the Talents."

Although Sir William had to spend most of the week in Ottawa, he still maintained his residence in Toronto and he usually went home over the week-end. It happened that Sir William and Mr. King senior were friends of long standing, and both, for many years, had been members of the Senate of the University of Toronto.

Perhaps King was concerned with the possibility that his disclosures in connection with the Post Office Department contracts might reflect unfavourably upon his father's old friend. Perhaps he believed that if he brought the matter directly to Sir William's attention the latter would take remedial action without undue delay. At any rate, he decided to withhold the article on the letter carriers' uniforms until he had discussed the matter with Sir William. But first he went to his father for advice. John King agreed that the proper course to follow was to bring the matter to Sir William's attention, and thus, one Sunday afternoon, father and son called on Sir William at his home.

"It was even better than I anticipated," wrote King, when referring to the interview some years later. "The Postmaster General walked the floor like a caged lion, and wanted to know what should be done to remedy immediately such an abuse of public patronage.

"I suggested that conditions might be inserted in public contracts to ensure to the labour employed a minimum wage which would be a fair compensation for the work performed; that wherever work for the government was being executed, the premises should be open to inspection; and that sub-contracting likely to lead to sweating on government contracts should be prohibited."

Mulock asked King, then and there, to draft out the conditions that he thought would protect the workers. Then he advised King to meet him the following morning at the offices of the firm which held the contract with his Department.

Sir William was as good as his word, and a few days later he officially requested King to make a report to the government upon the methods theretofore adopted in Canada in the carrying out of government clothing contracts. Special attention was to be given to the conditions of manufacture of uniforms for Canadian Post Office officials, the Militia and the North West Mounted Police. Early in January, 1898 King submitted his report. It revealed conditions that fully supported his earlier investigations and many of its recommendations were later to be embodied in the Fair Wages Resolution sponsored in the House of Commons by the Postmaster General.

Taking a post-graduate course in political economy at

Harvard, King won a travelling fellowship which took him to Europe in 1899. Here he continued to inquire into the social and labour problems of Great Britain, France, Germany and Italy.

In London, as in Chicago, he lived at a settlement house, the Passmore Edwards Settlement, and here, again, he came into close touch with the poor and the under-privileged and had the opportunity of observing the results of "sweating" and other unfair labour practices.

In this unique atmosphere, surcharged with all the militant sociology of the times, King's philosophies matured and flourished. He moved about amongst the poor, attended meetings of the famous Fabian Society, lectured at the settlement, and met such men as the late Ramsay MacDonald, whose home he frequently visited, and others who were devoting their time and effort towards the improvement of the worker's lot.

At Toronto University King had read Arnold Toynbee's *Industrial Revolution* and had been deeply impressed. In London he met Toynbee's sister, Gertrude. Arnold Toynbee, who was an uncle of the present Arnold J. Toynbee, had been dead for some time and the students of Oxford University had built Toynbee Hall in memory of the brilliant young social reformer. Years later, in 1919, when King returned to Britain to further his studies, he visited Toynbee Hall and again met and talked with Gertrude Toynbee. Many of his former acquaintances had passed away and he found things greatly altered. But Gertrude Toynbee was working as hard as ever, carrying on the work to which her brother had devoted the best years of his life.

King always went out of his way to meet worth-while people, men and women from whom he believed he could learn something. He never overlooked an opportunity to make the acquaintance of anyone who was interested in social reform. His first meeting with Ramsay MacDonald ripened into a friendship which lasted till the time of MacDonald's death. King met MacDonald at Toronto in 1897 when the latter and his wife were visiting Canada on their wedding trip. MacDonald was attending a meeting of the Association for the Advancement of Science when King, then working for the *Globe,* was asked to write an article about him. King wrote the article, and made a friend. No doubt this friendship had something to do with the appointment, many years later, of Ramsay MacDonald's son, Malcolm, as British High Commissioner to Canada. Certainly, with King, Malcolm MacDonald was *persona grata.* Malcolm and King met for the first time in 1924 when the former visited Canada as a member of the Oxford debating team. On that occasion King took him under his wing, entertained him at Kingsmere and went out of his way to show the young Oxonian that his father's friendship was a cherished thing.

King had many interesting experiences in France, Germany, Italy, Switzerland and other European countries when touring them on his fellowship from Harvard. During part of his wanderings he was accompanied by another young Harvard student, Max Trenholme, who was also travelling on a fellowship. There is one story that provides a revealing picture of the two young students abroad, young men not too sure of themselves, with not too much money in their pockets, but who were obsessed with the desire to see the world and at the same time eager to present as good a front as possible.

They had arrived at Interlaken in Switzerland and had put up at one of the big resort hotels. As they strolled along in the twilight admiring the beauty of the Geisbach

Falls, which were a feature of the district, the proprietor of the hotel approached them deferentially and asked them if they would like to have the falls lighted. King and his friend nodded a smiling assent. But of course!

A few minutes later the falls were brilliantly illuminated by electricity and the tourists gasped with astonishment and delight at the spectacle. During the course of the evening not a few of them approached the two students and shook them by the hand in most cordial fashion. Apparently they believed that they had been responsible for the illumination of the falls that evening and that they were persons of some considerable importance. Had not the manager turned the lights on at their bidding? And had not this been the friendliest and most thoughtful of gestures on the part of the two visiting Americans?

But King and Trenholme were more than a little puzzled. It was not until they went to pay their hotel bill the following morning that they discovered that the cost of lighting up the falls had been charged up to their account.

When they protested to the proprietor he raised his eyebrows in surprise. But had he not asked them if they would not like the falls lighted? Had they not said that they would be delighted to see them illuminated? Why, now, all this argument?

The two bewildered students pointed out that the manager had made no mention of any fee. They told him bluntly they did not intend to pay for the lights. They put down the money to cover the rest of the bill and prepared to leave.

In the meanwhile, however, word had spread that the two young Americans were persons of some means, although travelling quietly. Thus, when they gathered their kit together and made for the door they found the maître d'hôtel, the chef, the garçon, the femme de chambre and all the rest of the staff lined up in the lobby to bid them Godspeed. All stood with palms hopefully extended.

It called for some quick thinking, but the two young tourists rose to the situation. With all the dignity and condescension of departing royalty they shook hands all around and then withdrew in good order.

King was in Italy when his destiny caught up with him in the form of a telegram from Mulock offering him the editorship of the *Labour Gazette*. The editorship carried with it the position of first lieutenant in the Department of Labour, a branch of the government service which at that time was little more than an idea in the minds of Sir William and Sir Wilfrid Laurier. It came at a decisive moment in King's life. He had just received a most flattering offer, that of the position of instructor in political economy at Harvard. What should he do?

After some deep soul-searching he decided against Mulock's offer in favour of the opportunity to teach. But his refusal of the government position merely elicited another more pressing cablegram asking him to reconsider. On his way back to Canada King discussed the situation with Professor William Cunningham, at Cambridge.

"Take it," advised Cunningham. Without further delay King wired his acceptance and entered the Civil Service of Canada.

In September, 1900, only five years after graduating from the University of Toronto, King became Deputy Minister of Labour. He was twenty-five.

At the time of King's appointment, Sir William was acting Minister of Public Works, and in that capacity he authorized King to lease premises for the new offices in the Molson's Bank Building, just across the street from the

Langevin Block where the offices of the Postmaster General were located. To distinguish them from other offices, the new premises were designated as those of the Department of Labour. Before the end of September the first issue of the *Labour Gazette* made its appearance, the title page indicating that it was being published by the "Department of Labour under authority of parliament." From this time on Mulock became known as Minister of Labour as well as Postmaster General.

Indubitably, King owed his start in politics to Sir William. Long after the latter had retired from active political life he continued to give King the benefit of his knowledge and experience.

Sir William was one of those robust and salty men whose intellectual capacity and professional attainments were balanced by a wholehearted indulgence in all the minor vices. He liked big black cigars, and usually had one sticking out of the corner of his mouth. He enjoyed his Scotch-and-soda, and he was suspected of chewing tobacco occasionally. His close friendship with King lasted throughout the years and he was always fond of pointing out that he had been instrumental in launching King upon a political career. Upon his death he willed King the not inconsiderable sum of fifty thousand dollars, tax free.

IV

DEPUTY MINISTER OF LABOUR

WHEN KING WAS appointed Deputy Minister of Labour he was bursting with ideas that he had absorbed and developed in Chicago, London, Toronto and elsewhere, ideas which had to do largely with social reform and, in particular, conditions among the labouring masses. He was not long in translating some of these thoughts into action. Perhaps the most notable of his contributions to the labour legislation of the Dominion during the next few years was the Industrial Disputes Investigation Act. Broadly speaking, the object of the Act was to prevent strikes and lockouts in industries on which the public welfare depends.

The important principle enunciated by King, which is given effect to in the Act, had been expressed following the settlement of a strike in the Southern Alberta coal fields which began early in the winter of 1906 and which soon resulted in a most serious situation throughout the prairies where many municipalities found themselves suddenly without fuel.

The principle laid down by King was that: "In any civilian community private rights should cease when they become public wrongs . . . Either the disputants must be prepared to leave the differences which they are unable amicably to settle to the arbitrament of such authority as the state may determine as most expedient, or make way for others who are prepared to do so."

King had not been long in the position of Deputy

Minister before he sent for Henry Albert Harper whom he had known at the University of Toronto. Harper was a year King's senior and, like King, he had studied social economy and was interested in a career in the public service. Specifically, King appointed him secretary of the embryo Department and assigned him to the work of preparing economic articles for the *Labour Gazette*. Neither King nor Harper knew very much about running an office nor were they familiar with the intricate working of a government department; but they were both young and enthusiastic and they believed that they knew where they were going.

Two people, they worked as one. When King was absent from Ottawa on departmental business, Harper, left in charge of the office, did King's worrying. When King was successful, Harper was elated; when King failed, Harper shared his defeat and disappointment.

The two men had much in common. They were both awake to the urgency of the need for labour reform; they liked the same books and held similar opinions on many subjects; and they both loved the outdoors. They shared an apartment in the city and together they explored the shores of Kingsmere Lake where King was later to build his summer home.

As might be expected, during the early organizational days of the Department, King leaned heavily on the permanent civil servants who were assigned to work for him. One in particular, Francis Giddens, was later to serve as King's private secretary and follow him when he entered politics.

But Giddens' main duties as employee of the Labour Department were of a stenographic nature. He found King a slow, methodical, painstaking worker, who insisted on perfect typewriting and who would not let even a faulty visible rub-out get by. But King's insistence on perfection had its rewards. He himself became a careful and fluid dictator and Giddens became a shorthand expert and typist who made few errors.

King had a habit of striding up and down the room when dealing with a knotty problem, especially when preparing speeches or articles. When working on a speech he gathered material from many sources, piled it on desks and tables about him and then got down to work.

Most of his letters, however, King first wrote out in longhand. These, according to his stenographers, were always "infernally" long. He wrote with a stub pen in a small hand and after filling the page he would creep around the margins and go everywhere he could find some white, except on the back of the page. His newspaper training had taught him never to do that, but if there was a crack or a crevice where he could scribble in a word he would find it. The result was terrible copy and often Giddens was at his wits' end attempting to decipher it.

But if King was not the easiest man in the world to work for and demanded twenty-four-hour-a-day service when he was concentrating on a problem, if one happened to be caught up with one's work and wanted a day off one could usually get it.

Sometimes when King and Harper were concentrating on a departmental problem their thoughts would stray and they would become involved in an enthusiastic discussion of a philosophic or literary nature. As their two chiefs sat there quoting authorities to one another and unconsciously exhibiting their impressive erudition, Giddens and his colleagues sometimes pretended to be deeply absorbed in their own work; but once in a while they would look up and exchange a sly wink. Both King and Harper were particularly devoted to the poetry of Matthew Arnold and often they sat entertaining each other by quoting their favourite passages from *Literature and Dogma* or *The Buried Life*.

Very early in his career as Deputy Minister of Labour King began travelling about the Dominion adjusting industrial disputes.

Senator Charles Bishop, who was the dean of the Parliamentary Press Gallery before King appointed him to the Senate some years ago, recalls the first time he saw King in action as Deputy Minister.

A serious labour dispute had occurred between the employees and management of a lumber company at Hawkesbury, Ont. Bishop and a number of other newspapermen from Ottawa who went down to see what it was all about found that the men were in a very dangerous mood.

The lumber workers, who were mostly big, brawny French-Canadians, thought the newspapermen had been sent down to spy on them, and they were in favour of running them out of town. However, Bishop knew enough French to explain that they were only peaceful reporters. The next day, Easter Sunday, King arrived. He immediately called a meeting of the men and the management and had both sides state their case. Despite the mood of the employees and the fact that the trouble had been brewing for some time King managed to effect a settlement within a few hours. His unique gift for conciliation was to pay dividends time and again during the years to come. The King of those days is recalled as a pleasant affable fellow, a man who liked to work alone, who was strong-willed and self-sufficient.

As an example of the cold, clear logic which King learned to apply to industrial disputes one might cite the following incident. A certain textile firm was seeking damages from its employees in connection with losses incurred by the firm when a large quantity of cloth was allegedly ruined by the employees during a strike. King was asked to arbitrate the dispute and fix the damages, if any.

King, however, could not see that the material had been damaged. He examined it carefully, but it looked quite all right to him.

"But the damage is there," insisted the company's representative, "only it is invisible."

King grinned. "Is that so?" he observed. "Well, the damages will be invisible too!"

During the time that he was Deputy Minister King settled more than forty labour disputes, many of them of major proportions, involving important principles of labour relations. This work took him from one side of the Dominion to the other and it sometimes seemed that he was always travelling.

Few men were equipped so well for this work. Not only did King have the knowledge, but, it seemed, he possessed something very nearly approaching a genius for reconciling contrary elements. He had an easy way with working men and he was genuinely interested in their problems. He settled many disputes without the slightest bit of wrangling, appealing to both parties' sense of fair play and making his points with such fairness and logic that both employees and employers often gave way and compromised on the terms of settlement.

Sometimes, when discussions got out of bounds or it appeared as if things were reaching an impasse, King would turn to the men about the conference table and suggest:

"What do you say we just stop talking about this thing for a while and talk about something else?" A recess would be called and King would chat with the labour men in a way that demonstrated that he knew their problems and difficulties. During those days most of the labour leaders were socialists or had strongly socialist leanings and they were fond of quoting Karl Marx. But King could quote Marx, too, and he was usually able to quote it with considerably more authority than those who thought they knew all about the great socialist. For King had read Marx, not in the translation, but in the original German.

The men came to have great faith in his fairness and they were impressed by his willingness to see them at any hour of the day or night. Many a time they knocked at the door of his hotel room in order to confer with him for a few moments on some perplexing point, to find him in bed or having a meal. It didn't matter; the men were welcome. Sometimes he invited them to join him in a cup of coffee. This sort of thing built up trust and confidence and the word soon got around that this fellow King knew what it was all about and you could trust him.

When King was away on these trips he kept in close touch with Harper by letter. Their correspondence reveals that both men felt that in furthering the work of the Department of Labour they were carrying out a public trust. The letters which passed between them also indicate the extent of their personal regard for each other.

"You must not take my official daily notes as a measure of my interest in your affairs here, your progress yonder, or your thoughtfulness in writing me such refreshing letters as those which you have written en route," wrote Harper, in answering one of King's letters from the West.

"The dating of your last 'in the country of the foothills'

makes me think how eagerly you must be looking forward, as you wrote, to the prospect of the mountains. Perhaps you were fortunate to see them in the stern glory of a winter sunset. These things, like great pictures and noble thoughts, leave a permanent impress upon one's life, and I rejoice that the path of duty has led you through so much that is beautiful and sublime.

"But hold, I am probably several chapters behind your present thought and work, for by now you will be wrapped up in the affairs of a mining town, interested in its mushroom growth, its throbbing, ill-digested life, and in the main object of your mission, the strike. . . ."

Again, Harper wrote . . . "The Canadian Manufacturers' Association to the contrary notwithstanding, your work is neither superficial nor ephemeral. It is of the very essence of a force which is calculated to prove a strong lever in regulating the labour movement, and indeed other movements as well, in Canada. It is my happiness to be associated with you in that work. I think I comprehend its nature and its importance, immediate and even prospective, and I trust I may prove equal to its demands and purpose.

"But I must get down to my night's work, Rex. The house is singularly quiet, without any movement in the adjoining room, but that does not excuse the sacrifice of opportunity."

From these and other letters it would appear that King and Harper were, indeed, serious young men with few interests outside the work of the Department, their love for books, their deep appreciation of the outdoors. It is true that both of them interested themselves to some extent in the social life of the capital. There were dances and theatre dates, skating parties and dinner engagements. But one finds no light, idle prattling in their letters, no talk of "best girls" or "nights out" or "after-party headaches." Both apparently were completely engrossed in the deeper and wider spiritual and intellectual attainments of the "fuller life." Two serious young men, indeed.

During December, 1901, King had been out west settling a number of strikes. Running out of funds, he wired Harper who sent him $100. On his way home he again ran short and when he reached North Bay he had only a few cents left in his pocket, not enough, in fact, to buy breakfast. When the train stopped at Barrie, King was wondering if he should buy a sandwich or a newspaper. He settled for a newspaper. As he glanced out of the window his eye rested on Harper's old home which was visible from the train. For a moment he watched the old house on the hillside and then, as the train began to gather way, he turned back to his paper.

The first item that caught his eye was a story under an Ottawa dateline to the effect that Harper had been drowned in the Ottawa River the previous night while attempting to save the life of a young woman skater who had gone through the ice.

When King reached Toronto where his father was to meet him at the station he was exhausted. The tragic news, together with the fact that he had not eaten all day, proved too much for him. He collapsed on the platform and it was some minutes before he was able to proceed. Then he took the next train for Ottawa.

The story was a simple one. Harper had been skating on the river when the young woman had fallen through the ice into the swift current. When he prepared to dive into the river in an attempt to save her, other skaters warned him that his efforts would be useless.

"What else can I do?" he cried, and plunged in to his death.

The two bodies were recovered the next morning not far from each other.

Subsequently, a monument, a bronze Sir Galahad, was erected to Harper's memory. It stands in the shadow of the Parliament Buildings and carved deep into its granite base are Sir Galahad's words in the Holy Grail:

> If I lose myself
> I save myself!

It was four years before King could bring himself to put down on paper the tumultuous and tortuous stream of memories which bound him to his friend. Then, in a little memoir, *The Secret of Heroism,* he unburdened himself.

Referring to the happy days they had spent together at Kingsmere, and describing the spot itself, King wrote:

"It is a distance by road of twelve miles from the Capital, eight of which can be covered by rail. Harper's real sense of freedom began when, after a day's work in town, that eight miles of travelling was at an end, and the chance came for a four-mile walk across the fields, through the woods and along the country roads, or for a ride upon his wheel or by stage.

"Then came the evenings with their glorious sunsets, and the walks and talks in the twilight, and then night with its unbroken panoply of star-lit sky.

"It is, perhaps, impossible," continued King, "to convey, save to those who have known the experience, any conception of what a constant association of this kind with Nature really means. It proves, to use Harper's own words, 'how beauty, grandeur, sublimity and purity in God's world, find a ready response in the human heart unfettered.' Yet it is this perception of God, this communion of soul between the creature and the Creator as He is revealed in

53

Nature, that is the conscious or unconscious secret of all the refreshment and joy which comes from a contact of this kind. Harper's nature was one that could share and did share it to the full."

The next few years were busy ones for King. Following Harper's death he plunged into the work of the Department with increasing energy and concentration. He began to show more interest, too, in social life. He again took up horseback riding and, in the winter, skating, being a familiar figure on the big open-air rink at Rideau Hall. He joined the Rideau Club and the Canadian Club, taking an active interest in the affairs of both. He began to do a great deal of public speaking and, in 1905, was elected president of the Canadian Club. Slowly but steadily he was building up a competent staff about him. The Department of Labour was proving an effective division of government and its increasing usefulness was being demonstrated in many ways, particularly in the field of conciliation and arbitration.

The matter of immigration was one which received serious attention during King's early years as Deputy Minister. It was a complex problem. In 1905 he conducted an investigation into fraudulent practices which had been employed in Britain to bring men to Canada to act as strikebreakers. In 1906 he went to London to confer with the government on this matter and was successful in obtaining the enactment, in the British House, of legislation designed to prevent the continuance of such practices.

The Oriental immigration to British Columbia, however, was an even more serious problem. The United States had for some time recognized the danger of allowing any heavy influx of Asiatics. At first the Chinese coolies had been welcomed as constituting a pool of cheap labour, but later the danger had been recognized, the Americans passing an exclusion law in 1882. But Canada was slower to appreciate the potential danger of heavy immigration from Asia and at first the movement met with scant opposition. Finally, however, British Columbia became thoroughly aroused and expressed itself by the enactment of a number of exclusion acts. But the Dominion Government, looking towards Westminster, used its power of disallowance. This quarrel was to go on for some years and it was not until 1923 that legislation was enacted forbidding immigration of the Chinese coolie class.

In respect to immigration from Japan the situation was met in part by the making of a "gentlemen's agreement." Canada would not exclude Japanese labourers and Japan would see that not too many left the Mikado's shores.

King played an important part in the settlement of this problem. It was one of his first triumphs in the broad field of international relations. His investigations not only directed a flood of light upon the entire question of Oriental immigration but paved the way for its solution.

In 1908 King resigned his position as Deputy Minister of Labour to run for parliament. He successfully contested the riding of North Waterloo.

But Laurier did not move too quickly. The problem of Indian immigration had yet to be dealt with and Laurier advised King to go to India and consult with the authorities there.

King, thinking of his new parliamentary duties, was not keen to go. He felt that he should be in the House, getting the feel of things.

"You'll get enough parliamentary experience during

your lifetime," said Laurier with uncanny prescience, and King took the tip and made preparations to leave.

In 1907 King had prepared a report dealing with the need for legislation to suppress the opium traffic in Canada, and as a sequel to this report he was appointed by the British government, in 1908, as one of the British members of the International Opium Commission which was to meet at Shanghai. In 1907 he had been appointed as a Royal Commissioner to inquire into the anti-Asiatic riots in British Columbia, and later to conduct an inquiry into the methods by which 'Oriental labourers had been induced to come to Canada from India, China and Japan.

These various assignments thus necessitated a world tour which was to take him to Britain, across Europe to India, and, finally to China and Japan.

King decided to take Giddens along with him. Laden down with guide books and other volumes of reference they set out from New York on the *Lusitania*. King was in holiday mood once he stepped aboard the ship and Giddens was amazed to find that his chief was quite a different person away from the office. He made friends easily and was excellent company. The trip was a great education for young Giddens because through King he met people whom he had only read about and whom he had never expected to see or talk to in the flesh.

When they reached London King immediately began conferring with high government officials and public leaders. King met Lord Northcliffe and appeared to be deeply impressed. The two spent much time together. Somewhere King and Giddens made the acquaintance of the celebrated American humorist, George Ade. Giddens' eyes popped, but King wasn't particularly interested. It was the men with big ideas whom he wanted to talk to, not some magazine writer who wrote fables in slang.

They visited Sutton Green and King slept in a bed which was said to have been once used by Queen Elizabeth. Again Giddens was all agog, and again King failed to be impressed.

As they crossed over to France and continued their journey south King spent many hours studying his guide books, particularly those which dealt with India, its politics, geography and economic status. It was important, he pointed out, that they should know as much as possible about the country, its people and its customs.

The trip across the Mediterranean was a rough one. Both King and Giddens remained in their cabins not daring to try their feet on deck. The ship pitched and tossed like a ferry boat crossing the English Channel. The two men clung to their bunks, read some more about India and subsisted for the most part on a diet of grapes. From Bombay they proceeded to Calcutta where King spent three weeks conferring with the Viceroy. They then continued on to Shanghai, via Ceylon, to attend the International Opium Conference. After three weeks at Shanghai they went on to Hong Kong and Peking.

King obtained a tremendous amount of information wherever he went. Each night Giddens' notebook would bulge anew with dictation. King had also started to keep his own personal diary and when he had finished his departmental work he would jot down his random thoughts on the day's activities.

The trip was to have an amusing little sequel when, following his return to Canada, King addressed a large meeting at Hamilton. Speaking without notes, he gave an account of his round-the-world trip. Among other incidents he described the visit to Hong Kong. The reporter who was covering King's speech for the Hamilton *Times* decided that it would be easier to obtain a report from

Giddens than rely on his own notes, so after the meeting he sought out the secretary. Somehow the latter, who had taken a few notes of the speech, had got them tangled up. To satisfy the reporter he decided to do a bit of improvising. He had seen the beautiful view from The Peak across the harbour, had seen the Peak from Kowloon across the Bay, so he scribbled out a flowery description which satisfied the reporter.

It must have been fairly good, because later, when King checked over the newspaper account of the meeting he remarked'to Giddens: "You know, I made a pretty good job of that description of Hong Kong from The Peak, didn't I?"

Giddens enthusiastically agreed, but he wasn't flattering anyone but himself. King liked the passage so well that a number of times afterwards, when addressing small church organizations or similar groups, he worked it into his speeches.

The varied and extensive experience which King gained as Deputy Minister and while carrying out his Asiatic assignments did a great deal to broaden his mind and strengthen his hand. It added tremendously to his stature not only as an individual but as a government official, as a Canadian, and as a citizen of the world.

Soon after King returned to Canada Laurier took him down to Government House and had him sworn in as Canada's first full-time Minister of Labour.

V

A VICTORY AND A DEFEAT

IN 1908 WHEN King decided to run for parliament it was only to be expected that he should seek election in his home town. He expected real opposition, however, because for many years North Waterloo had been held by a Conservative, J. E. Seagram. Seagram, besides being one of Canada's biggest distillers, was a colourful personality and his influence throughout the riding was great. His celebrated stable of racing horses was known from one end of the country to the other and the Seagram colours—black-and-orange—had long been accepted as the district's official colours. Although he was not running in 1908 (the Conservative candidate was a school teacher by the name of Richard Read) it was assumed that Seagram's influence was behind the Conservative candidate and that it would swing the election to the Conservative side of the ledger.

King, however, felt that he knew his fellow Berliners and when he arrived to start his campaign he was suffering from no inferiority complex. He had decided that he would have to exert every effort, and he lost no time in getting down to work. He bristled with enthusiasm, and his self-confident attitude proved so infectious that in no time at all he had hundreds of townsfolk working for him. He organized the business men, gave inspiring talks to his workers, outlined the issues of the election at every opportunity and soon had his supporters busy on a house-to-house canvass.

King himself did his own share of bell-ringing. He

looked up all his old school friends, visited the Sunday school he had attended as a boy, went to church and sat in the old family pew. His remarkable memory for names and faces soon won him a great following. Everyone knew that Billy King was back home and almost everyone, it seemed, was anxious to see him win.

Finally, there came the day of the big outdoor rally in Victoria Park. Many prominent Liberals were present, including the great Sir Wilfrid himself. After Rodolphe Lemieux had softened up the crowd with one of his traditionally witty and persuasive speeches, Laurier took the platform.

He announced that King was definitely cabinet material and intimated that the young Deputy Minister had a great future ahead of him. All the electors had to do to make this possible, he suggested, was to choose King as their member.

Then King spoke! He delivered a brilliant oration and his wonderful command of English and his remarkable faculty for grasping detail and making it work for him had its results. The meeting was a great success. People had come from far and near to hear Laurier, but they remained to listen to King. As for Laurier, he charmed the ladies with his old-world gallantry and grace. No doubt he was responsible for a good many of King's votes.

When election day arrived King was in. When, in 1909, following his appointment as Minister of Labour he again presented himself to the electors of North Waterloo he was tendered an acclamation.

King worked just as hard in the Reciprocity election of 1911, but this time he was defeated. Like a good many other Liberal members who were personally popular in their constituencies he went down to defeat before the overwhelming opposition to the principle of free trade. There were some other factors, too. The Conservatives had chosen as their candidate W. J. Weichel who, besides being Mayor of Waterloo at the time, had a very wide association throughout the riding and had the advantage over King when it came to dealing with his fellow business men. In addition, it is possible that King made a few mistakes in his general attitude towards the electors.

The Reciprocity election was an outstanding example of how a political contest is sometimes won or lost on the strength of a slogan. The Conservatives advanced the entirely fallacious argument that free trade was synonymous with annexation and that the two were indivisible. Actually, the question was not "free trade" as such but "freer trade." Nevertheless the issue provided the anti-free-traders with the opportunity they required. From every political platform in the country the Conservatives thundered their battle-cry: "No truck or trade with the Yankees!" It was such a simple thing to sell to the public; one did not even have to give oral expression to the argument. Conservative candidates merely stepped to the front of the platform, produced a Union Jack and an American flag and held them before their audience, one in either hand.

Which flag did the elector want to live under? He was offered his choice!

So far as the majority of Canadians were concerned, there was only one answer. The fallacy of the argument implicit in the question was quite overlooked by the electorate. All that mattered was that they should remain under their own flag. The appeal won thousands of votes from those whose understanding of or interest in the nation's tariff policy was infinitesimal.

When the ballots were counted it was found that the two

old parties had switched positions in the House. The Liberals, who had won 133 seats in 1908 were now reduced to 86, while the Conservatives, who had mustered only 85 seats in 1908 now boasted 133 members. It was the mathematical as well as the political wonder of the day.

One incident which is said to have lost King some support during the campaign was his action in making public a number of letters which he had received from business men in the riding in reply to letters he had written them while he was still Deputy Minister of Labour.

While the Reciprocity debate was on in the House of Commons King sent out a questionnaire to every business man in Waterloo County soliciting a free expression of his views on the issue. The Conservatives moved in the House that government officials produce all correspondence between themselves and their constituents. The government, holding that such correspondence was of a private nature and as such was privileged, refused to produce it.

But at one of King's election meetings he held up a sheaf of answers he had received from the business men of the county. As he waved one letter in the air, signed by a prominent Conservative business man who had written that his business would not be adversely affected by Reciprocity, someone in the audience, as if by arrangement, called out: "Read it!"

"I will," said King, and he did so.

But this action of King's in making public a letter which the government had refused to produce in the House of Commons acted as a boomerang. The industrialists of the town organized against him, and no doubt his action in producing the letter at that meeting contributed to his defeat.

King worked frantically throughout the last days of the

campaign to stem the rising tide of opposition. At one Conservative rally Weichel was in the middle of his speech when Giddens walked into the hall and presented him with a letter from King in which the latter challenged the Conservative candidate to a public debate on the issues of the campaign.

"Mr. King wants an answer," Giddens explained.

"The best thing Mr. King can do," Weichel replied, "is to mind his own business and let me mind mine."

Giddens beat a hasty retreat. The Conservative crowd was definitely hostile and he lost no time in making his departure.

Most of the election meetings were held in the old skating rink in Berlin. Some of them lasted until well after midnight. The Berlin *Telegraph* was supporting King, and after the meetings, perhaps at two or three in the morning, King would arrive at the newspaper office to edit the report of his own speeches. Slash, slash, slash would go his pencil; grunt, grunt, grunt, and he would make revision after revision until he was satisfied that the report was an accurate one. Then he would wander off to his hotel, Giddens plodding wearily at his side. It was all very well for King, for he could sleep in next morning, but his secretary had to rise at nine to deal with the departmental correspondence that had come in the morning mail.

Another thing that possibly contributed to King's defeat was that although in his first campaign he did a tremendous amount of personal canvassing, in 1911 he appeared to rely too much on the fact that he was Minister of Labour and a person of some consequence. In his first election he had been Billy King, the home-town boy; in the next, Hon. William Lyon Mackenzie King, Cabinet Minister!

In other words, a good many people thought he had

gone high-hat, which is usually political suicide in an industrial riding.

For instance, after his election in 1908, King used to rent a furnished house in Berlin for a month or so. He had a telephone, but he kept the number private except to a few close friends and party workers. This antagonized many people, and it was only after some of his advisers pointed out that he was losing friends that the telephone operators received instructions to put everyone through.

King possibly realized some of the mistakes he had made, after the votes had been counted, because the morning after his defeat he appeared to be in humble and contrite mood.

Walking into the lobby of the Walpur House with a couple of his friends King noticed a little group of youths standing by the desk. One of them, Karl Homuth, was one day to represent Waterloo South in parliament. King recognized the members of the group as Conservative workers who had led the heckling at many of the public meetings. For a moment or so he stood looking at them gloomily, then his face broke into a big, good-natured smile and he walked over to them.

"Well, just because I lost the election is no reason why we shouldn't all be friends," he suggested, and he shook hands all around.

King always contended that the thing that defeated him in 1911 was Grand Trunk Railway money. During the years 1908 and 1909 there was a widespread movement throughout North America to promote the establishment of standard rates of pay throughout the industry. In 1910 an attempt was made to bring the Grand Trunk and the Canadian Pacific into line with railway companies in the United States. Despite the fact that the Canadian Pacific signed an agreement some difficulty was encountered in the case of the Grand Trunk. When at last the matter was settled, following a strike of Grand Trunk employees, one of the conditions agreed to was that the men should be reinstated in their former positions and that all seniority and pension rights should be respected.

But the Grand Trunk, although it reinstated the employees in their positions, refused to honour pension rights. King fought the railway on this question, and he maintained that in reprisal the Grand Trunk poured thousands of dollars into the riding to accomplish his defeat.

There is one 1911 election story which might be told here, because it indicates that not only did King possess a well-developed sense of humour as a young man but that his mental reactions were trigger-fast.

King was scheduled to speak at the Linwood School on a Saturday night, but something interfered with his plans—possibly the poor roads or the bad weather—and by the time he reached Linwood it was almost Sunday morning.

However, the chairman had managed to keep the meeting going until King's arrival. As midnight struck King told his audience that as a political meeting could not be held on a Sunday he would preach instead. There is no record of what text he chose for his sermon, but he no doubt managed to get in a few licks for the Liberal Party and his own candidature.

VI

"INDUSTRY AND HUMANITY"

FOLLOWING HIS DEFEAT at the polls King accepted the task of organizing the Liberal Information Office at Ottawa. His duties included editing the party publication, *The Liberal Monthly,* and, in addition, in 1912, he became president of the General Reform Association of Ontario, a position which he was to hold until 1914. These interests kept him occupied for the next few years. He did much writing and lecturing, maintained his university and political contacts, and continued to delve into the subject of social economy.

Just prior to the outbreak of World War I the King family suffered the first of what was to be a long series of heartbreaking misfortunes. John King, who had been carrying on his work at the university, as well as his private law practice, was stricken with blindness. He was obliged to give up all professional activity with the result that his income ceased. About the same time, Macdougall, who had built up a modest medical practice in Ottawa, developed tuberculosis. He, too, was obliged to relinquish the practice of his profession and for the greater part of two years to spend his time in a sanatorium. Later, he and his wife and two small children, took up permanent residence in Colorado.

There was no one left to share the responsibilities of the King home under these sad and trying circumstances but King and his married sister Janet, now Mrs. Morrison Lay. In addition, Janet had her own family to consider. King's unmarried sister, Isabel, was at home and this was

66

some comfort to her parents, but the financial burden lay squarely on Billy King's shoulders.

King did not receive a large salary as Chief of the Liberal Information Office and his financial resources were limited. It was soon apparent that his father would never again be able to practise his profession and that his brother's sanatorium treatment might be protracted and costly. An unexpected solution presented itself when King was offered the post of Director of Industrial Research with the Rockefeller Foundation. The position carried with it a substantial salary, the duties were in line with King's special training, and he had always wanted to be of service in the field of social welfare. It was a job to test his particular training and ability as an expert in the field of labour relations. He accepted the offer gladly and immediately took over his new duties.

His original assignment was to make a study of industrial relations throughout the world. The war altered these plans, however, and when a number of large companies in the United States which were turning out munitions of war and other vital supplies for the Allies found themselves facing possible shutdowns due to labour troubles King's counsel and assistance as a conciliator was sought. His intensive studies and experience in the field of labour relations, and the successes which he had achieved as a conciliator during his years as Deputy Minister and then Minister of Labour had won him international recognition, and marked him for the job.

No other Canadian, said one authority, in referring to King's studies in political economy, had ever spent so much time and talent on the subject.

In accepting the position with the Rockefeller Foundation King made it a specific condition of his employment that he be allowed to retain residence in Canada and, further, that he be permitted to participate in the political life of his own country. While, during the next four years, he spent some months in the United States, the bulk of his work was done in his apartment at the Roxborough, in Ottawa. This arrangement made it possible for him to take part in the general elections of 1917.

King's work with the Rockefeller Foundation was greatly complicated by the numerous personal difficulties he was called upon to face over a short period of time. No sooner had he become embarked upon the project when Isabel, his unmarried sister, died. The following year, in August, 1916, his father passed away. After spending a few weeks with Macdougall in Denver and two or three weeks with Mrs. Lay, Mrs. King came to Ottawa to stay with Billy. She was critically ill most of the time she was with him at the Roxborough. Shortly before the 1917 elections, although very ill, she insisted that King carry out his plan to contest the riding of North York. On December 18, the day after the election, while King was on his way back to Ottawa, Mrs. King died. King was disconsolate at the fact that he had failed to be at his mother's side during her last hours. At the same time he knew that his mother had hoped that he might win the election and thus become the Member of Parliament for the constituency which had returned her father nine times to parliament.

When King took over the position of Director of Industrial Research he recalled to his side one of the two men upon whom he had leaned so heavily during his early days with the Department of Labour, F. A. McGregor, his former secretary. McGregor, who had returned to college to complete a course in economics, had graduated and was now teaching at McMaster University. He gave up his professorship to work at King's side again.

LAURIER AND KING

"He announced that King was definitely cabinet material."

During the first three years of the war King was instrumental in settling a number of serious labour disputes in the United States. Probably the most outstanding instance was the Colorado Fuel and Iron Company strike in 1915. When King accepted the task of finding a solution to the disagreement which had resulted in a two-year tie-up of the industry a condition closely approaching civil war obtained.

One of his first moves was to enlist the personal interest and co-operation of John D. Rockefeller, Jr. King found that unfortunately the management had kept young Rockefeller in ignorance of much that had gone on and had discouraged his natural desire to familiarize himself with the actual problems of management. King immediately took steps to correct this situation. He brought the facts to Rockefeller's attention.

When King arrived in Colorado he immediately set about establishing friendly relations with the employees. This accomplished, he persuaded Rockefeller to come west and to take a personal interest in the negotiations. Together they made a tour of the mining towns affected. They donned miners' togs and went down into the mines and talked with the men who toiled at the face of the seam. They attended the miners' meetings and conferred with their leaders.

The miners were amazed that Rockefeller was actually interested enough in their problems to spend so much of his time among them, and soon an entirely new spirit made itself evident. A firm basis for negotiation was laid and, eventually, an agreement acceptable to both parties was effected.

The period of negotiation was marked by many interesting and sometimes amusing incidents.

On one occasion when Rockefeller was visiting a mine

for the first time he undertook to shake hands with a group of workmen. The members of his party could not suppress a smile at the mingled delight and bewilderment experienced by a giant negro who, along with the other miners, had had the opportunity of stepping up and shaking hands with the famous industrialist.

Holding out his great black palm to his comrades the big negro exclaimed: "Look at it! Look at it! Dat hand hab' held de hand of de great Rockefeller!"

But it was this sort of thing, this personal contact with the men, this unbending of authority from the very top, which resulted in a tremendous change of feeling on both sides. King had inspired it, and he continued to foster and encourage it.

It was not long before Rockefeller suggested that the front-office men and the miners should get together in a social way. He planned a big company dance. It was attended by all the employees and their wives and sweethearts, and Rockefeller had a grand time dancing with the miners' womenfolk. The following year Rockefeller brought his wife out to Colorado and together they toured the mines and visited the company towns. Never before had relations between the workers and the company been so satisfactory.

Actually, it had not taken King long to discover that young Rockefeller was sincerely interested in his employees and their problems. King's talent for conciliation was best demonstrated when he worked to bring Rockefeller and the men face to face. That accomplished, understanding and reason prevailed. Rockefeller realized that something must be done and he lost no time in taking remedial action.

One of the miners' leaders and spokesmen was "Mother Jones." She was a colourful and dynamic personality who exercised great influence over the men. King cultivated her friendship from the first and the two soon learned to know and respect each other's views and objectives. Samuel Gompers, president of the American Federation of Labor, was also much in evidence during the period of negotiation. Gompers and King met frequently. The great labour leader was impressed by King's youthful enthusiasm and determination to end the strike and, in turn, King profited from his association with Gompers.

Conferences with the miners or the company officials usually consumed most of the day, and it was sometimes late in the evening before King was able to sum up the day's activities and discussions. Every night when he returned to his hotel he dictated to McGregor, summarizing the arguments which had been advanced by both sides, setting forth his own conclusions, and preparing for the next day's meetings.

King's successful work in obtaining an agreement between the Colorado Fuel and Iron Company's 12,000 employees, and the management, was only one of his many wartime achievements in the field of labour relations in the United States. He did equally effective work in dealing with the labour problems of the Bethlehem Shipbuilding Corporation which at the time was employing 70,000 men.

The Bethlehem Steel Company, another large industry, which was employing 50,000 workers, and which was also producing war supplies, paid tribute to King for the part he played in promoting harmony and co-operation between capital and labour in that industry. King also gave his services as an expert to the General Electric Company, the Youngstown Sheet and Tube Company, the International Harvester Company and a number of other giant corporations, working out the details of labour-management plans which resulted in the establishment of more cordial relations between the parties concerned, and which were reflected in the substantially increased production of war materials.

Industry and Humanity—A Study in the Principles Underlying Industrial Reconstruction, was completed by King in 1918. It embodied the results of his experiences in the United States and set forth his principal social ideas. It was to go through almost a score of editions and to be translated into a number of foreign languages including the Japanese.

King went to considerable pains to develop the proposition, which he had advanced when he was Deputy Minister of Labour, that there are actually four parties to Industry—Labour, Capital, Management and the Community.

"One of the aims of the book," he wrote, "is to show that the war, in the last analysis, is but the expression upon a world scale of conflicting forces at work in the relations of industry . . .

"Wherever in the affairs of the state one class has sought to maintain a monopoly of government, there, sooner or later, conflict has been inevitable. It will be the same in industry so long as reasons which are identical persist, and human nature does not change.

"In the struggle for a wider freedom mankind will not rest until in industry, as in the state, autocratic government, whatever its form, is superseded by a form of government representative of all the parties in interest, and, ultimately, by a system the cornerstone of which is responsible self-government.

When King wrote *Industry and Humanity* he did not know that one day he was to become leader of the Liberal

Party and, later, Prime Minister of Canada. The book has occasionally been a source of embarrassment to him because it has been held up to him as a blueprint of what he had promised to do for Canadians. Actually the book was not a promise to anyone, although it did contain his ideas of what reforms were overdue in respect to labour and social conditions generally.

That King was unable to carry out all the suggestions contained in his book goes without saying. It was a very comprehensive and ambitious programme of what he hoped might some day be achieved. That he was able to see implemented even some of its main proposals must have afforded him considerable satisfaction.

Although the book was sometimes cast up to him as an example of unfulfilled aims and aspirations, often the shoe was on the other foot and King was able to quote his work to the discomfiture of his critics.

Once, in the House, when a member had been lecturing the government long and tediously on the question of social reform, King grew bored and then amused in turn.

"I put all that in a book once," he advised the garrulous member, at last, with a grin.

Charges were made in the House, shortly after King's return to political life, that during the war he should have spent less time in the States and more in Canada, or that he should have shouldered a gun.

These charges cut King to the quick and he never forgot them or quite forgave those who brought them forward or seized upon them for political purposes.

Part and parcel of the charge was that King had gone over to the "big monied interests", that he had deserted Canada in her hour of need in search of the Standard Oil millions. This, of course, was a palpable untruth. King turned down more than one lucrative offer when he was Deputy Minister of Labour making only $2,500 a year. One offer came from a group of Canadian industrialists who promised him $8,000 a year to act on their behalf in the field of labour relations. King refused it without even consulting his chief, asserting that he preferred the $2,500 a year he was receiving from the Department of Labour because he could be independent of one side or the other. He was not willing to be associated exclusively either with Labour or with business. He believed he could be most useful as conciliator and intermediary.

The Rockefeller Foundation, it should be remembered, was an institution which had as its goal the betterment of humanity, and any results of King's studies as Director of Industrial Research were made freely available to the public. Far from working for the big vested interests, King was making a valuable contribution in the field of public service.

Undoubtedly, as is generally admitted, King's efforts in settling many wartime labour disputes in the United States contributed to the increased production of war supplies, and to victory.

King could have carried a gun, but it would have been a woeful waste of manpower.

The actual writing of *Industry and Humanty* consumed the best part of a year. King and McGregor worked side by side at the Roxborough, King drafting out his chapters in longhand, McGregor typing and retyping them until King was satisfied with the results. It was a case of revise, revise, revise! After King had written a chapter he would settle down by himself and study it word by word, while at the same time McGregor, in his own room, would also hunt for flaws. Then they would meet again, discuss the chapter's merits and demerits. King was unhappy if even a comma was out of place and sometimes spent many minutes pondering over the placing of a period or a semi-colon.

Finally, King came to McGregor one afternoon with the last long paragraph of the book in his hands. "McGregor," he said, proudly, "you won't be able to find anything wrong with this." McGregor read it over carefully. At first sight it appeared to be without imperfection. Then he looked again.

"Sorry, sir," he said, half-apologetically, "but I'm afraid you've got a dangling participle here."

"A dangling participle!" exclaimed King. "For goodness sake, whatever is that? I never heard of one."

THE LEADERSHIP

WHEN MEMBERS OF the Liberal Party gathered in Ottawa in August, 1919, to choose a successor to Sir Wilfrid Laurier, who had passed away in February of that year, the people of Canada were giving their attention to such residual war problems as the rehabilitation of veterans, the high cost of living, the Bolshevist menace, a growing labour unrest which had made itself felt throughout the world, the future of the League of Nations, and what to do about prohibition which, in half a dozen different forms, was being tried out by the various provinces.

It was a time, however, of general prosperity and expansion. Those who had profited from the war—and there were many such—were spending their money freely, secure in the belief that there was plenty more where it had come from. Shiny new automobiles, expensive radios, trips to Florida and California were the order of the day.

Sir Vincent Meredith, president of the Bank of Montreal, in his usual address to the shareholders on December 1, 1919, gave an excellent description of the period when he said: "The deprivations of the past five years have induced an orgy of self-indulgent expenditure by the general public, to which has been added lavish outlays by many people who amassed fortunes during the war."

As to labour troubles, the organization of the One Big Union which was to have its repercussions in the famous Winnipeg Strike of May, 1919, a series of sympathetic strikes throughout the Dominion, a sedition trial, the arrest and conviction of J. S. Woodsworth and other labour leaders, and a general wave of labour unrest from Halifax to Vancouver, gave the more thoughtfully-inclined individual ample cause for concern.

"Though marked by a high degree of prosperity," said Sir Vincent, "the year has also been one of world-wide labour unrest, with demands for increased wages and shorter working hours, culminating in strikes and disorders, with resultant decreased efficiency, lessened production and greater cost of output.

"This unrest may be in a measure attributable to unsatisfactory pre-war conditions, but probably in a greater degree is the result of unsettlement due to the abnormal nervous strain of the Great War."

For the most part Canadians were being carried along on the crest of the post-war boom. They were still paying 75 cents a pound for butter and $80 for a ready-made suit. But in the main they were happy and contented with their lot.

Young people were beginning to carry hip flasks, were singing *Swing Me in the Moonlight, If You Were the Only Girl In the World,* and *How Are You Going to Keep Them Down On the Farm After They've Seen Paree.* Rudolph Valentino, Wallie Reid, Pauline Frederick and Mary Pickford were still making cinema history, while returned soldiers, in nostalgic mood, were packing theatres across the country to witness revivals of *Chu Chin Chow* and *The Maid of the Mountains,* the wartime musicals they had flocked to in London while on leave. Morley Plunket, with his all-Canadian *Dumbells* was touring Canada and playing to jam-packed houses.

By the end of June, 1919, the majority of Canada's

armed forces were back home, there having been a steady repatriation of about 3,400 a month since the end of the war. All in all, there was no reason to suppose that Canada was not facing a prolonged period of unprecedented expansion and prosperity.

These, in brief, were the economic and social conditions which obtained in Canada at the time of the Liberal convention. To the good times that the people were enjoying was added the deep sense of liberation from the stress and strain of war and this feeling made itself apparent during the convention. Spirits were high, and hospitality generous and unrestrained.

The convention had been called for three specific purposes: (1) to draft, discuss, and adopt the platform of the Liberal party; (2) to deal with the question of party organization; (3) to select a leader in succession to Sir Wilfrid Laurier.

But it was the selection of a leader which seemed the most important matter to the rank and file of the party, and prior to the convention it was naturally the chief topic of discussion. Should he be French-speaking or English-speaking? Should he be an elderly, experienced statesman, or should he be young, active, with fresh ideas and a new approach to old problems? Should he be from the West or from the East?

As the opening date of the convention drew near it was apparent that there would be a number of candidates for the leadership. Hon. D. D. McKenzie, a former member of the judiciary and a well-known Nova Scotia lawyer who had been chosen House leader following the death of Sir Wilfrid, was, of course, considered to have an excellent chance owing to the fact that he was the man on the job. Other possible candidates were: Hon. W. S. Fielding,

Premier of Nova Scotia for 12 years and Minister of Finance for some 15 years; Hon. George P. Graham, who for some time, had led the Ontario opposition and who had been a member of the Dominion government in 1907-11; Hon. William Martin, a member of the House of Commons for eight years and Premier of Saskatchewan since 1916; Hon. Sydney Fisher, a staunch Laurier Liberal; and W. L. Mackenzie King.

Most of the speculation centred around McKenzie, Fielding and Graham. McKenzie, it was said, had come to the point where he thought well of himself and his performance. He was ready to serve, even if this meant personal sacrifice.

As for Fielding, he was a man of outstanding ability who enjoyed the general respect of the party. However, the loyalty of some of his friends had been somewhat shaken by the fact that he had parted with Laurier on the conscription issue.

George Graham was an able, jovial and friendly man, but he was suspected of having been friendly towards the idea of union government. One of the factors which from the first militated against his chances of success was the circulation of a report that he was being sponsored by Sir Clifford Sifton, one of the architects of union government. The report enraged Graham, but there was little he could do about it. Denial seemed to lend support to the possible truth of the story.

In view of the result of the convention, the pre-convention comments of the press are of particular interest. They indicate, on the whole, some inability on the part of observers close to the scene to forecast with any great degree of accuracy the final result.

"It cannot be said," wrote Charles Bishop in the Ottawa

Citizen, some three days prior to the opening of the convention, "that Mackenzie King is pressing himself forward; but some are doing it for him a bit. When Sir Wilfrid died he was prominently mentioned to succeed him, but the boom faded later on, particularly when King went to England to pursue problems of industrial research. His great ability is conceded. One recognition of it is his employment by the Rockefeller Foundation. He has been the subject of vicious onslaught in certain papers because his war work was not in the trenches. It is not known that Mr. King wants the job. Probably no one wants it unless there is unanimity."

On August 5, the day the convention opened, there was a flurry of interest in the possibility that Hon. William Martin might win the backing of important groups in the party. Fielding's stock had declined, while Graham's had gone up. It was conceded that Mackenzie King was still in the race!

In the spring of 1919 King was in England pursuing his sociological studies. Whether the matter of the Liberal convention was to the forefront of his thoughts at that time it is difficult to say. Certainly he had given no promise to any of his political friends to stand for the nomination. Instead he was possibly seriously considering two very flattering offers of employment which had come from the United States. One held out the inducement of an important post with a large philanthropic organization, while the other came from an industrial corporation which was ready to employ King as an industrial adviser at a handsome salary.

Apparently King decided to reject both these offers in favour of remaining in his own country. At any rate, he made last-minute plans to sail for Canada.

As it was, he very nearly missed being present at the convention. McGregor had booked a passage on a boat which would get them to Canada in good time for the convention, but a seamen's strike broke out and all reservations were cancelled.

King told McGregor not to bother booking another passage, that they had plenty of time to make the trip, that the strike would be over in a few days and that they would be able to sail as scheduled. But McGregor went ahead on his own and made arrangements to sail on another ship. They arrived just in time to attend the convention. The first boat did eventually sail, but had King waited for it he would not have reached Canada in time.

When King got to Ottawa there was little to indicate how the convention would go. The fact that King had been considered by most people as the heir-apparent to the great Liberal chieftain was certainly a point in his favour. Efforts were made to offset this by the circulation of a report a day or two before the convention that Laurier, before his death, had expressed the opinion that the Hon. W. S. Fielding would be the best choice as successor to himself.

This was a piece of pure fiction. Laurier's wishes in respect to a successor were well known by all within the intimate circles of the party. He had wanted King to succeed him, and to this day King believes that the desire of the delegates to follow out their chief's wishes was the deciding factor in his election.

The day before the big convention the news of the meeting at Howick Hall was competing with headlines announcing that the Prince of Wales had sailed for Canada aboard H.M.S. *Renown,* that the British labour situation was again serious, and that Canadian dairymen were seeking government assistance in selling their cheese to Britain at 25 cents a pound.

Speculation as to the outcome of the leadership race had now reached a new high level of intensity Some thought that Fielding, Graham and King would likely be in close running, if Premier Martin was not a candidate. The order of precedence is interesting in view of subsequent events. It was believed that the Ontario vote would be divided between Graham and King. It was admitted that Graham was stronger in Ontario but that King would make up for this support from Quebec. Graham's boom was creating the most noise and had the support of the most systematic organization.

When the opening day of the convention arrived and Liberal speakers began to outline the new planks of the Liberal platform, interest reached a high pitch. Keynote speeches by Liberal bigwigs pledged the party to lighten the cost of living. Imperial Federation was opposed as a danger to Canada. The party was enthusiastically described as a bulwark against Bolshevism.

It was not until King had had the opportunity of addressing the convention on the evening of the sixth that his stock soared. When he appeared on the platform to speak the tumultuous reception he received far exceeded in enthusiasm the receptions which had been accorded the other candidates. Not less impressive was the round of applause that followed his address to the resolution on the principles embodied in the covenant of the League of Nations respecting labour. Observers, suggesting that the reception might have been staged and that all who cheered for King might not vote for him, nevertheless had to admit that he looked like a winner.

In his address King paid tribute to the memory of his

late chief. It was a fine bit of oratory and it went well with the old Laurier Liberals. But equally impressive was that part of his speech in which he dealth with the principles of labour relations to which he had already given expression in *Industry and Humanty.*

"The resolution," he declared, "is based on the assumption that human personality is more important than any consideration of property. It is founded on the belief that ethical and human considerations ought to stand above considerations which are purely business or national. It is an expression of the belief that industry exists for the sake of humanity, not humanity for the sake of industry."

Government in industry, he asserted, should be shared by the four parties: Labour, Capital, Management and the Community.

It was a good speech, and it was a long one, setting the pattern for a good many King speeches that were to be delivered over the years. Even then King's style was somewhat involved and extended. He has never been able to make a good short speech, except on those few unexpected occasions when he has been angry or has had his back up against the wall. Usually, like a freight train, he took a little time to get under way.

At all events, he considerably exceeded his time that evening back in 1919. And, of course, they couldn't stop him, even had they wanted to, because he had left his tribute to the great Laurier to the end.

Voting took place on the afternoon of the seventh, a total of five names having been placed in nomination. They were: King, McKenzie, Graham, Fielding, and Alexander Smith, of Ottawa, the latter a prominent Liberal organizer and party stalwart whose nomination was purely complimentary.

83

The result of the first ballot gave King a substantial lead. He received a total of 344 votes out of the 949 cast. Fielding received 297 and Graham and McKenzie 153 each. There were two spoiled ballots. Under the rules governing the convention the balloting was to continue until a candidate received a majority of the total ballots cast. When the second ballot was counted it was found that King had received 411 votes, Fielding 344, Graham, 124, and McKenzie 60.

Graham then announced that he was retiring in order to expedite proceedings and shortly afterwards McKenzie also retired. This left the field to King and Fielding. When the third ballot was counted it was found that King had received 476 votes and Fielding 438. It was close enough, but without hesitation Fielding moved that the convention unanimously confirm the nomination.

Those near King when the ballots were being counted said that he didn't seem at all anxious as to the outcome. When the scrutineers passed by on their way to the platform to announce the final result one of them leaned over as he passed King and in a stage-whisper announced: "You're it!" King didn't register any more emotion than if someone had remarked it was a fine day. He admitted later, however, that he had been excited enough.

As Fielding put it in his congratulatory speech, "to win was a triumph of which any man might be proud." King, in his forty-fifth year, had been chosen to succeed one of Canada's greatest statesmen. True, he found himself in opposition, but perhaps this fact served only to whet his appetite for action. There was much to be done.

It was characteristic of King that he could not let this moment of triumph pass without a sentimental reference to the memory of the man who had been as a guiding star

KING WHEN CHOSEN LEADER

"Never before had one so young been chosen
to direct the destiny of the Liberal Party."

to him throughout the years, William Lyon Mackenzie. Referring to Sir Allen Aylesworth, who had nominated him for the leadership, King recalled that Sir Allen, when in Sir Wilfrid's cabinet, had been a member for North York. Before that Sir William Mulock had represented the constituency.

"The Liberals of North York who honoured these men," said King, "did me the honour of tendering me their nomination at the last election. There we fought together the same old battles for the control of parliament by the people, and of the executive by parliament, which our forefathers had fought years ago, and which helped to establish the foundation of the Liberal party in this country.

"I can never forget—and I hope you will permit me to mention it on this occasion—that my grandfather on four or five different occasions, was chosen as their representative by the electors of North York in the days of the early struggles for responsible government in Canada, when he, in Ontario, and Papineau, in Lower Canada, were seeking to bring about that change in the relations of the executive to parliament which would subject the executive to the will of the people as expressed through their representatives.

"Ladies and gentlemen, I hope that in making mention of these things, which are part of the traditions of our party, and also a part of the history of this country, I utter words that are prophetic of that greater unity which is to prevail between the sister provinces of Quebec and Ontario—indeed, between all the provinces of this Dominion."

When, on the following morning, the newspapers carried the streamer: "Hon. W. L. Mackenzie King Chosen Liberal Leader," a new era in the history of the party had begun.

Of his own lack of parliamentary experience and training in public life, King was aware. "I should despair altogether of being able even to attempt to discharge its obligations," said King, in thanking the convention, "were it not that I know that one who is called upon to accept the office of leadership must first and foremost be the willing servant of all, and that in seeking in the spirit of service to meet the wishes of those who have chosen him as their leader, he may look for guidance and counsel to the great forces assembled about him."

Never before had one so young been chosen to direct the destiny of the Liberal party in Canada. Sir Wilfrid Laurier had been 52 when he had been selected for the same position in 1893. If King was young, however, he was able.

On one occasion Laurier had said: "Young Mr. King has the best brains in the country."

Apparently the delegates who attended the convention thought so too.

VIII

BACK IN HARNESS

Soon after King re-entered parliament as leader of the Liberal party he found the government forces led by the man whom he had often opposed in university debates: his old rival, Arthur Meighen.

Meighen and King had crossed swords in parliament before, of course, because Meighen had been first elected to the house in 1908, the same year that King made his parliamentary debut. But, unlike King, Meighen had been re-elected in 1911, and again in 1913 and 1917. While King had been out of the House pursuing his investigations into social and labour conditions, Meighen had been rolling up a great back-log of valuable parliamentary and administrative experience, first as Solicitor General in 1913 and, later, in 1917, as Secretary of State and Minister of Mines. Still later, the same year, he had been sworn in as Minister of the Interior and Superintendent General of Indian Affairs, and in 1918 he had proceeded to Britain with Sir Robert Borden to attend the Imperial Conference.

Thus, by the time King got his feet solidly set once more on the floor of the Green Chamber he found himself facing a government leader who already had enjoyed some 12 years' experience as parliamentarian, who had achieved distinction as a first-rate fighting man, and whose parliamentary equipment included a prodigious industry, unquestioned ability as a legislator and debater, and physical and intellectual courage of a high order.

Even the traditionally Liberal Winnipeg *Free Press* paid

high tribute to Meighen's qualifications upon his ascension to the leadership. "Since the passing of Sir Wilfrid Laurier," commented that newspaper, "he has been easily the first figure in the chamber as a master of the parliamentary arts; and these qualities of readiness, combativeness and all-round capacity have bred faith."

Indeed, Meighen had won his spurs, had proved an able debater and an adroit parliamentarian. He had given leadership in many important debates and had handled such contentious questions as the Naval Bill, the tariff and the railway problems with extreme tact and good judgment. The Military Service Act, the Land Settlement Act, and the Wartime Elections Act had all afforded him an excellent opportunity to display his wares and demonstrate his genius for handling complicated and involved technical debates.

Meighen was then only 44, the youngest man to hold the position of Prime Minister since Confederation. He was in his prime, and he was already a veteran parliamentarian. King, on the other hand, with but a few short years in the House, found himself somewhat at a disadvantage in this respect. But he brought with him a dogged determination to succeed, the ability to think coolly and methodically, and a passion for study and research which was to confound many an opponent in the future. His vast experience in labour matters was to prove invaluable to him.

It was a time when labour problems were coming increasingly to the fore, and King, with his natural gift for compromise and conciliation, was probably, in all Canada, the man best equipped to cope with them. In addition, he was ambitious, full of physical and mental drive, and eager to come to grips with the enemy. It was not going to be all clear sailing, however.

Following his election as leader, King declined an invitation to run in Stormont-Glengarry, against a Farmers' candidate, and then accepted the Liberal nomination in Prince County, P.E.I., where he was given an acclamation. In the meanwhile he had accepted a nomination to contest North York in the next federal elections.

The wartime coalition was dissolving when King took over the Liberal leadership and the first task which faced him was the reorganizing of the party, which had been split asunder on the conscription issue. While it is true that the premiers of eight out of nine provinces were present, the 1919 Liberal convention had been ignored by a good many old-line Liberals who had entered the Union government in the belief that they were taking the only proper course in respect to the successful prosecution of the war. By the dyed-in-the-wool "Laurier" or "Anti-Conscription" Liberals these Unionists were regarded as having been guilty of an abandonment of true Liberal principles, and they had been denounced as apostates to the cause.

In turn, these Unionist Liberals charged that the 1919 convention had been dominated by the anti-conscriptionists of the party. Whatever the basis for these charges and counter-charges, there seems little doubt that the convention had been controlled by a substantial majority of the party, and whether they were "Laurier" Liberals, "Anti-Conscriptionists", or just plain "Liberals" with a capital L matters but little. Whatever they were, they were ready to welcome back those members of the party who had sat in the Unionist government throughout the war, and who were still, in many instances, wavering between loyalty to the party of their fathers and this new Unionist coalition which had proved so effective during the war.

In the words of Hon. D. D. McKenzie, in his address to

the convention, there was "a light in the window" which it was hoped would guide the return of those who had wandered.

Scarcely had the echoes of the convention died away before King was barn-storming up and down the country making the most conciliatory gestures to these "black sheep" who had strayed from the fold. The door was wide open for their return, he declared, the welcome mat was out and the fatted calf was being prepared. No embarrassing questions would be asked.

"Are we to believe," said King, "that these men and women of Liberal convictions numbering themselves by thousands, were not honest, were not conscientious, were not patriotic in the votes they cast, in the light of the knowledge they had at the time, and the circumstances as represented to them?"

Having been "good" Liberals once, one gathered, they could be "good" Liberals again.

As for King and his supporters, King indicated that they were ready to be magnanimous. "The Liberals who stood with Sir Wilfrid in 1917," declared King, "if they are to be true to the first principles of Liberalism, must be as ready to accord sincerity of purpose to those who differed from them as they are to demand like attitude towards themselves."

Holding out the olive branch to agrarian movements, King argued that these were the results of Liberal thought and feeling. However, he warned farmers, war veterans, and labour that political movements founded on class antagonisms and class struggles could only result in confusion and retrogression. On the other hand, within the fold of the Liberal Party, all could find the fulfilment of their desires.

His direct appeal was for the return of the old two-party

system of government as opposed to union government and a coalition system which, to use his own words, led only to "compromise, subterfuge and inaction."

Only through the existence of permanent parties could stable government be provided, he argued. He was unalterably opposed to government control by railway, manufacturing, or financial interests. No less was he opposed to monopoly of control by an essential element of the national economy, whether it was representative of farmers, labour, war veterans or the newly-enfranchised female voters.

The year 1921 was a momentous and inspiring one for King. It provided him with his first real opportunity to tour the Dominion from coast to coast, and to come into personal touch with the people. He addressed scores of meetings, speaking to hundreds of thousands of Canadians, and wherever he went he hunted out and attacked the enemy with much vigour and vehemence. The government, he charged, was a group of autocrats who wanted to usurp the powers and the privileges of the people. He spoke of an "invisible government" composed of the great financial interests of the country, which, he alleged, had placed Meighen in power and had enabled him to "usurp" the powers of the government, and to "defy the people in their just rights of political control of their own affairs."

"They constitute the real government in this country today," he asserted, "the invisible government of the big interests of which Mr. Meighen and his cabinet are but the visible embodiment."

The war, he said, had made the rich richer and the poor poorer. He advocated "not free, but freer trade," taxation of profits and luxuries, a union of "all progressive forces" under the banner of Liberalism to save the people from their "all-powerful enemy," the government.

And wherever he went he demanded a general election

on the ground that the government had no mandate from the people, that it was a war government and had not been voted into power to deal with post-war problems.

In December, 1921, following the election, King found himself heading the largest group in the House. A total of 117 Liberals had been elected as against only 50 Conservatives and 64 Progressives. In addition, three Labour members and one Independent had been successful at the polls.

King, although heading the largest numerical group, found himself with an actual minority. It was clearly a case of wooing the support of the Progressives. If the balance of power was in the hands of the Progressives it certainly operated in King's favour as he was able to remain in control of the House for the best part of a decade. The interruption which occurred in 1926, when Meighen and his shadow governmenut were in power for a short period, merely served to provide King with the authoritative mandate which he had lacked in 1921.

The results of the 1921 election elated King. He had been chosen leader of the party only two years before. Now he was Prime Minister. He had, indeed, good reason to feel satisfied with his progress to date.

The Conservatives were surprised at the turn of events. They had expected to win. One in particular, John Bayne, the party's director of publicity, had been so sure that the election was "in the bag" that he had personally wagered Mr. King $1,000 that the Liberals would be defeated. This was too much for King, canny Scot though he was. He accepted the wager. When the votes were counted John Bayne sat down and wrote King his personal check for $1,000. Perhaps King was flushed with victory, perhaps he felt that it was beneath the dignity of the Prime Minister to indulge in any form of gambling. With a fine gesture of magnanimity which probably had much the same effect on Mr. Bayne's sensibilities as rubbing salt into a wound, King returned the check uncashed, with the proviso that he would cancel the debt if Mr. Bayne contributed a stipulated and substantial part of the $1000 to a local charity. Mr. Bayne accepted the suggestion.

No sooner had King been sworn in as Prime Minister than he began to be importuned by party hangers-on. He was still living in his apartment at the Roxborough and this address soon became the target for an unending procession of callers. Many of them, it is true, were Liberals who had valid reasons for calling upon King, but too many of them were persons who were merely seeking to serve their own selfish interests and who thought that in the excitement of the moment they might be able to influence King on their own behalf. In fact, a good many Liberals who had actually worked against King at the 1919 convention were now attempting to ride the band-wagon.

King stood this for a time, then he realized that it would be best to lighten the load before the wheels became inextricably mired in the mud. He decided that if he could not rid himself of those who sought to direct his actions he could at least preserve an effective inaccessibility, see and talk with only those in whom he could safely confide. The news went out that young Mr. King was seeing no one who had not been sent for.

No longer was the door of his apartment ajar to callers; no longer was the telephone at the Roxborough answered. If King wanted to see some one he sent McGregor out to fetch him. As a result McGregor's movements were carefully watched by those who had reasons for wanting to know what King was up to.

Actually, King needed a breathing space in which to put his house in order. He found himself, a young man, comparatively inexperienced in the intricacies of political techniques, embarrassed at times by the superior attitude of the much older senior members of the party, and yet, withal, in the seat of responsibility. He realized that while it would be wise to listen to men like Fielding and Graham whom he had been forced to take into his cabinet because of the support they commanded in the ranks of the party, he must not, at the same time, delegate his powers to such advisers but make his own decisions and, in the final analysis, accept the full burden of responsibility that he had knowingly shouldered. He realized too, that when it came to all major decisions, state and not personal considerations must prevail. As desirous as the next person of having friends, he knew that in politics friendships can sometimes prove not only embarrassing, but often fatal obstacles to the attainment of one's objectives.

"I've always found that you can control people better if you don't see too much of them," he once told a political colleague whom he thought was seeing too many Liberal supporters.

Cavalier as such an attitude of mind might at first appear, King decided that he must stand solitary and alone because he dare not do otherwise.

There were a few in whom he had the utmost confidence, including Sir Allen Aylesworth, who had moved his nomination at the convention, Senator Haydon, Dr. Oscar Skelton and, of course, Ernest Lapointe. Senator Raoul Dandurand, whom King appointed Minister of State in 1921, was also an anchor to windward. These, and a few others, King gathered into the fold. But to the rank and file the door was closed.

Thus, with a few notable exceptions, King maintained a certain intangible but effective distance between himself and those who were about him. He discovered that this formula worked exceeding well. True, the legend of his unapproachability, of his coldness, of his emotional aloofness, soon took root and flourished, and it was a legend that did not win friends.

This official privacy which King insisted upon was only exceeded in degree by the privacy he maintained in respect to his personal life. It was traditional that no one but King's personal friends ever called at his home unless invited, or unless they were paying their formal respects on some special occasion such as King's birthday.

In 1921 Lady Laurier died. She willed Laurier House to King.

Possession of this fine old home meant much to the young Liberal leader. He was, essentially, a deeply domesticated person and the prospect of having a comfortable home in which he could entertain his friends and acquaintances, in which he could keep his books and paintings, and to which he could attach himself with some degree of permanence appealed to the conservative side of his nature.

The contents of the house had been left to Lady Laurier's nephews and nieces and thus, when King took over, the place was unfurnished. Not much had been done to it for some years and it was badly in need of renovation. King did not have the money to cover the cost of the work but, fortunately, among his political friends there were those who did. Hon. Peter Larkin, who had built up a substantial fortune in tea, and a number of other prominent Liberals, came to King's assistance. The house was completely renovated and redecorated. Finally, it was appropriately furnished and the receipted bills were handed to King.

King never ceased to express his gratitude for this kindness. Had it not been for his friends it is probable that he would have been unable to occupy the house.

On April 26, 1922 King held his first big party at Laurier House. It was for his parliamentary colleagues. It was a formal occasion to the majority of those who attended, but to the young Prime Minister it was something else, too. It was his first "house warming." He felt that he had really arrived.

IX
IN MEMORIAM

It SEEMED THAT some perverse and malevolent fate was forever catching up with King in the moments of his greatest triumph. He had barely been appointed Deputy Minister of Labour and had begun to get the work of his department organized, when he had lost his beloved friend and departmental associate, Harper. Later, following his experiences as a labour conciliator in the United States and just before the results of his years of work had been given concrete form in *Industry and Humanity* he had lost both parents, and a beloved sister.

Now, in 1922, following his election as leader of the Liberal party and his subsequent ascension to the Prime Ministership, he was to lose his only brother, Macdougall.

Macdougall, whose long illness had been the direct result of hardships he had undergone while serving with the Canadian Medical Corps in the South African War, had waged a brave fight against tuberculosis. When he abandoned his practice in Ottawa and moved to Denver it looked as if the change in climate might result in his eventual return to health. Indeed his health did improve for some time and he managed to find the strength to write two books: *The Battle with Tuberculosis and How to Win It,* and *Nerves and Personal Power.*

In his first book Macdougall attempted to pass on to others afflicted like himself the benefit of his experience in fighting tuberculosis. He particularly had in mind veterans of the South African War by whose side he had served, who had suffered privations similar to his own. For a time it seemed as if he had won his fight; but then he suffered another illness. This time muscular atrophy developed. After a losing battle of another year he eventually succumbed.

King and his brother had always been very close to each other, and as the family circle narrowed this affection became even more pronounced. King visited Macdougall frequently, and every week, without fail, he wrote him a long, newsy letter filled with cheerful chat calculated to bring Macdougall out of himself and help him forget his troubles. He would recall their days together at "Woodside", the year when Macdougall had starred with the University of Toronto Dominion football championship team, and he would give his brother news of his own activities.

Because King had already published two books of his own he was aware of some of the pitfalls into which a writer can slip and he did his utmost to assist his brother in the preparation of his two manuscripts. He spent long hours revising Macdougall's work, making suggestions which he believed would result in improvements. He, himself, had become deeply interested in the writings of Louis Pasteur and he felt that his brother was making a not unimportant contribution to the history of medicine.

As a matter of fact, it was through his brother that King developed such an intense interest in the life and work of Pasteur. Pasteur's philosophy formed the basis of much of King's thinking in *Industry and Humanity* and, indeed, he prefaced the book with a quotation from Pasteur: "Science will have tried, by obeying the law of Humanity, to extend the frontiers of life!"

When King received the news of his brother's death he

immediately left for Denver to accompany the body back to Canada and to make arrangements for the care of Macdougall's widow and twin sons. He was accompanied on the trip by W. H. Measures, who had recently been appointed to his staff.

King was deeply affected by his brother's death and although he took some routine work along with him to put in the time he failed to get much accomplished. It was late in March, and as the train sped over the dreary landscape King became more depressed and introspective. One afternoon he surprised Measures by suddenly beginning to recite Tennyson's *In Memoriam*. From this he went on to *Locksley Hall* and *Mort D'Arthur*. King had always been a lover of Tennyson and on this occasion the poet's words seemed to provide a suitable outlet for his mood. For Measures, too, it was a somewhat doleful journey. He never forgot the incident for it disclosed to him an unexpectedly human side of King's nature.

Macdougall had not lived to see his second book, *Nerves and Personal Power,* published. It went to the printers some little time after his death and King wrote an introduction to it in which he referred to the extremely difficult circumstances under which it had been written.

"Apart from the scientific value of the treatise," said King, "to know of the suffering which inspired its conception and the fortitude which made possible its publication, is to glimpse something of those higher levels of human greatness to which men and women are capable of rising in adversity, and which uplift all who pause to dwell upon the secret of spiritual attainment in human lives."

Macdougall was buried in the family plot in Mount Pleasant Cemetery, in Toronto. Recalling his brother's tremendous admiration for Louis Pasteur, and seeing in

Macdougall's life the same devotion to science and medicine which typified the career of the great French scientist, King had a special stone prepared to mark his brother's grave. It is an exact replica of the slab which lies over Pasteur's grave in Paris.

X

THE JOB BEGINS

WHEN KING BECAME Prime Minister in 1921 the period of prosperity which had followed the war had already begun to wane and a definite recession appeared to be settling in. The boom had lost its momentum in the middle of 1920, business had begun to slip, dragging down prices, and Canadian farmers were looking gloomily to the future. There was some unemployment. It looked as if the next few years would be difficult and uncertain ones.

However, to the south, the people of the United States, despite the collapse of business, were hopefully looking towards President Harding's new administration to bring that nation out of its depression and this feeling of optimism was reflected throughout the Dominion. Everywhere people were doing their utmost to relieve their minds of the tension and excitement which had carried over from the war years. President Harding, who had been sworn in on March 4, had promised the people a "reign of normalcy" and business was looking forward to a revitalizing freedom from governmental control and interference. The Red Scare was taking up less and less space in the newspapers, the Dempsey-Carpentier fight was scheduled for the following summer, radio broadcasting had been inaugurated, the flapper and prohibition were still subjects which were receiving attention from the press and the pulpit. All was not shadow, then, and if times were not so good as they had been they were at least interesting and lively.

In Canada the country was still saddled with substantial

debt accruing from the war years. Increased taxation by the Union Government and by Mr. Meighen's Conservative administration had failed to provide the money to meet expenditures and serious deficits had resulted. King moved cautiously at first in respect to any reduction of tariff rates, concentrating on a programme of curtailment of public expenditures in an attempt to balance the budget, plus an effort to increase exports.

By the end of 1922 production had greatly increased, Canadian credit was higher than it had been for some years, the Canadian dollar gained in purchasing power in almost all markets of the world and there was a gain of 23 per cent in exports for the first eight months of the year as compared with the corresponding period in 1921. On the other hand imports increased by only one per cent over the corresponding figure for 1921. Domestic trade was less encouraging, however, and commercial failures were still on the increase. But there were signs of more employment and better days in the varied trade activities. The depression was felt most keenly in the farming communities, the unsettled European situation being the most unfavourable factor in the marketing of agricultural products.

Soon after forming his government, King announced his policy in respect to the Canadian National Railways.

"We intend," he declared, "to give government ownership of the national system . . . the fairest treatment and under the most favourable conditions it is possible for a government to secure. So far as it is possible for the government to demonstrate what can be done under government ownership, it is our intention to see that it is done." Administration of the railways, he promised, would be freed from all political influence. It was not long before the Canadian National, which had been running regular deficits, began to show a profit. The road was extended and improved.

As to state intervention generally, however, King expressed the view that Canadians should stand on their own feet and not look towards the government for a solution to all their problems. "The tendency is becoming too general," he told a gathering in Toronto, "to look to the state to do things which individuals should do for themselves."

When he visited his home town, which during the war had been re-named Kitchener, King took the opportunity to deliver a sermon directed towards the flask-carrying, jazz-happy young men and women of the country who, while in a minority, gave a certain tinge of irresponsibility and abandon to the adolescent population as a whole.

"It is not the girls who drink cocktails and smoke cigarettes and spend their evenings between movies and the dance halls, any more than it is the women who spend their afternoons at bridge who make the mothers of men who rise up and call them blessed," sermonized the Prime Minister. "It is not the men who are striving to subvert old established customs and institutions, to break with traditions and provide a rule of anarchy, that are making either our country or the world a better place in which to live . . . We must return to the quiet and more refined modes of living if we are to ensure our nation's future along the paths of happiness and peace."

Mr. King's indictment of Canadian youth was to result in a good many indignant protests from women's and young people's organizations from one side of the Dominion to the other. His condemnation of subversive activities, however, evoked little criticism.

Throughout most of 1923 King and his administration

had had to face a fair amount of criticism from the opposition and the Tory press. The Montreal *Star* had been particularly active in this respect and in a series of editorials under the caption, "The Whisper of Death," the *Star* had belaboured the Prime Minister and his government with considerable zest. On September 21, speaking at Quebec on the eve of his departure for Britain, to attend the Imperial Conference, King answered his critics by announcing that Canada's revenues and expenditures would be made to balance at the end of the year, for the first time since 1913. During 1923-24 the budget was indeed balanced, and this successful operation was followed by a reduction in tariff rates on the implements of production in the basic industries of agriculture, mining and lumbering. A number of special war and post-war taxes were also removed or substantially reduced.

Canadians were eager to see how Mr. King would conduct himself at the Imperial Conference. He had already established the reputation for independence and far-sightedness in the handling of Canada's international affairs and this had won him not only the admiration of his followers at home but the respect of British statesmen and other Commonwealth leaders.

It had been during his first year as Prime Minister that the crisis with Turkey had arisen and King had established the principle of Canadian autonomy in international affairs by refusing to be stampeded into supporting some members of the British cabinet in their intention to "resist" Turkish aggression in Europe.

In effect, what had happened on that occasion was that King had told Mr. Lloyd George that Canada would not consent to the sending of a contingent to fight the Turks without authority from parliament and that he wanted to know the facts before deciding whether or not it would be necessary to call a special session of parliament.

His firm stand had taken much of the wind out of the sails of Mr. Lloyd George and the cabinet ministers who had supported him, and the announcement of Canada's attitude towards the suggested military operations had the net effect of discouraging precipitate action which might have resulted in war.

As King stepped aboard his boat at Quebec on September 22 he told reporters that it was his privilege to go to the Imperial Conference "in the name of the people of Canada, without a single grievance, and to say that our relations with Britain and all parts of the Empire are of the best."

This was not to say that Canada had no problems to bring before the conference. Already, over the objections of the British government, the Dominion had actually established her right of full powers of negotiation in international affairs. She assumed this right when she signed a treaty with the United States in respect to the Pacific fisheries. This was the first treaty signed by Canada alone and with full powers from His Majesty the King. The precedent was to result in Canada now pressing the matter of the principle of independent status with increased vigour. Largely owing to the representations advanced by King and the Hon. Ernest Lapointe, Canada's right to negotiate treaties was now confirmed. The Dominion, which along with the other self-governing Commonwealth countries had been granted national status at the conference of Versailles, and upon whose behalf Britain herself had demanded separate representation to the League of Nations, now moved one more step along the road to complete and independent nationhood.

King returned home late in November satisfied that

Canada's position had been strengthened as a result of the conference. Certainly influences were now at work which were one day to result in significant changes in the Commonwealth structure. During his stay in Britain King received honorary degrees from Oxford and Edinburgh Universities and was given the freedom of the cities of London, Edinburgh and Sheffield.

By 1924 Canada was sharing in the general world improvement which had begun to evidence itself in an increased purchasing power on the part of those countries whose reservoirs of wealth had been drained off during the war, and a resumption of world trade on a more encouraging scale. Farm prices in Canada rose encouragingly and farmers were reported to be paying off mortgages, liquidating bank loans, and even adding materially to their bank accounts. The Canadian Merchants' Association, while admitting that conditions were improved, put this improvement down to the influence of better world conditions and continued to criticize the government's tariff policy, claiming that tariff reductions had already afforded "painful proof" of the imperfections of a low-tariff policy.

XI

THE STORM BREAKS

WHEN, AFTER THE general elections of 1925, King found himself in a position to lead the government once more, a good many sceptics shook their heads, convinced that he would be unable to carry on in the face of his greatly reduced following. King, himself, along with eight of his ministers, had lost their seats. The Conservatives had increased their membership from 50 to 116, while King's following had shrunk from 117 to 101. The Progressives upon whom King had relied for a measure of support and with whose assistance he had managed to remain in power since 1921, had now only 28 members as against some 68 in the previous House. Redistribution having gone into effect, the total membership of the House had been increased from 235 to 245.

Throughout the country the general feeling was one of dissatisfaction with the indecisiveness of the elections. A few newspapers, including the Ottawa *Citizen,* expressed the view that although Mr. Meighen had the largest single group in the House, Mr. King, with almost certain support from the Progressives, had just as much right to attempt to form a government as Mr. Meighen; but for the most part the press thought Mr. King should step aside.

"The hope of amalgamating the Liberals and Progresives and forming a coalition ministry, which the Progressives would control," said the Montreal *Gazette,* "is not open to Mr. King who has been left no right to seek to maintain his place as Premier, even if he has the desire . . .

The sooner Mr. King retires from a position he never was suited to fill the better will it be for what reputation he has left."

Said the Toronto *Telegram:* "Canadians went to the polls yesterday and submitted designs for a new National government for Canada, the design not to include Hon. W. L. Mackenzie King . . ."

And the Toronto *Globe:* "The people of Canada have rendered their electoral verdict. Its meaning is unmistakeable—a severe vote of want of confidence passed upon the administration. The Prime Minister and . . . his cabinet colleagues have gone down to defeat in their own constituencies. With almost ruthless thoroughness the citizens have set about making changes."

Still holding the balance of power, despite the reduction in their numbers, the Progressives remained King's one hope. They were still the arbiters of the situation and in a position to call the tune. Had the Progressives not been prepared to continue to support King, Meighen, with the largest group in the House, could have formed a government. But the policies of the Progressive party were more in line with Liberal than with Conservative thought, and the party pledged its continued support to King who thereupon refused to resign and clear the way for Meighen.

The House met in January, 1926, and then adjourned in March to enable King to find a seat. The members returned to parliament on March 15. Throughout the entire session the government was constantly being threatened with defeat, retaining the confidence of the House by only the slimmest of majorities. These were 3, 10, 10, 1, 7, 8, 11, 13, 6, 9, 13, 13, 15, 1, 6, 8.

The situation was a precarious one. King would be able to maintain control only so long as he could hold the

Progressives in tow. It was far from being a healthy state of affairs and in the end King was to capitulate as a result of the customs scandal disclosures, and tender his resignation following the Governor General's refusal to grant dissolution.

Had Meighen been wise he would have joined King in the latter's demand for dissolution. Instead, against his better judgment and upon the advice and insistence of some of his closest advisers, he clutched at the straw provided by King's resignation and accepted Byng's invitation to form a government. It was a forlorn hope. Had Meighen taken his chances with the electorate he could have capitalized on the government's vulnerable position in respect to the customs disclosures. Instead he sought to grasp power the easy way and went down before King's brilliant handling of the situation. King made the constitutional question which resulted from Byng's refusal to grant dissolution the major political issue of the day. The customs scandal was forgotten as King wrapped the Union Jack around himself and demanded that British constitutional practices be upheld and British justice done. The appeal won him the support of Western Ontario as well as that of other sections of the Dominion and resulted in his return to power with a substantially enhanced majority.

To view the events of 1926 in their proper perspective one must go back to 1925 when the situation which was to result in the customs disclosures was reaching a climactic stage.

The Volstead Law was still in effect in the United States, but there was no prohibition in the Province of Quebec, a circumstance which resulted in the rapid growth of an extensive smuggling trade which assumed very serious proportions. Rum-runners crossed the Quebec border into the United States in the dead of night, and sometimes even in broad daylight, their heavy trucks and lorries laden down with valuable shipments of liquor. Returning, they smuggled into Canada shipments of cigarettes, silks, radios, automobile parts and a wide variety of goods which, being thus freed of duty, were sold on the Canadian market to the detriment of legitimate Canadian manufacturers and dealers. Much stolen property from the United States was also disposed of in Canada through "fences" who operated on a large scale. It was the hey-day of the gangster, the rum-runner, the hi-jacker. The cooperative customs official was paid off in bills of large denomination. Laxity and dishonesty crept into the Department of Customs and Excise as examiners and other officials at important border points fell victim to the lure of easy money.

Canadian manufacturers, alarmed at the situation, pressed for a full investigation. They did much of the spade work themselves and then, on February 5, 1926, a special committee of the House was set up to inquire into the matter of smuggling. The committee made its report to the House some four months later and the conditions, as disclosed, were such as to give cause for alarm, not only to the public, but to the government.

In its report the committee recommended the dismissal of six customs officers whom it had found to be "delinquent in their duties", the retirement of R. R. Farrow, Deputy Minister, and further investigation into the conduct of all officials in all important ports of entry.

Also recommended was the re-organization, under a separate chief, of the preventive service and amendments to the regulations which would permit preventive officers to arrest without a warrant persons found committing any act declared by the Customs and Excise Acts to be an indictable offence.

The findings of the committee revealed that the theft of motor cars had frequently been associated with the smuggling racket, that it had been the common practice of customs officials to grant clearance papers to vessels wholly or partly laden with liquor for the United States, or allegedly bound for a foreign port but admittedly sailing to "rum rows" and that false landing certificates had been produced to obtain cancellation of bonds given for foreign export of cargoes so cleared.

The report was tabled in the House on June 18. On the 22nd Hon. H. H. Stevens, speaking for the Conservatives, moved an amendment to the motion for "concurrence" in which he asserted that the findings of the committee indicated that "the Customs and Excise Department had been degenerating in efficiency for some time, and during recent years at an accelerated rate" and that the conduct of the Prime Minister and the government in failing to take remedial action at a time when they were conversant with the facts was "wholly indefensible."

"As to the ex-minister," said Mr. Stevens, "I have this to say. He perverted his opportunities of service to the state to the distribution of indulgences to his favourites. The vast revenues of the country collected by this department and amounting to over $300,000,000 annually, which he ought to have jealously guarded, were left unprotected, the easy prey to mendacious individuals. High officials with a long career of faithful service to the country were debauched by him and must now pass out of the picture under a cloud more or less of shame.

"His conduct and the conduct of these officials influenced, debased, I might say, by him as the responsible head, were well known to the Prime Minister and his associates. Yet he was allowed to resign his seat and his position as minister and he was rewarded with a seat in the Senate while his puppets have been driven out of the service in shame."

Mr. Stevens declared that King had received representations as early as a year before investigations were begun pointing out that smuggling and under-valuation for duty purposes were resulting in immense losses of revenue and serious interference with the business of legitimate traders and manufacturers.

"It is high time for this unholy partnership between the government of Canada and a gang of bootleggers to be dissolved," he declared.

On June 23, J. S. Woodsworth, who was one day to become leader of the C.C.F. party, but who at that time was the Labour member for the old constituency of Winnipeg Centre, moved a sub-amendment. The amendment proposed the setting up of a judicial commission to continue the investigation but would have removed Mr. Stevens' condemnatory reference to the actions of the Prime Minister, the Minister of Customs, and the government.

This was accepted by the government but was opposed by the Conservatives, and on June 25, when it came to a vote, it was defeated by a majority of only 2. A second sub-amendment was moved by Mr. Fansher of the Progressives which would have left the Stevens' amendment much as it was with the exception that it would have added Mr. Woodsworth's proposed condemnation of other persons and provision for the establishment of a judicial commission. This was ruled out of order, but the speaker's ruling having been challenged and overruled by a majority of 2, it was subsequently carried without division.

That was a hectic evening in the House of Commons with the division bells ringing far into the small hours of the morning and with the whole House tense with the drama and suspense of the situation. During the early hours of the morning a motion to adjourn, supported by the government, had been defeated by one vote. A second motion for adjournment made by the government just around five o'clock in the morning carried by one vote. When the House rose, the hands of the clock stood at 5.15. Many members had gone to sleep in their chairs or were occupying sofas in the lobbies. Only the division bells kept them straggling into the House from time to time as the various votes were recorded.

As Mr. King left the Chamber with his colleagues the handwriting on the wall was clear to see. The government no longer commanded effective support in the House and it was apparent that when the Stevens' amendment came to a vote the government would be defeated on a motion of censure.

On Saturday King drove down to Rideau Hall to ask Byng for dissolution. The actual conversation which took place is not, of course, a matter of permanent record. But from a letter which King addressed to the Governor General on the morning of the following Monday, the day upon which he announced his resignation in the House, it is clear that King advised Byng that his refusal to grant dissolution might result in "very serious consequences". He urged Byng to seek to ascertain the views of the Secretary of State for the Dominions as to how a Governor General should proceed in considering advice tendered to him by his Prime Minister. But Byng could not see the propriety of following this course. He was adamant in his stand.

There is reason to believe that the matter of dissolution had been gone into very thoroughly by the Governor General and King immediately after the election in October. Certainly, at that time King urged Byng to let parliament decide who should form a government. A motion of want of confidence in King's government was moved but was defeated and thus parliament was established.

It is conceivable that at that time, with only 101 members at his call, King may have felt that it would be difficult for him to carry on the government, even with the assistance of the Progressives. But from first to last he was ready to abide by the decision of parliament.

Soon after the election, King announced that he had decided to meet the new House at "the earliest practical moment." He explained that he had reached this decision after carefully considering the three courses which were open to him, namely: to resign at once; to meet the new House of Commons; or to advise an immediate dissolution.

As has been stated, King's visit to Rideau Hall, following the fateful session of June 25, took place on a Saturday. At two o'clock Monday afternoon King informed the House that shortly after noon that day, he had advised His Excellency that the public interest demanded a dissolution, and that upon His Excellency's refusal to grant it he had thereupon tendered his resignation which His Excellency had seen fit to accept.

On Monday morning, King had written to the Governor General as follows:

"Your Excellency will recall that in our recent conversations relative to dissolution I have on each occasion suggested to Your Excellency, as I have again urged this morning, that having regard to the possible very serious consequences of a refusal of the advice of your First Minister to dissolve parliament you should, before definitely deciding on this step, cable the Secretary of State for the Dominions asking the British government, from whom you have come to Canada under instructions, what, in the opinion of the Secretary of State for the Dominions, your course should be in the event of the Prime Minister presenting you with an Order in Council having reference to dissolution. . . . I shall be pleased to have my resignation withheld at Your Excellency's request pending the time it may be necessary for Your Excellency to communicate with the Secretary of State for the Dominions."

But Byng was making his own decisions, as he always had, and he did not choose even to communicate with the Secretary of State for the Dominions. He insisted that parliament had voted against the government no less than three times and he did not seem to be able to appreciate the fact that the votes in question had been taken on private members' motions and were not, in effect, government defeats.

In informing the House of his resignation Mr. King said: "May I make my position clear? At the present time there is no government. I am not Prime Minister; I cannot speak as Prime Minister. I can speak as only one member of this House and it is as a humble member of this House that I submit that inasmuch as His Excellency is without an adviser, I do not think it would be proper for the House to proceed to discuss anything.

"If the House is to continue its proceedings, some one must assume, as His Excellency's adviser, the responsibility for His Excellency's refusal to grant a dissolution in the existing circumstances; and until His Excellency has an adviser who will assume this responsibility, I submit that this House should not proceed to discuss any matters whatever."

At two o'clock the following afternoon, Sir Henry Drayton rose in his place and announced that, immediately following the resignation of the Prime Minister, His Excellency had sent for Mr. Meighen and asked him to form a government.

Mr. Meighen had undertaken the task. In order to conclude speedily the work of the session, and to obviate the necessity of ministers having to vacate their seats and stand for re-election Mr. Meighen had decided to constitute a temporary ministry composed of seven members who would be sworn in without portfolio, and who would assume responsibility as acting ministers of the several departments.

Sir Henry then read the list: Sir Henry Drayton, Hon. R. J. Manion, Sir George H. Perley, Hon. H. H. Stevens, Hon. Hugh Guthrie, Hon. W. A. Black, Hon. R. B. Bennett.

Mr. Meighen, he explained, having accepted an office of emolument under the crown, namely that of Prime Minister, had thereby vacated his seat and had asked him to assume temporarily the duty of leading the government in the House.

These preliminaries having been concluded the House proceeded with its work, debate on the customs inquiry.

In the meanwhile, Mr. King and his colleagues had been busy. After considering the situation from every possible angle they hit upon what they believed was a chink in the Conservative armour: the vulnerability of Meighen's temporary cabinet in respect to the validity of their appointment.

"Let's sit quiet until they come for supply," King advised, "then we'll go after them."

It was an approach that appealed to King and its elaboration offered an excellent opportunity for the exercise of his exceptional talents as a parliamentary tactician. His devastating cross-examination of Meighen's newly appointed cabinet ministers on the evening of the 30th was to stand as one of the most impressive political performances of his career.

The attack came out of the blue, as the House was dealing with routine matters in the Committee of Supply, and it found the government utterly unprepared. Like a cyclone that flattens everything in its path, it struck with such lightning-like suddenness and ferocity that the hastily-improvised structure of government, which Mr. Meighen had erected so hopefully, was reduced, within the space of a few brief moments, to a heap of twisted wreckage. Mr. Meighen and his ministers stood bewildered and lost amidst the litter of their hopes. Their moment of triumph had been pitifully brief.

Someone once recalled having been present when an aide brought King word that the opposition intended to take a certain line of attack in respect to a particular issue. The situation called for a counter-attack. After due consideration King made up his mind. "If they do that I shall be good and mad," he decided. What he intended to convey was that he would meet the arguments of his opponents with a show of righteous indignation and anger. Having schooled himself all his life to keep his temper in check, King had likewise learned how to put on a show when the occasion demanded one. The studied performance he now gave the House was a case in point.

"We are now voting large sums of money to different

hon. gentlemen opposite who are supposed to be administering several departments of the government," commenced King in his usual stodgy manner. "Before we proceed any further I would like to discover from those hon. gentlemen to what extent they have complied with constitutional practice in the matter of assuming office. I would like to ask my hon. friend who is leading the House whether he has taken any oath of office of any kind since he undertook to lead the House, or even before doing so."

This elicited from Sir Henry Drayton the admission that, while each of the different formalities prescribed in the office of the Privy Council had been observed, he frankly did not know how many they were. He admitted he had taken no oath of office during the year.

Sir George Perley on being "examined" said he had taken no oath of office during the year, but had taken his oath as a Privy Councillor many years before.

One by one, King put Mr. Meighen's "ministers" to the test. He sought to make the point that, having failed to take the usual oaths of office in respect to the departments which had been placed under their administration, they were each and all guilty of a patent breach of constitutional propriety. The effect of this argument on the Progressives and Independents was profound. It was obvious that they were not prepared to commit themselves to such a flouting of constitutional practice.

"This country," declared King now putting real fire into his words, "today is being governed with all the great responsibilities of government, by a cabinet in which there is not a single minister of the crown in parliament and in which there is no Prime Minister with a seat in the House. With such a sequence of events I say that if ever a Prime Minister was justified in tendering advice urging that the conditions demanded dissolution I have been justified in this instance.

"We find the affairs of the country being administered by a group of gentlemen not one of whom is a minister of the crown—and this while parliament is in session."

"Look at the spectacle!" he went on. "Here you have all these gentlemen being made acting ministers, and how have they been made acting ministers? By themselves, all sitting around one table, not one of them sworn to office."

Sheepishly, in answer to King's questioning, the temporary ministers rose and listed the departments they had been placed in charge of. Many of them had been entrusted with no less than three separate divisions of government.

Smarting under the cross-examination, Mr. Cahan described King's failure to advise the House of his intention to resign at an earlier date as an "unparalleled dereliction of duty."

"Keep cool, boys," Ernest Lapointe suggested, "it is only beginning!"

The cross-examination lasted until one in the morning. Next day King took up the task again and this time he really got down to work, quoting every available authority to support his contention that the appointment of the acting ministers was clearly in violation of the Canadian Constitution.

About two o'clock the following morning by a majority of 96 to 95 the House agreed that: "the actions in this House of the honourable members who have acted as ministers of the Crown since June 29, 1926, are a violation and infringement of the privileges of the House for the following reasons: 1. That the said honourable gentlemen have no right to sit in this House and should have vacated their seats therein, if they legally hold office as administrators of the various departments assigned to them by Orders-in-Council; 2. That if they do not hold such offices legally they have no right to control the business of government in this House and to ask for supply for the departments of which they state they are acting ministers."

And to add a tragi-comic note to the proceedings the vote that defeated the government was cast by Mr. Bird, the Progressive member for Nelson, who broke his pair and voted with the Liberals. Some said that Bird was asleep in his seat when his name was called and that he jumped up and voted 'without thinking of what he was doing.

However, it was all over. Just before the House rose Mr. King said he assumed that the Prime Minister would advise His Excellency that the House had declared that the government had no right to be in existence and that he had found it impossible to carry on.

The following day Mr. Meighen so advised the Governor General. Dissolution was granted and the House was dissolved without prorogation.

XII

BACK ON THE HUSTINGS

BYNG'S REFUSAL TO grant King dissolution provided him with the ammunition he needed to wage a successful campaign. Although, at first, public interest in the issue was lukewarm, King kept hammering away until the electors began to sit up and take notice. The issue, as it was presented by King, was whether or not the Canadian government should be dominated or interfered with by Downing street. Although the Conservatives tried to make the most out of the customs probe exposures, the people were now tired of hearing about something that had already been thrashed out in parliament. It was an old story. On the other hand, the international implications inherent in the Byng issue and Mr. King's insistence that he be placed in the position where he could attend the Imperial Conference and advance Canada's demands for a still greater degree of national autonomy caught the people's imagination. Mr. Meighen's stand that the Governor General had not in any way been at fault and that no important constitutional issue was involved failed to win popular support.

In his campaign, Meighen charged that King, after the 1925 election, had tried to buy the support of the Progressives by promising the enactment of legislation sought by the Progressives but upon which the country had not had an opportunity to express an opinion. This, King replied, was untrue. The support given the Liberal Party by the Progressives and other members had been "a matter of honest co-operation with respect to a known programme of legislation arrived at in the open and openly avowed by all the parties concerned." To Mr. Meighen's charge that King had sought to evade the consequences of the customs disclosures by diverting attention to the constitutional issue involved in the Governor General's refusal to grant dissolution, King replied that he had not sought dissolution to evade a vote of censure in respect to the disclosures; and he maintained that, not only did Hon. Mr. Stevens' amendment to the Customs Committee report not constitute a vote of censure, but that the amendment, had it been put, would have been defeated.

As to tariff policy, much was heard of it during the course of the campaign. Admitting that he was a protectionist and had never been anything else, Mr. Meighen nevertheless declared that he was not the apostle of high and onerous protection. He was in favour of a tariff policy that would give all classes in the country a fair chance. King described Meighen's policy as impracticable. Best results could be obtained, he said, through the operation of the Tariff Advisory Board. Some tariffs might be essential for the upkeep of some industries, he admitted, but these were matters the tariff board had been created to deal with.

Other issues came up during the course of the campaign but the constitutional question and the government's fiscal policy were the two main subjects of debate. To some extent the Conservatives' attempt to capitalize on the customs disclosures misfired, largely because the public was tired of hearing about them and also because fresh charges brought forward by the Conservatives remained unsubstantiated.

Commenting on the situation in 1926, Hector Charlesworth said: "Never was the political adroitness of Mr. King more remarkably demonstrated; but I do not think it would have availed him if it had not been that the public believed in his own personal honesty. The way in which he managed to shift the attention of the public away from the issue [of the customs disclosures] to the intricate constitutional question involved in the fact that Lord Byng had refused him a dissolution and granted one to Mr. Meighen in 1926 was a remarkable example of political skill."

King had always enjoyed his election campaigns and this one was no exception. He was elated over the fact that he had effectively disposed of Meighen's "shadow government" and that the Governor General had been forced, in the final analysis, to do exactly what he had advised him to do in the first place.

King and his entourage spent a total of 50 days on the train. During all that time King did not sleep off the train more than half a dozen times. The late Senator Andrew Haydon used to say that King could lie down on the pavement and before one could snap one's fingers be asleep. There was a good deal of truth to this. Before a big meeting, an important speech, King used to lie down, fall asleep for a quarter of an hour, and then wake up refreshed and with every faculty alert.

Throughout the long and trying campaign King's powers of recuperation astonished his companions. He would wind up a big political meeting late at night or early in the morning, climb aboard his train and within a few minutes be fast asleep. In the morning he would be as fresh as a daisy. He could go to sleep at any time he wanted, and whenever he got the chance he did so. It did not matter whether the train was bumping along over a rough road-bed or was being shunted around in a noisy switching yard, King could snore through it all.

During the trip King overlooked no opportunity to pick

up a few votes wherever he was. When the train pulled in to some little flag station to take on or let off passengers, or for a supply of water or fuel, King would saunter out on the rear platform and if anyone happened to be about he would make a speech. Sometimes it was only to a chance group of railway workers or the usual little company of townsfolk who had come down to see the train arrive. But if there was more than a baker's dozen King would go to work on them. Naturally these brief addresses usually ran along the same lines and the reporters on the train soon got to know them by heart.

One afternoon the train stopped at Orillia where Mr. King was to speak in the evening. King and some of his friends went into town on some business, but the majority of the newspapermen remained in their car putting in time. For want of something better to do, one of their number, Edgar March, announced that he intended to deliver one of King's standard speeches from the observation platform of King's car. It was not long before a little group of station attendants and passers-by had gathered to listen to March's rhetorical effort.

Suddenly March's colleagues, who had joined the "audience" and who stood facing him, saw his jaw drop, and his gaze freeze to a spot over their heads. Turning, they saw that King had returned and had joined their group. March gulped, grinned and quit.

"I think," suggested King, with a chuckle, "that you had better come down to the hall tonight and take my place. You make that speech better than I do."

When newspapermen get together, especially when they become bored or listless from listening to the same speeches day after day, there is bound to be horseplay.

Harvey Hickey, city editor of the *Globe and Mail,* was

the victim of one harmless joke engineered by one of his older colleagues. Hickey, who was then a youngster, had joined the train somewhere in Ontario. When he happened to say that his clothes had become badly creased while travelling his companion suggested that he go up the track and ask King's confidential messenger, John Nicol, if he would be kind enough to press his trousers.

"John does all our pressing and he'll be glad to look after you," explained his friend.

Hickey took his spare trousers and went up to King's car. Nicol's bewildered look informed Hickey that he had been the victim of a practical joke.

"Oh, I'm afraid I can't do that, sir," said Nicol with considerable embarrassment. "I do Mr. King's things, but if I did someone else's things I am afraid he would be annoyed."

King had acquired Nicol shortly after becoming leader of the Liberal party. At first Nicol had acted only as confidential messenger, but he was such a handy fellow that soon he was looking after most of King's personal affairs, including his wardrobe. It was an association that was to last for almost thirty years.

Just before King started out on his tour he called in Ralph Campney, one of his secretaries, and showed him a big, black wooden box. "That contains all my speeches and speech material," King explained. "Look after it, and make sure you get it on the train."

Campney took charge of the box, arranged for it to be placed on the train and then busied himself with a multitude of other chores. He thought no more about it until late that night when the train was roaring through the hinterlands of Northern Ontario. When he checked up he found that the box was not on the train. For a few frantic moments Campney thought of pulling the communication cord, getting off the train, and disappearing into the night. King was asleep and he dared not disturb him. He spent a sleepless night wondering what he would say to King next morning. When finally King awoke about ten o'clock Campney went in to see him.

"Mr. King," he began, "you know that black box . . .?"

"My box of speeches?" nodded King.

"Well, sir, I'm afraid we haven't got it!"

Suddenly King's face broke into a big, broad smile. "You know, Campney," he said, "I knew something like this would happen some day and so (he reached under his berth and began dragging something out) I took the precaution of having a duplicate box prepared. Here it is!"

To Campney's amazement and relief King produced a second "black box" containing copies of his campaign speeches.

Towards the end of the campaign there were indications that the Liberals were moving into the lead. During the last two weeks both leaders made an intensive tour of western Ontario. Meighen, in a last desperate effort to save the day spoke at every little hamlet, sometimes making two or three major speeches a day. He wore himself out. But King took things more easily towards the end. When the election was over and the ballots were counted it was clear that he would be able to form a government. He was still fresh and ready for new fields to conquer. When he got back to Ottawa he immediately began preparing for the work of the Imperial Conference.

The Imperial Conference of 1926 was probably the most important that had been held since the meeting which had taken place between the Commonwealth leaders on the occasion of the celebration of Queen Victoria's Golden

Jubilee. So far as Canada was concerned, the constitutional question which had arisen earlier in the year had given rise to a great deal of debate throughout the Dominion on Canada's status in general, and there were those who thought that a great many Canadians desired to sever completely the constitutional or other ties which bound the country to Britain. On top of this, the Nationalist government of South Africa, headed by Prime Minister Hertzog, had proclaimed the view that South Africa had the right to secede from the Empire should a referendum of the people indicate the desirability of such a step.

The most pessimistic talked of the dissolution of the Empire and saw Imperial unity hanging in the balance. In actuality, the members of the Commonwealth were merely growing up, seeking the independence of thought and action which comes with maturity, and demanding a status in conformity with the responsibilities of empire which they had been accepting to an increasing degree, as witness their participation in World War I.

Attending the Conference were the representatives of Australia, New Zealand, Newfoundland, the Union of South Africa, the Irish Free State, India and Canada.

King was accompanied by Mr. Lapointe, Minister of Justice, and by a staff which included Dr. O. D. Skelton, Under Secretary of State for External Affairs; Jean Desy, Counsellor, Department of External Affairs; Major General J. H. MacBrien, Chief of the General Staff; Commodore Walter Hose, Director of the Naval Service; L. C. Moyer, his private secretary; and W. H. Measures, assistant private secretary.

The Conference opened on October 19. At a dinner given by the Canada Club to mark the occasion Mr. King told the gathering that his disagreement with Lord Byng had not been one involving Imperial unity. He believed the constitution of the Empire was in the development stage and that its evolution was a matter not of a few years or a decade, but of centuries to come. Presiding over the dinner, which was attended by H.R.H. the Prince of Wales, the Duke of Connaught, Rt. Hon. Winston Churchill, and many others, was King's old friend of university days, Sir Hamar Greenwood.

During the course of the Conference King leaned heavily on Dr. Skelton. While King supplied the driving power behind the Dominion's struggle for national recognition, Skelton was particularly successful in harmonizing the situation with the other Dominions.

King continued the fight for national autonomy which he had waged at the 1923 Conference and this time it was to result in the Balfour Declaration in which document the Dominions were declared to be "autonomous communities within the British Empire, equal in status, in no way subordinate one to another in any aspect of their domestic or external affairs, though united by a common allegiance to the Crown, and freely associated as members of the British Commonwealth of Nations."

Also, as a result of the Conference, and as a direct product of the Byng controversy and the stand which King had taken in respect to the powers of the Governor General, the latter became the personal representative of His Majesty in Canada and no longer an official of the British Government.

"In our opinion," the Conference reported, "it is an essential consequence of the equality of status existing among the members of the British Commonwealth of Nations that the Governor General of a Dominion is the representative of the Crown, holding in all essential respects the same position in relation to the administration of public affairs in the Dominion as is held by His Majesty the King in Great Britain, and that he is not the representative or agent of His Majesty's Government in Great Britain or of any department of that Government."

While this change in the status of the Governor General served to dignify and exalt his position, it likewise emphasized the need for the appointment of a direct representative of the government, and this need was to be met by the appointment of a High Commissioner to Canada.

"Were I to express in a single word my feeling as to the significance of the appointment to Canada of a High Commissioner of Great Britain," said King, "I would say that it is by far the most important step that has yet been taken to further effective consultation and cooperation between the Government of His Majesty in Great Britain and the Government of His Majesty in the Dominion of Canada with resultant benefits to both; also, and this is even more important to the unity of the Empire as a whole, that it is the most important means thus far devised of securing the crown against any involvement in any possible controversy which may arise between the different governments of which His Majesty is the head."

King celebrated Canada's increased status as a nation a year later when he appointed Hon. Vincent Massey as first Canadian Minister to the United States. This step was the first of many subsequent ones which were to give Canada independent representation throughout the countries of the world.

Speaking of the part King played in the development of the principle of responsible government, the late Norman McLeod Rogers said: "Giving full expression to what was formulated at London by Sir Wilfrid Laurier, and affirmed by Sir Robert Borden at Versailles, he brought to completion the concluding chapter of the evolution of responsible government and assumed for Canada the rights and responsibilities of full membership in the community of nations."

King's love of symbolism is well known. Thus when he was present when one of the big bells for the Peace Tower carillon was being moulded at Croydon, England, he leaned over and with a twinkle in his eye tossed a Canadian one-cent piece and an English half-penny into the running metal with the observation: "Equal status!" Incidentally, King borrowed the coins from one of his secretaries!

XIII

GOOD TIMES, BAD TIMES

THE NEXT THREE years were to be ones of continuing prosperity for the Dominion, marked by generous crops, the rapid and extensive development of the mining and newsprint industries, unprecedented expansion in construction, high employment, and increased immigration. By 1928 the country had reached the highest point in industrial and trade activity in its history. New high records were achieved in that year for wheat and newsprint production, the country's two leading exports. A total of 532,000,000 bushels of wheat and 2,381,102 tons of newsprint were produced.

The stock market crash, the imminence of which was suspected and feared by only a few, was just around the corner; but during the three-year period from 1926 onwards there were few storm signals flying. Financial institutions expressed much confidence in the future.

Sir Herbert Holt, president of the Royal Bank of Canada, presenting his report for 1926, expressed the view that the country had "definitely emerged" from the discouraging conditions of the post-war period.

"The year just closed has been one of steady and substantial improvement in almost every department of Canada's business life," he reported. "It is gratifying to know that our greater prosperity is well grounded on the solid foundations of expanding production and commerce."

Sir John Aird, president of the Canadian Bank of Commerce, saw the return of the Liberal administration as having a definite stabilizing influence on business. Pointing out that 1926 had been a year of general progress, and, indeed, the most satisfactory year for business since the temporary set-back of 1921, he expressed confidence that the return of the existing government, with a strong parliamentary majority, would enable it to devote its full energies to the important tasks that lay ahead, "without the consciousness of insecurity of tenure which exerts such a paralyzing effect on the practical usefulness of a government."

Following his defeat at the polls in 1926 Mr. Meighen indicated his intention of resigning from the leadership. Accordingly, Hon. Hugh Guthrie was appointed to lead the party until a permanent leader could be found. A convention was held at Winnipeg on October 11, the following year, and Mr. R. B. Bennett, who had been Minister of Finance in the Meighen government, was chosen leader. When King and Bennett faced each other across the floor of the House the public had an opportunity to observe two opposing types of personality in action. King was determined, stubborn, dogged in debate, somewhat given to deviousness and unpredictability in respect to his political manoeuvring. He was a supreme tactician possessing an uncanny sense of timing. Bennett, on the other hand, scorned the oblique approach. He was a hard-headed executive type with a solid professional background of legal training. Even his colleagues were to find him, at times, strong-willed and domineering. Honesty and sincerity of purpose, were, perhaps, his two most notable qualities. A non-drinker, and non-smoker, he had a deeply religious side and at times he could become quite sentimental over old friends and associations. He had, too, a terrific temper. King and Bennett may have had a professional respect for one another's capabilities, but for the most part there was little love lost between them. Bennett was the irresistable force, King the immovable body. The clash of their dissimilar and conflicting temperaments was to lead to many a tense and electrifying situation in the House.

From 1926 onwards King's tariff policy continued to be one of moderate reduction in tariffs coupled with an effort to further promote inter-Imperial trade. He continued to describe the Liberal policy as one based on "the greatest good to the greatest number." Anything in the nature of provincial or regional tariffs he deplored as an expedient that was certain to result in disunity and confusion. He pointed out that regional tariffs could not be introduced without altering the basis of Confederation, that the rights of the respective provinces were involved. The 1927 budget contained no tariff changes, upwards or downwards, and was heralded by many as contributing very materially to stability in industry and to the revival of trade generally. Mr. Robb, the Minister of Finance, described the government's tariff policy as one which was "neither high nor low."

It was true that the substantial reductions in duties on automobiles and trucks provided for in the 1926 budget aroused a storm of protest from those Canadian manufacturers who believed they would be affected either directly or indirectly, and hundreds of automotive workers and representatives of the industry organized an impressive motorcade and drove to Ottawa to wait upon the government.

The Canadian Manufacturers' Association saw this reduction as "a severe blow" to the automobile and truck industry which, they pointed out, supported 100,000 Canadians and brought into Canada the tremendous sum of $107,000,000 annually.

When the automotive workers who had come to Ottawa

gathered in a local theatre to discuss what immediate representations should be made, King walked in on their meeting
unannounced and spoke to them. He predicted that the
industry would not only survive the reduction in tariff rates
but that it would continue to expand and that the competition resulting from the importation of American cars and
trucks would have the effect of improving general conditions throughout the Canadian industry. In the meanwhile, he asserted, thousands of Canadians would directly
benefit from reduced prices.

In the 1928 budget there was a reduction of tariffs on
implements of production in the mining and fishing
industries. The textile tariff was revised, providing for a
reduction of the maximum duty under the general tariff
from thirty-seven and a half per cent to thirty per cent, with
one single exception. At the same time fertilizers were
placed on the free list as an aid to agriculture. These
revisions were made only after they had been considered by
the Tariff Board which King had set up in 1926. By the
time the King administration came to an end in 1930 the
board had dealt with a total of 200 applications for revision
of the tariff.

The tariff question came to the fore to an increasing
extent in 1929 when it was learned that the United States
was considering the imposition of restrictive tariffs against
Canadian natural products and manufactured goods which
would have a serious effect on the export of these products
of farm and factory.

To the suggestion that Canada, as a warning, should
prepare to raise retaliatory tariffs against American goods
Mr. King replied that it would be undesirable to make any
changes in view of the measures to be introduced by Congress.

"In the condition of prosperity which Canada is today enjoying," he asked, "would it be desirable on the part of the administration to take any action in respect to the tariff in Canada at the present time which would be regarded as provocative by those across the line who may be interested in seeking to raise the tariff in that country?"

Any raising of tariff barriers at this time, he reiterated, would help to create in the minds of the American people the very sentiments which would cause them to raise their tariffs higher, perhaps, than it had ever been their intention to raise them.

"We do not intend to take any action of that provocative character," he declared. Even to increase the British preference at such a time might be misconstrued by the United States, he believed. It was true that the British preference had always been part of the policy of the Liberal party, and year after year the government had considered carefully wherein it could justifiably extend and increase it, but now was the time for cool heads and calm consideration.

Nevertheless the fears of a good many Canadians that the proposed U.S. tariff changes would seriously affect the export of Canadian agricultural products were realized early in 1929 when the Hawley-Smoot tariff, as it had come to be known, passed the House of Representatives. Among the Canadian products on which duties would be raised were cattle, with beef, hides and leather; sheep, with wool and lambs; swine and pork; potatoes and all garden produce; flaxseed, dairy products, hardwood lumber, and shingles. A last-minute amendment placed an import duty of 20 per cent ad valorem on Canadian wheat entering the country under bond when milled and shipped to Cuba.

King expressed the government's reaction succinctly when, speaking in Winnipeg in the fall of 1929, he said:

"The government is fully prepared in the interests of Canada to re-adjust its fiscal policy from time to time to meet any changes in existing fiscal structures which may affect home markets.

"If the United States or any other country does not want to trade with Canada except on unequal terms, then surely we can look as never before to the rest of the world and particularly to the rest of the British Empire."

Following the 1929 session it became apparent that an election was imminent. Mr. King and Mr. Bennett toured the Dominion. Canada's trade position and her tariff policy were dealt with by both leaders.

King expressed hope that the movement for inter-Imperial trade would grow as the result of another Imperial Conference, which he hoped would be held the following year.

There should be in Canada the heartiest co-operation on the part of all parties to seek within the Empire new markets to replace any that may be lost elsewhere, and to place within the Empire, at home and abroad, as many of the purchases now given to any country that penalizes our trade as can be transferred without penalizing Canadians," he declared.

The Canadian position in respect to the United States was clear, he added. In nothing had Canada been provocative. The Canadian tariff would continue to serve Canadians.

Mr. Bennett expressed alarm at the large volume of goods still coming into the country from the United States. He condemned the government for allowing New Zealand to flood Canada with butter, for permitting the United States to dump fresh fruits and vegetables in the Dominion, to the detriment of Canadian farmers and fruit-growers. So far as free trade with the Empire was concerned, said Mr. Bennett, it was obvious that the Liberal administration was prepared to sacrifice the industrial life of individual parts of the Empire.

Referring to the New Zealand agreement, Bennett declared that his party would never consent to any transaction or treaty "that will destroy any industry indigenous to Canada."

"It matters not whether it is with New Zealand or any other country," he added. "My concern is Canada, so is yours."

Speaking at Calgary, in January, 1930, Bennett scored the government for holding the view that relief was the responsibility of the provinces and municipalities. This was the attitude the government had taken, said Mr. Bennett, at a time when the United States was organizing to provide employment for its citizens.

"So long as the present economic system is pursued," he warned, "we will have to answer for it. The right to work is the right of every man and woman in Canada, or should be. We have been content since 1922 to send out of Canada into other lands, free, the resources of the country, and buy back from them the manufactured materials. Thousands in the United States have been given employment fabricating Canadian goods.

"They've got the jobs and we've got the soup kitchens," he said.

As for his own party, it proposed a tariff not for exploitation, he asserted, but to provide Canadians with an equal chance in their own country against the dumped products of other nations.

King gave his answer to the Hawley-Smoot tariff when Mr. Dunning brought down his 1930 budget. It made allowances for an important extension of the British preference which had the two-fold objective of diverting Canadian imports from the United States to Britain, thus providing Canada with a stronger market for her wheat.

The Times expressed the opinion that the 1930 budget was "the most important preparatory step which has been taken by any government since the Imperial Conference of 1926 toward the ideal of closer Imperial economic co-operation." The spirit of the budget, said *The Times,* was an indication of the spirit in which the Dominion would approach the forthcoming Imperial Conference.

As a result of the extension of the British preference Canadians benefitted from the removal of the duty on tea, free entry of porcelain and chinaware, and an opening of the fruit and vegetable trade with the West Indies.

"We do not intend," said Mr. Dunning, "to meet the other countries of the British Commonwealth of Nations in a spirit of petty bargaining, but rather in the broad spirit of willingness to become in ever-increasing measure good customers to those who treat us in like manner."

The stock market crash of October and November, 1929, took the United States and Canada by complete surprise. At first its full significance was lost upon the public. It had followed on one of the most favourable years in the Dominion's history, a period which under the stimulus of three years of general prosperity had been marked by new records in industry and trade. In addition the country had enjoyed bumper crops.

Hand in hand with the prosperous conditions which characterized the great part of 1929, however, had developed a mania of stock-market speculation which swept the entire continent to an extent and on a scale without precedent in previous financial history. With inflation in stock values had gone its inevitable concomitant—inflation in credit on which the stocks were carried.

Now, in October and November, came the collapse of values, and losses to individuals on a scale, as to magnitude at least, never before witnessed.

Yet some experts in the financial world still remained optimistic. Sir Thomas White, President of the Bank of Commerce, reporting to his share-holders, viewed the collapse as a "necessary and fortunate event." Had it continued longer, he thought, general business throughout the world must inevitably have been seriously affected.

"With the underlying conditions of production and commerce thoroughly sound," Sir Thomas assured his shareholders, "there is every reason to believe that a recession due to this cause will be but temporary in character."

Perhaps Sir Thomas and some of his optimistic colleagues were merely whistling in the dark.

King went to the country in the summer of 1930 on the principles of his budget and, in particular, on his policy of extending Empire preference and seeking trade with those countries which would accord Canada equal trading terms. With the Imperial Conference approaching, he believed that the government which would represent Canada should have the full confidence of the people, and he held that the only way this confidence could be re-affirmed was by the expedient of an election.

Unemployment resulting from the depression, which was now revealing itself in all its bleak and forbidding colours, was increasing. Mr. Bennett promised to end unemployment by putting everyone to work and finding immediate markets for all farm products.

Apparently Mr. Bennett's promises carried considerably more appeal than Mr. King's elaboration of the Liberal tariff policy, for on July 28 when the votes were counted the Conservative party found itself in office with a substantial majority. It had elected a total of 137 members as compared with 91 in 1926. The Liberals, on the other hand, who had won power in 1926 with 116 members, now saw their numbers reduced to 88. The United Farmers returned 10 members, the Progressives 2, Liberal Progressives 3, Labour 2, Independent Labour 1, and Independents 2.

By one of those strange little quirks of fate which sometimes exert a tremendous influence over the course of human events, King, unwittingly, contributed to his own defeat. In an unguarded moment, during a House discussion on relief, he let drop one of those unhappy catch-phrases which an alert opposition is always waiting to seize upon and turn to their own advantage. It was a slip of the tongue which the opposition transformed into an offensive weapon of razor-like sharpness, and with a stubborn perverseness which he could not afterwards rightly explain, King gave the phrase unnecessary emphasis by repeating it.

It soon came to be known as "Mr. King's five-cent speech," and he was never to hear the end of it.

King had been arguing that as the relief problem affected only certain municipalities and widely separated sections of the Dominion he did not think the federal government was obliged under the Constitution to collect taxes from the people at large to meet conditions which affected only certain groups. He denied the existence of a national unemployment problem, the existence of an emergency. He declared that he did not think it was ever intended that the federal government "should become the agency through which problems which are primarily municipal and provincial should be dealt with."

Then, prodded and goaded by the opposition which asserted that the federal government was being niggardly in doling out unemployment relief, King blurted out:

"So far as giving money from this federal treasury to provincial governments is concerned, in relation to this question of unemployment as it exists today, I might be prepared to go a certain length, possibly, in meeting one or two of the western provinces that have Progressive premiers at the head of their governments . . . but I would not give a single cent to any Tory government."

Over the shouted protests that came from the opposition side of the House, and Mr. Bennett's cry of "Shame!" King continued:

"May I repeat what I have said? With regard to giving moneys out of the federal treasury to any Tory government in this country for these alleged unemployment purposes, with these governments situated as they are today, with policies diametrically opposed to those of this government, I would not give them a five-cent piece!"

Actually, while King's remarks were quite understandable, they were susceptible of being shortened up and distorted. The opposition claimed that King had stated he would not give anything towards relief. Thousands of men and women throughout the Dominion who were drawing the dole flocked to the polls and voted Conservative. In vain King told the electors that the federal government would be ready to consider assisting with relief if and when the provinces indicated that the situation had got beyond their control. He was plainly ticketed as the man who would not give a five-cent piece towards relief, and that was that!

Just why King went out of his way to make the "five-cent speech" has never been fully explained. He said, later, that he had been tired at the time, and no doubt his nerves may have been a bit edgy.

As to his unfortunate choice of words, he had been having luncheon with Howard Ferguson, and Ferguson had expressed the view that relief was up to the provinces and that if he were Prime Minister he would not give the provinces a five-cent piece. When King was speaking in the House the phrase just popped into his mind and he used it.

"It defeated us," King admitted later, "but as it turned out, it was the luckiest thing that could have happened from the standpoint of the future of the party."

Indeed, it was a good time to hand over the reins of government and sit in the seats of the critics. Mr. Bennett, in winning the election, inherited all the trials and tribulations of the depression years. He found himself saddled with a situation which was beyond the control of any Canadian government. Yet in 1935 the Canadian electorate, apparently dissatisfied with what Bennett and his government had been able to do by way of remedying the situation, was to return the Liberals to power.

But the five-cent speech taught King something. It taught him to be on guard against making snap statements in the House. This caution, born of experience, resulted in the development of a style of speaking which became unique for its extensive circumlocution and indirection. Those who sought to coerce or trap King into making an ill-advised statement, a too-definite commitment, a pronouncement of policy which might circumscribe his future actions, found themselves wasting their time and effort.

In his nine years in office King had not only demonstrated his ability as a leader and administrator, but he had given abundant evidence of his unusual virtuosity in the field of political strategy. During his first four years as Prime Minister the Liberal party had a majority of only one over the combined membership of the opposition parties. In addition the Senate was predominantly Conservative. Yet King managed to carry on, holding the Progressives in tow by adroit and masterful handling. The situation was considerably improved from 1926 on, but throughout those uncertain years there had never been a time when he could completely relax his vigilance in respect to the problem of maintaining a majority.

King had been successful in office; how, now, would he stand up in opposition?

The new parliament met in special session on September 8 to deal with the unemployment emergency.

King opened the Speech on the Address by asserting that the government's victory was "much more apparent than real." He attacked Mr. Bennett in respect to the latter's allocation of portfolios, Mr. Bennett having delegated to himself the responsibilities of both Finance Minister and Secretary of State for External Affairs. This, said King, looked like a lot of work for one man.

Bennett lost no time in placing his plans for the relief of unemployment before the House. He brought forward three main measures to meet the existing emergency: unemployment relief, tariff amendments, and amendments to the Customs Act designed to prevent the dumping of U.S. goods. He asked the House for a vote of $26,000,000 for the relief of unemployment. This was to be spent on the construction of public works, improvement of existing government roads and other undertakings, railways, harbours, etc.

Mr. Bennett admitted that the measure was palliative in its application. It was not intended, in any sense, as an attempt to deal with the problem as a problem in economics, but, he believed, it would provide, within a few weeks, employment for from 25,000 to 30,000 workers and sustenance for twice that number of Canadians.

His tariff changes, on the other hand, he explained, were in the nature of "remedial" action. When they were brought down on the 15th the Prime Minister explained that they were not in the nature of a general revision of the tariff, but dealt only with such items as it was believed would ensure additional employment to a large number of Canadians. The end result, however, was an increase of about 50 per cent in the general tariff.

The Prime Minister declared that it was not for the purpose of protection that the tariffs had been raised. The government was merely giving Canadians "an equality of opportunity" with others who were building up their countries, to enable Canadians to build up theirs.

But actually the tariff changes were the most sweeping which had been made since 1879 when Macdonald had initiated his National Policy, and Mr. King saw them as prejudicial to the success of the forthcoming Imperial Conference to be held in Ottawa in the summer of 1932. Before and during the Imperial Conference King refused to discuss the tariff question in public. Perhaps he did not wish to embarrass the government. Perhaps, on the other hand, he wanted to see just how deeply the government could involve itself.

In 1933, however, King took advantage of every opportunity to attack the government's policies. A number of by-elections provided excellent openings. He suggested that the problem of unemployment relief could have been effectively dealt with by a national committee or commission which would co-ordinate the efforts of the federal and provincial governments, supervise expenditures and give a national cohesion to the work. Over Mr. Bennett's protests that it would be an insult to the provinces to demand a federal audit of them in respect to moneys spent on relief, Mr. King asserted that vast amounts from the public treasury had been mismanaged and misspent. Nothing in the nature of a national plan had been developed, he contended.

In respect to the administration of government generally King charged that Bennett was usurping more and more authority as time went on, that ministers of the crown were being ignored in respect to matters pertaining to their several departments. There was a growing tendency away from free, democratic government towards a police state. The government's manner of doing business brought to mind methods employed by Hitler, Mussolini and Stalin. As to Mr. Bennett's action in restoring titles, this was a return to feudalism tending to emphasize class distinctions, and it had been effected when parliament had not been sitting and despite the fact that the House had gone on record as opposed to the principle of the granting of titles to Canadians.

Mr. Bennett was doing his best, but he had been unable to fulfill his 1930 election promise to end unemployment. By the fall of 1933 a total of $122,552,000 had been spent by his government on unemployment relief. Bennett assured the country that the world was slowly recovering from its economic depression. He promised to introduce a new public works programme at the next session of parliament that would provide further unemployment relief, and the following January he presided over a federal-provincial conference at which relief problems were discussed. In July, 1934 the conference was re-convened and Bennett announced that the federal government had decided to discontinue its former policy of assuming responsibility for the administration of much of the direct relief, and would, instead, allocate to each province a lump sum which each would be directly responsible for and would administer according to its particular needs. This proposal, which was accepted by the provinces, relieved the Dominion government of the responsibility of administering relief expenditures and placed that responsibility squarely on the shoulders of the provinces.

On the whole, however, the unemployment situation was anything but encouraging. Communist elements had infiltrated the ranks of the unemployed and had found a fertile field for the exploitation of their doctrines. In particular, they concentrated their efforts in the various work camps which the government had established throughout the country and where single men were employed on government projects on a twenty cent per diem basis.

While Mr. Bennett and other members of the cabinet declared that they had visited many of the work camps and had found conditions excellent, undoubtedly they saw the brighter side of the picture. In the main, the camps were well administered. Many of them were well equipped with recreational facilities and under capable management. Unfortunately, as is often the case when attempts are made to provide shelter, food, and recreational and intellectual outlets for human beings in the mass, the government had failed to satisfy everybody. Admittedly too, abuses of one kind or another had crept in. The majority of the men in the camps were decent citizens, young men who for the most part wanted only an opportunity to earn a living. They felt their position keenly, they were suffering from a natural feeling of frustration and neglect, and a good many of them were only too ready to lay the blame for their enforced idleness at the door of the government.

In May the men in a number of British Columbia work camps went on strike. Organized by the Communists, they began a march on Ottawa. Some 1,500 of their number reached Regina early in July, and their presence in the city led to a riot in which a city detective was beaten to death and a number of R.C.M.P. constables were so seriously injured that they had to be removed to hospital. Bennett laid the entire blame for the outbreak on the shoulders of Communist agitators and branded the march on Ottawa as a definite attempt to disturb the peace, order and good government of the country. He recalled that Arthur H. Evans, one of the marchers' spokesmen, had warned that "blood would flow in the streets of Regina." The police, said Bennett, had not been issued any ammunition for their guns and thus when the riots broke out were not in a position to use them.

It is difficult to believe that the situation would have been much different had the Liberal party been in power. The Conservative government was dealing with a condition of unemployment that was world-wide, and the undercurrents of distrust and discontent engendered by the unfortunate economic conditions that existed were intangibles beyond the control of any governmental authority.

The year 1934 was a particularly black one for the western provinces. Drought swept the prairies and wheat production sank to a mere 267,000,000 bushels as compared with the peak production of 567,000,000 bushels in 1928. Again, in 1937, drought was to take its toll and wheat production was to sink to a new low of 182,000,000 bushels. The situation in 1934 was further aggravated by the fact that the world carryover of wheat in that year amounted to

1,200,000,000 bushels, resulting in a sharp decline in demand. The price, which had been $1.60 in 1929 had, by 1932, dropped to 36 cents.

In 1940, disbursements by the federal government for assistance provided under relief legislation amounted to $17,728,000, but by 1935 this annual contribution had increased to over $51,000,000, and for the ten-year period 1930-39 inclusive it was to total the not inconsiderable sum of $374,153,000. When one considers that in 1949 the government budgeted for an expenditure of $270,000,000 for family allowances alone and another $67,000,000 for old age pensions then the federal relief expenditures of those depression years seem ridiculously small.

In January 1935, Mr. Bennett announced a sweeping programme of economic reform. Admitting that the capitalist system stood in need of a thorough overhauling and that such reform depended to a large extent upon a measure of government intervention and control, he announced a programme which, in his own words, would be "more comprehensive, more far-reaching, than any scheme of reform which this country has ever known." The programme envisaged the establishment of an Employment and Social Service Commission and of a Dominion Trade and Industry Commission. The foundations of earlier measures in respect to farm credits and the marketing of natural products were considerably broadened, while a 48-hour week, minimum wage legislation and a scheme of unemployment and social insurance were enacted.

Bennett announced his plans for economic and social reform over the radio. With an election in the offing it appeared that the government's action would considerably enhance its chances of being returned to power. But if Bennett expected King to take immediate issue with the programme he was doomed to disappointment. King had always believed that the opposition should sometimes flatly agree with government action and that it was not necessary to go out of the way to seek grounds for disagreement. He was to take this stand now. His stratagem took the government completely by surprise. When Bennett's radio announcement made a deep impression on the electorate, King's advisers urged him to rush to the microphone and speak up because the Tories were taking a lead. But King waited patiently until the programme was formally outlined in the Speech from the Throne. Then he rose in his place in the House and, in effect, told the government: "Good. That's just what this country needs. We will do everything we can to help you put it into the law."

But King knew that the government had not yet drafted its legislation. It was months before the bills were ready for the House and in the meanwhile King was able to sit in his place and criticize the government for its tardiness in implementing its own programme. Eventually it was introduced, but most of it was to be declared unconstitutional in 1937 on the grounds that it infringed the rights of the provinces. While its validity was being tested in the courts the legislation was held in abeyance.

Throughout the session, however, King managed to convey the impression that he was forcing the government to enact legislation which it seemed to be postponing unnecessarily.

It was an example of the shrewd political manoeuvring for which King was becoming famous.

The period of Conservative power witnessed a number of important political developments which were to have important repercussions not only in the immediate future but throughout the years to come.

One of these was the evolution, perhaps as the direct result of the depression, of a new party definitely committed to socialism—the Co-operative Commonwealth Federation. The C.C.F. first saw the light of day in Calgary in 1932. In July the following year it met in convention at Regina and produced its famous 13-point programme or manifesto. It was a radical pronouncement of intentions calling for socialization of financial machinery and industries and services essential to social planning, public organization of health, hospital and medical services, and government assumption of responsibility for unemployment and its solution.

Core of the party was a small coterie of labour members and a larger group formerly identified with the Progressive party and the United Farmers of Alberta. It was sparked by a hierarchy of forty odd politically-conscious social planners, including no less than six Rhodes scholars, under the direction of Professor Frank Underhill, of Toronto.

"The C.C.F. manifesto," commented the Toronto *Globe,* following the Regina convention, "is nothing more or less than a 4,000 word expression of a wish without giving any explanation of how it can be obtained."

Nevertheless the party was to become a sounding board for the opinions of all those who had lost their trust in the ability of the two old parties to find an acceptable solution to the country's economic ills. It battened on the growing discontent of the western farmer and made a direct appeal to the labouring masses. Because it was well-led and well-organized it was to assume, at times, the functions of the official opposition. Under the leadership, in the House, of J. S. Woodsworth it became a vital, articulate force and as the years went by, under the cool, capable direction of its new leader, M. J. Coldwell, it was to continue to exert a powerful influence on government policy and action.

The appearance of a third party in the House did not make things any easier for King. While in sympathy with many of the social reforms advocated by the C.C.F. he could not accept some of its extreme views and tendencies.

He had called Mr. Bennett dictatorial and autocratic and had warned the people that the Conservatives were tending towards government by the big interests. He now asserted that the rising power of the C.C.F. was leading to class dictatorship.

Concurrent with the rise of the C.C.F. party, the farmers of Alberta had turned to the gospel of Social Credit as propounded from the pulpit of the Prophetic Bible Institute in Calgary by one William Aberhart. Mr. Aberhart advocated the payment of a dividend of $25 monthly to every man and woman in the province as a means of overcoming what he maintained was the basic flaw in the economic system—the inadequate distribution of wealth.

Another political development which took place towards the end of the Conservative administration was the apostasy of the Hon. H. H. Stevens, Mr. Bennett's Minister of Trade and Commerce, in his efforts to establish his "Reconstruction" party.

Stevens had been named chairman of the special parliamentary committee set up in 1934 to inquire into price spreads in natural products and manufactured articles, the effect of mass-buying by chain and department stores, and labour and wage conditions. Towards the end of the session, and before the committee had reported to parliament, Mr. Stevens, speaking before a Conservative study club, disclosed evidence which had been adduced before the committee. Clearly such an action was not consonant with his duties as chairman of the committee, and late in October Mr. Bennett questioned him on the matter in the presence of other members of the cabinet. He demanded that Stevens make a public explanation for his actions, whereupon Stevens tendered his resignation as minister.

It was not long before Stevens decided to set up his own party. Promising a tremendous development and construction programme if his party came into power, Stevens appealed particularly to the youth of the country whom, he declared, should be given an opportunity to surmount the obstacles and handicaps forced on them by the older generation. He waged a magnificent campaign but time was against him and his opportunities to organize were limited.

Stevens was re-elected in East Kootenay, but he was the only "Reconstruction" candidate to find a seat. Actually, on the basis of the popular vote the newly-established party deserved a fairer share of representation in the House than the one lone seat, as it had polled 384,215 votes. The Social Credit party with only 182,767, less than half the number given to Reconstruction candidates, found itself with 17 seats in parliament, while the C.C.F. party with a total of 390,860 votes elected seven members. The Conservatives with a total vote of 1,311,459 found themselves with 39 seats, while the Liberals with 1,955,727 swept back into office with 171 members.

It was a situation calculated to arouse considerable apprehension as to the effectiveness of the Dominion's electoral system.

An incident which occurred in 1931, and which for a time caused a considerable stir throughout the country was the investigation into the activities of the Beauharnois power company which had obtained permission from the

Liberal government in 1929 to proceed with the development of a power project on the St. Lawrence River. After the company had given its assurances that navigation rights would be safeguarded the government gave its permission to proceed. In conducting its negotiations with the government, however, some of the company's officials had apparently thought it advisable to make contributions to the campaign funds of both the Liberal and Conservative parties. The Liberals received a large contribution, the Conservatives a smaller one. Other power companies had been interested in the power sites, and when it was learned that the company had been contributing to party funds criticism of the negotiations was heard in the House, with the result that a parliamentary committee was set up to conduct an inquiry. But no evidence of any bargain between the government or its officials and the company was produced, although there were indications that "loans" and "gifts" had changed hands in some instances, and it was evident that the Liberal government had acted in good faith.

Many of Mr. King's followers were taken aback, then, when he rose in the House and declared that the Liberal party was in "the valley of humiliation." While he held that the party was not disgraced because individual members might have done what they should not have done, King spoke of himself as humiliated and of the party as having been placed in a similar position.

But the Conservatives, it developed at the time, were not entirely in the clear either in respect to Beauharnois and Liberals felt that King's own reputation for honour and integrity was too well established to be sullied. It was thought that he went further in his remarks than the situation warranted.

This, apparently, was the reaction of the public also for by the time the 1935 election rolled around the incident seemed to have been completely forgotten.

King, however, was apparently deeply concerned with the situation inasmuch as he saw in it the results of unsound party practices and consequently the need for a measure of electoral reform. The Conservatives, on their part, indicated no desire to push the inquiry further and they renewed the agreement with the company with some minor modifications.

King was no sooner back in power than, in an attempt to revive trade, he negotiated a reciprocity treaty with the United States, again opening up trade between the two countries. The intermediate tariff was applied to U.S. imports, replacing the higher general schedules, and there were reductions in the tariff on farm machinery, automobiles and other items. Canada, in all, obtained a reduction of U.S. duties on some 200 items. While the trade in cattle, lumber, and some other natural products was not opened as widely as it had been at one time, certain reductions were provided for where quotas were established.

In 1938 three-way pacts between Canada, Britain and the United States were negotiated in a further effort to stimulate trade. Canada again benefited by further U.S. tariff reductions to the extent that duties on over half Canada's imports from the States and on four-fifths of her exports to the U.S. were materially reduced. Trade was springing up again between the two countries. A workable reciprocal tariff was at last in effect.

One of King's first steps in 1935 was to establish a National Employment Commission to study the problem of relief and, subsequently, negotiations with the provinces resulted in agreements which proved mutually beneficial.

King also took immediate steps to cancel a number of relief construction projects and at the same time increased the federal monthly grants to the provinces for direct relief to the extent of 75 per cent.

In 1937 the government established the Rowell Commission to re-examine "the economic and financial basis of Confederation and the distribution of legislative powers in the light of the economic and social developments of the last seventy years." But co-operation with Ontario, Quebec and Alberta was not achieved. The report, when it was presented in 1940, recommended that the Dominion assume full responsibility for unemployment relief, that provincial debts be assumed by the federal government, that the provinces surrender to the Dominion the sole right to income and corporation taxes and succession duties, and that the system of paying provincial subsidies be replaced by a system of adjustment grants to the several provinces. Discussion on the report was to carry into the war years and beyond, and the failure of Ontario and Quebec to reach a basis of agreement with the federal government continued to embarrass the latter in its efforts to institute a national system of health and welfare services.

When King took over the reins of office again in 1935 the country was still in the depth of depression. But again he was riding the crest of good fortune. By 1938 prices were rising and unemployment was tapering off. Canada was beginning to clamber to its feet, dust itself off, and look about with some hope for the future. The clouds had not yet rolled away, but there was already a spot or two of blue on the horizon.

XIV

THE KING LEGEND

By now King had begun to take on the stature and dignity of the elder statesman. He was 65 years of age, for over two decades he had successfully led his party, and during that period the Liberals had been in power for some 14 years. Those in his own party who had taken his leadership for granted now began to appreciate the fact that they were being led by a man who possessed unusual talents and capabilities. Even members of the opposition parties began to pay King grudging tribute on the score of his political acumen and statesmanlike approach to domestic and international problems. His physical and intellectual durability was, in itself, impressive. He had outlasted Meighen and Bennett and a number of interim Conservative leaders. Now he dominated the House. In addition he continued to exercise a firm control over the sometimes diverse elements of his own party. At a time of life when many men in public affairs begin to think seriously of retirement he brought to the task of government a degree of physical vigour and intellectual enthusiasm that completely belied the circumstance of his advancing years.

Slowly but surely the King legend began to take shape. Wherever the politically-minded gathered to settle informally the affairs of the nation, whether around the pot-bellied stove in the crossroads general store or in the plush precincts of such milieus of political controversy as the Rideau or Manitoba Clubs, sooner or later, King's record as a politician and a man was sure to be subjected to microscopic examination. As his policies were attacked or defended, his virtues extolled or discounted, his shortcomings emphasized or excused, a hundred and one incidents of his career were recalled by way of illustration.

There were those who asserted that King was a cold, callous individual interested only in the advancement of his own career. There were others who knew him as a man possessing a warm, friendly personality which was unfortunately hidden to the public by a cloak of shyness and sensitive reserve. There were those who called him fearless and aggressive, and there were those who claimed he had revealed himself as timid, and over-inclined to seek the path of compromise and evasion.

The stories they told! They left no corner of his public or private life unexplored. What they actually knew they enlarged upon; what they merely suspected they proclaimed as fact; what was hearsay sooner or later took on the colour of actuality. But here and there, out of the welter of fact and supposition and wishful thinking, a little of the truth emerged.

Those who sought to humanize the Prime Minister invariably spoke of his attachment for his little Irish terrier, Pat. Pat was King's constant companion for some 17 years. He was the only one whom King could talk to in confidence. Pat probably was the repository of more state secrets over the years than one could shake a stick at. Many a time as Pat snoozed happily at King's feet in the dimly-lit library at Laurier House the Prime Minister would turn to him and solemnly ask his advice on some important problem of state. Pat invariably agreed with his master, demonstrating his adherence with a decisive wag of the tail. He had to listen to a good many of King's speeches, too, cocking his head with interest as his master paced up and down the room memorizing his sometimes diffuse and dreary declamations. To give Pat due credit he never broke a confidence but always displayed a polite interest and exercised a discreet silence.

When King left Laurier House during the day Pat was last to see him to the door and wag his tail in farewell, and when, late at night, the Prime Minister returned from Parliament Hill Pat was on hand to welcome him.

When King was absent from the capital for any length of time, and could not take his dog along, the little terrier used to lose his appetite and mope around the empty house. Upon his return King's first question invariably was: "How is Pat?" Pat always accompanied King on his nocturnal walks about Sandy Hill during the winter, and in the summer he had the run of the countryside at Kingsmere.

King always claimed that his dog had an uncanny political sense, that he seemed to know if the day had gone well or badly for his master. He believed that a man could learn a great deal from a dog's sense of devotion and loyalty. "That dog taught me much," he declared on one occasion.

That the religious side of King's nature is highly developed is fairly well known. He reads his Bible every day, and every morning, before starting his work, he spends a few quiet moments in his study contemplating the work and thoughts of men and women who have made great and lasting contributions to mankind He may spend these moments studying the Bible, or again he may read Pasteur or Emerson or Ruskin. He believes that a few moments of such contemplative study relaxes and refreshes the mind and helps one start the day right.

King's views on life, death, and the hereafter are very definite and clear. He believes that during life one is exposed to spiritual influences, and that these influences can be either good or evil. He believes that the spirit is indestructible and that one's loved ones who have passed on can and do exert an influence over the living. "I believe," he said, on one occasion, recently, "in the reality of a spiritual world, that this life is merely an antechamber to eternity."

King has publicly stated that he believes in "the survival of the human personality." He has always felt that his friends and loved ones are near him. He believes that anyone who has lived alone as much as he has is more likely to commune with his own soul than is the person who enjoys the privilege of family life. Lacking wife, children, and close relations such individuals as himself, he contends, develop a community of spiritual affections. They live with the memories of their loved ones; the picture of a beloved parent takes on a new quality; one is more apt to reach out for the spiritual support and affection which one feels is ever-present.

On one occasion, when addressing a gathering of party friends, King observed: "I am proud to believe there is no separation between those who are nearest and dearest to us, and I believe in the survival of the human personality. Thus I know that if I have had any success in life it has been due to my father and mother, and that they share the tribute paid here tonight."

King admits to an intense interest in psychical research, a branch of scientific study which he contends cannot be overlooked by any thinking man. He knew the late Sir Oliver Lodge personally and he has studied all Sir Oliver's books. He believes that as one grows older the desire for more information in respect to spiritual things, for some form of scientific proof of the existence of a spiritual world, takes on an increasing significance. He feels that a number of universities are now moving in the right direction in respect to psychical research and that the day may come when man will find himself faced with incontrovertible evidence of the existence of a spiritual world, evidence so strong and irrefutable that it will provide a new and compelling sanction governing the conduct of mankind.

"If I were a young man," King remarked some months after his retirement as Prime Minister, "I believe I would be impelled to go out and crusade against the trend of materialism which is so evident about us today." He believes that today throughout the world evil has the upper hand, that, unfortunately, to some extent, mechanical progress and atheistic beliefs have developed side by side. He is afraid that many people have become far too materialistic in their approach to life and have lost their faith in the hope of a spiritual life to come.

King's views on the hereafter, he has stated, are identical with those which were held by the late Arthur James Balfour, the first Earl of Balfour. King has pointed out that these were outlined by Balfour's niece in a biography as follows: "From his young manhood onwards he had followed with the very closest attention and knowledge the scientific investigations, with which some of those nearest to him were connected, into the evidences of survival of personality after death. The very nature of those investigations precluded discussion of their results with those who were not engaged upon them. Therefore my own first-hand knowledge of his beliefs on that subject is far from complete.

"Nevertheless, since first-hand knowledge is the only right way of approaching so intimate a question, I will here record my conviction that he utterly rejected the idea of death as an end of personality or of service, and that he did not think of its partings as eternal. I believe too that as his own death approached he dwelt more and more upon the prospect of recognizing, and being recognized by, those whom he had loved."

"My interest in psychical phenomena and my views on life after death couldn't be better expressed," observed King, referring to these excerpts from Balfour's biography.

The subject of King's state of bachelorhood was always one that was good for at least a brief discussion. Single men saw nothing extraordinary in the fact that King had never married and, indeed, probably thought that his single state indicated a high degree of discernment. But on the other hand, married people often expressed the view that marriage would give King a different and more-balanced outlook upon life, that it would make him more sympathetic to the domestic problems of the average householder, that it would have a softening and humanizing effect.

As a matter of fact, King probably was too busy most of the time to give much thought to marriage. Early in his career when some of his married friends would drop in at Laurier House they would bluntly ask him when he was going to marry.

"I haven't got the time," King usually explained. Then, after further consideration, he would add: "In my opinion if a man is married he is entitled to give his family some attention. Maybe I'll get married sometime—later on."

"You ought to get married," a friend told King on one occasion. "It would do you a lot of good if you had a wife to come home to who would tell you what a poor Prime Minister you were and who would cut you down to size."

"I admit the value of marriage," said King, a trifle ruefully, "but when I was younger and might have married I didn't have the opportunity, and now nobody would have me."

"Just put an ad or two in the papers," suggested his friend, "and see how long you will last."

Despite the fact that King never got around to marriage he always enjoyed the company of women. In their presence he loosened up, expanded, glowed. He possessed a natural gallantry, was a charming conversationalist, and handled a compliment with a deftness that displayed an almost continental appreciation of female susceptibility to a neatly turned phrase.

He possessed, too, that understanding of the subjects which interest most women which is said to be singularly lacking in the American male. He had a flair for colour and design, an appreciation of women's clothes, of interior decorating, of many other things that interest the average woman. As a result he was never at a loss for a word when in their company.

King had always been cat-like in his love for comfort. He liked well-upholstered chairs and sofas. Modernistic furniture held no appeal for him. The older he grew the more completely he became attached to familiar objects. He did not care if the furnishings in his office were getting old or down-at-heel, so long as they were comfortable and serviceable that was quite enough. Thus it was that when they tried to take his old private railway car away from him and replace it with a new, modern streamlined model combining all the modern conveniences, King balked.

The new car had venetian blinds, mona-metal fittings, and was equipped with an expensive air-conditioning system. King looked it over and grunted, said the old one was quite good enough for him, and then grudgingly consented to try out the new one. But he soon asked for the return of his old car. He said the air-conditioning system in the new one gave him colds.

So they gave him back his old car with its plush, Victorian comfort, its bright slip covers and its dark, handsome panelling of circassian walnut. Perhaps it was not as fancy as the new one, perhaps it lacked some of the new gadgets and alleged conveniences, but it was comfortable and home-like and familiar.

Once in a while someone who thought he knew King would say that he completely lacked a sense of humour, that he could not take a joke. The record would seem to indicate otherwise. For instance, when James Oastler of the Montreal *Star* was covering an election meeting he noticed that King appeared to be having trouble with his teeth. His dentures seemed to be slipping and sliding about, and Oastler thought something should be done about it. So he sent one of King's secretaries a note suggesting that King should see his dentist and get a new set of teeth. On election night, after the returns were all in, Oastler received a wire from Ottawa. It was terse and to the point: "Got them!" it read.

As for those who claimed that King was selfish and thoughtless in his dealings with those about him, for every story of neglect or forgetfulness there were half a dozen to refute such testimony.

Barney Wise, a political worker in Ottawa, was lying ill in hospital. He was under the impression that he was dying. Somehow King learned of his illness and he left an important session of the House to visit him.

"Barney," he told the discouraged man, "I've left the House at one of its most hectic moments to come down here and cheer you up." Wise was so delighted that he forgot how ill he was and was soon up and about.

When Fred McGregor's father and mother were celebrating their sixtieth wedding anniversary King heard about it. He sent no gift, no letter of congratulation. Instead he went out into his garden at Kingsmere, picked some flowers, drove down to Ottawa to present them in person, and then spent a few hours chatting with the elderly couple.

When two children were burned to death in a tenement fire in Lower Town, Bennett, whose softness of heart was concealed beneath a brittle exterior and who was not the type of person who could find words to express himself at such a time, put $1,000 in bills in an envelope and sent them to the bereaved parents as an anonymous gift. King, who could make no such sizeable donation, wrote the parents a letter of sympathy, then attended the funeral, trudging unobtrusively in the funeral procession.

Thus the King legend grew. Despite the fact that King sought to keep his private life to himself, to draw a clear line of demarcation between those matters which he felt were entirely personal and those which he deemed were the proper concern of the public and of the nation, his fellow Canadians were adamant in their determination to penetrate this carefully manipulated curtain of personal anonymity.

THE COURSE IS SET

"The basis for action was a master plan
devised by General A. G. L. McNaughton."

PART TWO

I

THE WAR CLOUDS GATHER

KING HAD NOT been a student of international affairs for so many years without being alive to the fact that war with Germany was not only inevitable but imminent. Nor did he entertain any doubts as to what part Canada should and would play in the event of the outbreak of hostilities between Britain and Germany He realized that Canada, as a free and independent nation, would have to accept a free and independent nation's responsibilities and obligations. In a battle against the pagan ideologies of the aggressor the Dominion would, indubitably, unfurl her banner on the side of freedom and of right. There was not the slightest question in his mind but that Canada would align herself at the side of Britain, at the side of all freedom-loving nations.

So far as King was concerned this would not have been the case had the compulsion for participation been of a different kind, a war of British aggression, for instance, or one in which the moral issues involved were not clear-cut and imperative.

"I do not hesitate to say," he declared, when speaking in New York early in the war, "that Britain or no Britain, Canada would never have entered the war if, at the outset, our country had not seen the issues clearly for itself, and believed it to be what all free peoples know it to be."

Long before Munich, King had made up his mind as to the inevitability of Canadian participation.

Visiting Hitler in 1937, King had told him bluntly that

if Britain were attacked in war Canada would be at her side.

"That would be the case, even if Canadians had to swim the Atlantic to get there," he informed Hitler.

It is true that like Chamberlain, Roosevelt, and millions of the "little people" who yearned for peace, King did not abandon until the very last the hope that some unexpected, perhaps divine form of intervention might avert the impending conflict. During King's visit to Berlin in 1937 Hitler casually remarked that he was having difficulty getting things accomplished. So long as he was in Berlin he explained fretfully, he was subject to continuous pressure from officialdom, from his ministers, from the military, from one quarter or another. Under these conditions he found it most desirable to escape from Berlin whenever he could and seek the silences and solitudes of his mountain retreat at Berchtesgaden. Only there, he explained, could he give unhurried, contemplative consideration to the great problems confronting him; only there could he find the correct answers.

There is no doubt that this bit of information impressed King, and he may have drawn some analogy between Hitler's love of seclusion and his own habit of seeking the solutions to perplexing problems while enjoying the atmosphere of detachment from departmental routine and red-tape provided by his own mountain retreat at Kingsmere.

At all events, when the Munich crisis was approaching, King, brooding over the unsatisfactory state of the world's affairs, in his library at Laurier House, sat down at his desk and addressed a personal wire to Hitler.

Short, cryptic, and possessing a hidden connotation which only Hitler could have understood, the message said, simply: "Get out of Berlin!"

It was King's way of pleading with Hitler to make a

last, final effort to seek a solution which would prevent the outbreak of a world war. No doubt he recognized the futility of making this personal appeal and realized that Hitler was not likely to be influenced by it; but at the same time King's conscience dictated that, as an individual, he must do what he could to avert war. He must not fail to grasp at any passing straw in the extremity of the moment.

Hitler never answered the message. Eventually its receipt was formally acknowledged through the German embassy in Ottawa. Whether it ever came to Hitler's attention will probably never be known.

King found the year immediately preceding the outbreak of hostilities even harder to endure than the actual war years that were to follow.

Nor were the gloomy forebodings of those who were still closer to the scene of developments calculated to dispel the feeling of frustration and helplessness which marked the position of the leaders of the smaller nations, including those of the Commonwealth countries.

In Britain, Churchill was being criticized as an apostle of gloom.

"What kind of a hush is it?" he asked. "Alas! it is the hush of suspense, and in many lands it is the hush of fear. Listen! No, listen carefully; I think I hear something— yes, there it was quite clear. Don't you hear it? It is the tramp of armies crunching the gravel of the parade grounds, splashing through the rain-soaked fields, the tramp of two million German soldiers and more than a million Italians . . ."

Churchill, too, along with King, harboured no doubts as to the imminence of war. Nor, again along with King, did he entertain any misgivings as to the part the Commonwealth countries would play when the day of decision arrived.

"... There is no part of the British Empire," he declared, early in 1939, "there is no free country, which would not feel able to share in the struggle—the hard struggle—without the slightest self-reproach of blood-guiltiness. Some foreigners mock at the British Empire because there are no parchment bonds or hard steel shackles which compel its united action. But there are other forces, far more subtle and far more compulsive, to which the whole fabric spontaneously responds. These deep tides are flowing now. They sweep away in their flow differences of class and party. They override the vast ocean spaces which separate the Dominions of the King."

During all these months and years of fear and anxiety, of confusion and muddled thinking in Britain and in France, of the onward march of Nazi aggression in Europe, King and his government had not been entirely inactive.

As early as March, 1937 King had visited President Roosevelt at the White House and had discussed plans for the joint defence of the American continent on both the Atlantic and Pacific coasts. In the fall of 1937 Roosevelt visited Victoria, and plans were laid for talks between staff officers of both countries. These took place in Washington in January of the following year.

The defence of Canada was again the subject of conversation between King and Roosevelt in August, 1938, when the latter visited Kingston, and on this occasion the feelings of the people of the United States towards Canada were admirably expressed by Roosevelt in his Kingston Declaration when he said that the people of the United States "would not stand idly by if the domination of Canadian soil was threatened by any other Empire."

When King visited Washington to sign a new Canadian-United States trade agreement later in the year these common problems of defence were again discussed, and in the summer of 1939 when Roosevelt paid a visit to Canadian waters off the Atlantic coast he was chiefly concerned with the problem of coastal defence.

Thus was laid the groundwork for the historic Ogdensburg Agreement of August, 1940, which was to establish the Permanent Joint Board on Defence.

It is significant that the announcement of the Ogdensburg Agreement was followed a few days later by an announcement by Mr. Churchill to the effect that Britain had offered to the United States vital destroyer and air bases in the British possessions in the western hemisphere. On September 3 the President announced that an agreement on this matter had been reached and that sites in Newfoundland, Bermuda, the Bahamas, the British West Indies and British Guiana had been made available to the States.

The important role which King played in the negotiation of this bi-lateral defence agreement has never been fully revealed, but in actuality he played a most effective role in promoting the interests of both parties. The extent of Canada's participation in the plan, however, was hinted at by Mr. Churchill when he told the British House that "in all this line of thought we found ourselves in very close harmony with the government of Canada." Indeed, in this instance, as was the case time and again during the war, King was instrumental in harmonizing the views of Churchill and Roosevelt—two men who invariably held very definite and rigid opinions and who sometimes found difficulty in reaching a common ground of understanding. King sat between them, and his conciliatory and moderate approach to many of the problems that arose, and his ability to interpret Britain to the United States, and vice versa, often won the day.

King's long personal friendship with Roosevelt and the

friendly relations which had been growing up between the people of the United States and Canada over the years were about to pay tremendous dividends. King was happy to think that his own personal contact with the President and his own political policies were not unimportant factors in these neighbourly relations. Referring to the Ogdensburg Agreement, King later said: "In reality the agreement marks the full blossoming of a long association in harmony between the people of Canada and the people of the United States, to which, I hope and believe, the President and I have also in some measure contributed."

In 1941, following informal meetings between Roosevelt and King the Hyde Park Declaration was to come into being. Described by King as a "simple and logical extension, to the economic sphere, of the Ogdensburg Agreement," it provided for economic collaboration between the two countries in respect to the production and exchange of war supplies. It provided also that Canadian purchases of parts and components for equipment being manufactured for Britain would come under the provisions of the American lease-lend agreement with Great Britain. If Canada could provide the United States with between $200,000,000 and $300,000,000 worth of defence articles during the ensuing twelve months then Canada would obtain U.S. dollars which were so urgently needed to ease the serious exchange situation which had developed.

The agreement entered into between Roosevelt and King at Hyde Park, on behalf of their respective governments, was outlined by King and Roosevelt in separate press announcements. Actually no documentary evidence of the existence of the agreement, other than the formal press announcements which had been made, could be produced until after the war, when the agreement was expressed formally in an exchange of notes between the two countries. Roosevelt and King had merely scribbled out the details of the agreement on the back of an envelope and had affixed their signatures. It was in such an informal but none the less effective manner that the two friends conducted much of their state business.

The story behind the Hyde Park Declaration is an absorbing one. For weeks Canadian experts had been in Washington consulting with the U.S. authorities in an attempt to iron out their common financial difficulties. They were making little if any progress, the U.S. experts spending their time pointing out the various physical obstacles which stood in the way of an agreement. Suddenly King decided to visit Roosevelt at Hyde Park. Before lunch one day they discussed the problem. "This is what must be done," said King. "If that is what is needed then we'll do it," said Roosevelt. The details of the plan were scratched out on the envelope and while the two friends ate lunch a secretary typed out a number of copies.

A few weeks later the American experts were still being difficult, were still harping on the mechanical and constitutional obstacles which they declared made impossible the complete implementation of the plan. Once again King got in touch with Roosevelt who called in two of his ablest key planners. "This is what I want done," he told them bluntly. "Don't tell me why it can't be done; just do it!"

That was the last that was heard of the unworkability of the plan.

While the provisions of the Hyde Park Agreement were especially applicable to the war years and designed to meet a specific situation, yet the measure itself was to have far reaching effects which were to extend far beyond the period of the wartime emergency. It was apparent to all that if the two countries could assist one another during wartime by way of economic collaboration then similar collaboration which would result in a more efficient utilization of the resources of both countries could be mutually advantageous in time of peace. It is now patent that the principles embodied in the Hyde Park Agreement have not only been applied successfully in a number of outstanding instances in respect to the peacetime operation of the economy of the two countries, but that the general principle of economic collaboration and integration will continue to dominate Canadian-U.S. relations to an ever-increasing degree.

If, during the immediate pre-war period, King and Roosevelt were working out the details of a plan for joint defence, the Canadian government, on its own behalf, was projecting plans for the mobilization of the nation's manpower in the event of war.

The basis for action was a master plan devised by General A. G. L. McNaughton many years before, when he was Chief of the General Staff during the administration of the Bennett government. McNaughton, who had risen to the post of artillery commander in World War I, was strictly a "Canadian Army" man. He was an enthusiastic and determined exponent of the principle that in any future war Canada's armed forces should operate as a single fighting unit under the direct control of a Canadian commander.

Roughly, the overall plan provided for the formation of a completely equipped and highly mechanized Canadian corps of possibly two or, perhaps, three divisions, enlargement of the air and naval services as convoy and defence groups, and utilization of the bulk of the nation's remaining manpower for the production of the implements of war and the providing of food, clothing and other supplies which would be required by the Allied nations.

There seems little doubt that McNaughton's planning, and in particular his desire to avoid British corps and divisional command, was influenced to some extent by his own personal feelings in respect to the attitude of the British high command towards "colonial" troops in the first war. McNaughton, who was generally conceded to be Canada's finest military tactician, had no particular love for those members of the British general staff with whom he had come in contact as a Canadian commander, a sentiment which he shared with many other high-ranking Canadian soldiers who had seen service during 1914-18. In fact his lack of respect and regard for the "General Blimps" of World War I had led to an open rift between Bennett and himself. Bennett replaced McNaughton and appointed him President of the National Research Council in June, 1935, but when King took over in 1935 the Liberal government apparently saw eye-to-eye with McNaughton on the question of the autonomy of the Canadian military forces and accepted his overall plan with unequivocal approval.

In respect to the second part of the plan, that involving the mobilization of manpower for industrial production, it must be remembered that McNaughton was not only a soldier but a practical scientist. Thus he visualized the next war as a contest in which machines rather than men would play the most important role. He was able to aproach the problem somewhat more objectively than the average headquarters' officer. He believed that in the event of another European war Canada and the United States could best serve by contributing munitions, food and other supplies. A too-ambitious military programme, he was convinced, would hamper the nation's industrial effort.

II

THE COURSE IS SET

FROM THE OUTSET there were those who said that King would never make a war leader, that he was too old, that he was pre-eminently a man of peace, physically and emotionally unequipped for the task of marshalling the nation's manpower and leading the country into war. King was now 65, but he was in the prime of life and at the peak of his mental powers. Whatever his triumphs and successes had been up to this moment, he believed that he was now facing the greatest test of his career. The political philosophies, the policies, the stratagems of leadership which he had evolved, developed and practised over the years were now to be subjected to a final, exacting test. Everything he had learned and thought and done up to the outbreak of the war had been merely a preparatory course in statesmanship which now equipped him to meet the colossal problems posed by a world at war.

It was now that his friendship with the United States, his efforts to preserve national unity at home, his work in extending the status of the Dominion were to find justification and reward.

It was not long before the people of Canada began to realize that their peacetime Prime Minister possessed a hard core of resolve and determination that eminently fitted him for the long, bitter struggle that lay ahead. The crusading spirit which had animated his early efforts towards social and industrial reform now found new and broader avenues of expression. His peculiar talents for compromise and

174

moderation, his ability to forecast and calculate the probable results of immediate action, his happy gift of recognizing the strategic moment when it arrived, all were now to serve him well.

If, when Britain declared war on Germany on September 3, any doubt existed as to the legitimacy of Canada's claim to the status of a completely free and independent nation then that doubt was effectively dispelled by the Dominion's refusal to identify herself automatically with Britain's action.

This was not 1914, when Canada had been automatically bound by Britain's declaration of war; and King had not led his country up the rocky, uncertain slope towards complete self-government to overlook now this golden opportunity to proclaim to the world Canada's state of complete and uninhibited nationhood.

So it was not until September 10 that the proclamation declaring the existence of a state of war between Canada and the German Reich was given formal approval by the King.

This, in itself, was proof positive, if that were required, of Canada's complete autonomy in respect to international relationships; but even more interesting from a constitutional point of view had been the action taken by the government on September 1, when, availing itself of the authority granted under the War Measures Act of 1914, it proclaimed a state of "apprehended war."

Thus, even before Britain had entered the war, Canada had tacitly given notice of her own intentions.

The few extra days of neutrality which elapsed between Britain's declaration of war and Canada's official entrance were not without their beneficial results. Because Canada was not an active belligerent the United States, under her

Neutrality Act of 1937, which she invoked on September 5, was able to ship arms and ammunition into Canada for a brief but effective period, although at the same time being compelled to place an embargo on the shipment of such supplies to Britain and all other belligerents.

King was sitting in his office in the East Block when the telephone rang. It was President Roosevelt.

"We are having a discussion here," he told King, "and you can settle it. Is Canada at war?"

"No, we won't be until parliament says so," King replied.

"Well, you will be soon, won't you?"

"Yes."

Then Roosevelt turned for a moment to his Attorney General. "You see," he told him, "it's all right."

The question under debate in Washington, of course, was whether the United States, under her neutrality law, had the right to send munitions to Canada. In the week that followed Roosevelt saw that planes, guns and everything else that he could lay his hands on which might prove useful to Canada were rushed across the border.

King had summoned parliament to meet on September 7. In the meanwhile steps were taken to place the armed forces on active service. Certain provisions were made without delay for the defence of the coasts, internal security precautions were adopted, the Wartime Prices and Trade Board was established, and the Defence of Canada Regulations were brought into force. Thus, by the time parliament met on the seventh, Canada, while not yet a belligerent, had turned the switch putting into motion her wartime machinery.

When parliament assembled there was some criticism of the indefiniteness of the government's intentions as expressed in the Speech from the Throne, which merely asked that the government be given authority for the enactment of measures necessary to the defence of the country, and for "co-operation in the determined effort which is being made to resist further aggression, and to prevent the appeal to force instead of to pacific means in the settlement of international disputes."

But King was feeling his way. The translation from peace to war was to be accomplished quietly and smoothly; parliament was to have its say, and King was not going to risk stampeding public opinion by any bellicose and bombastic clarion call to arms.

There is no doubt that the course taken by King was dictated, in large measure, by his confirmed belief that the war would be very much different from the previous one, that sound planning and a steady, consistent war effort would be of greater advantage in the long run than a showy, emotional effort which might later collapse for want of a sound foundation.

He knew, too, that while the people of Quebec might be led, they could not be driven blindly into supporting the war. He was acutely conscious that he would have to face opposition from the people of Quebec and their political leaders. Thus it was that he decided to move slowly and cautiously, allowing the fateful implications of the situation to seep into the minds of the public, affording them ample opportunity for calm consideration and cool judgment, in the hope that they would realize that this time it was not a case of whether or not Canada should become embroiled in a European war, but whether or not Canada was to do her part in preventing the Nazi hordes from engulfing the entire world.

When he rose to speak in the House on the 8th, King

stated that if the Address in reply to the Speech from the Throne was approved a formal declaration of war would be issued immediately. The government's position was now clear. The Address was approved after only slight debate and without sufficient opposition to necessitate a standing vote. The ship had passed the harbour shoals and was headed out to sea.

Ten measures were enacted during the next few days. An Act was provided for the establishment when necessary, of a Department of Munitions and Supply; under a War Appropriation Act, the sum of $100,000,000 was provided for "national defence, securing peace, order and welfare"; and a number of special taxes were authorized. Two days after the country had declared war parliament rose.

On September 19 the government's immediate war policy became known when the Department of National Defence issued a press statement.

It was explained that the government had been in consultation with the United Kingdom and that based on information received as to the methods of contribution and the order of importance of the various forms of contribution which Canada could make, the government of Canada had developed a programme which endeavoured to put "first things first" and to co-ordinate Canada's effort with that of the United Kingdom in the most effective way.

The British government had indicated that Canada could be of most immediate assistance by facilitating the purchase in Canada by the United Kingdom of essential supplies. This would involve the immediate gearing-up of Canadian industry and an arrangement by which Canadian dollars would be made available to the British government. This would probably involve repatriation of Canadian securities held in London and, later, the granting of credits.

It had been indicated that in regard to the services, the greatest need was for naval craft, naval personnel and naval facilities, trained air personnel, and, in the militia field, primarily men with technical training and those attached to such special services as the medical, engineering and ancillary branches.

"With regard to general enlistment, the policy is to avoid indiscriminate recruitment and to proceed along well ordered lines as circumstances render desirable," the statement added.

It was announced that Canada's naval forces were already on duty on both coasts, that they were co-operating with the British naval forces for the protection of east coast Canadian ports, were assisting in the protection of departing convoys, and were aiding in mine-sweeping operations. Measures were being taken for progressive enlistment of naval personnel up to a number approximately double the present strength. Policy in respect to the construction of new vessels had not been fixed and would be co-ordinated with those of the United Kingdom. The government was making an immediate contribution of trained air personnel, and had authorized a plan of intensified air training in Canada.

"In regard to the militia service," the statement continued, "the regular mobilization order was issued in anticipation of a declaration of war. Fifty thousand men are now serving. Vulnerable points throughout the country are being protected in co-operation with the Royal Canadian Mounted Police, and with the provincial authorities, in accordance with a pre-arranged plan.

"In view of intimations recently received from the United Kingdom more definite plans can now be made regarding our militia services. As already announced it has been decided to organize and train a division to be available as an expeditionary force, if and when required. For that purpose those now enlisted will be permitted to volunteer for service in Canada, or elsewhere, and will be re-attested. A second division will be similarly re-attested and kept under arms as a further measure of preparedness. Pending the organization of these two divisions further recruiting will be deferred. This will mean that there will be training in Canada, two divisions, plus the troops required for protecting vulnerable points, and for coast and fortress defence."

This, then, on September 19, constituted the Dominion's tentative and immediate plan for mobilization of its fighting forces. Norman McLeod Rogers, who on that day had been appointed the new Minister of National Defence, gave notice that the army would not take key men from industry.

Before another month had elapsed the swift domination of Poland by the enemy had demonstrated the paramount importance of superior air power, and on September 26 the British presented their proposal for the Commonwealth Air Training Plan to the members of the Commonwealth. Canada, which some little time previous to the war, had made an agreement with Britain for the advanced training of British pilots at R.C.A.F. establishments, was to be chosen as the field of operations.

There was, however, one important point to be decided: who should have the administration of the plan? In 1938 Sir Francis Floud, British High Commissioner to Canada, had approached King on behalf of his government in respect to the possibility of sending British pilots to Canada for advanced training in long distance flying and gunnery practice. At that time King pointed out that the ownership, maintenance and control of British establishments in

Photo by Canadian Army

LONDON, SEPTEMBER 1941

"This time Canada was playing the role of a major world power."

Canada would involve "important questions of jurisdiction and administration." He made it clear that Canada's position as a free nation in the British Commonwealth demanded that all military establishments in Canada should be under the control of the Canadian government. Finally, King offered to have the necessary facilities provided at once under the control of the Canadian Department of National Defence. An agreement was reached covering a period of three years; Britain undertook to send fifty pilots a year, and subsequently parliament provided a special appropriation of $6,000,000 to cover the cost of training.

Many Canadians, some Liberals among them, considered that King took too narrow a constitutional view in not acceding promptly and enthusiastically to the request of the British government in 1938 to establish and operate the training schools. By no stretch of the imagination, it was argued, could Britain be defined as a "foreign power" and many felt that the matter might readily have been adjusted under the Visiting Forces Act.

But King, as always, was jealously guarding against any infringement of the Dominion's constitutional rights.

The establishment of the Commonwealth Air Training Plan involved questions of jurisdiction and administration similar to those which had been raised in 1938. King now told the British authorities that since Canada was to supply four-fifths of the pupils and over one-half of the expenses she was obviously the one to provide the management. He believed that Canada's prestige entered greatly into the eventual success of the plan and he was determined that the Dominion should have full administrative and jurisdictional authority.

The Commonwealth Air Training Plan was signed by Great Britain, Canada, Australia and New Zealand on

December 17, but before the signature of all four parties were affixed King had to overcome strong opposition from certain members of the British delegation who believed the United Kingdom should retain control.

One of the most dramatic incidents relative to the negotiations took place at a midnight meeting in King's office in the East Block. After long hours of bargaining King persuaded Lord Riverdale to sign the agreement giving Canada administration of the plan. The signing took place while one of the die-hards of the British delegation who had wandered afield was rushing back to Ottawa to prevent this "dire" happening.

When the agreement was signed it was planned that Canada's share of the cost would be $531,000,000 of a total cost of $823,000,000. But the extension of the plan and other additional responsibilities undertaken during the course of the war was to increase Canada's contribution to $1,281,000,000. During the time the plan was at its peak there were to be some 154 air and ground training schools in operation—more than twice the original estimate.

III

CLEARING THE DECKS

THE EMERGENCY SESSION of parliament which met in the fall of 1939 had scarcely concluded its business when deep undercurrents of distrust and antagonism—distrust in Quebec, antagonism in Ontario—began to shape themselves. Seething and eddying, these constantly shifting streams of public opinion were not long in rising to the surface.

Only two weeks from the time Canada declared war Premier Maurice Duplessis of Qubeec called a provincial election. The Liberal government at Ottawa, he asserted, was using the war as a pretext to deprive Quebec of her autonomy. At first he declared that a vote for the Union Nationale would be a vote against conscription and against active participation in the "European" war. Later he modified his stand slightly and explained that he favoured participation only if Quebec's rights were protected.

This was not the kind of challenge that Mr. King and his ministers could afford to ignore. Not only did it constitute a threat to national unity but it endangered the entire war effort. Mr. Lapointe, as the senior minister from Quebec, immediately accepted the challenge, along with Mr. King. Lapointe referred to Duplessis' action in calling the election "an act of national sabotage." He was joined by his French-speaking cabinet colleagues from Quebec who, one and all, declared they would resign their portfolios in the event of a Union Nationale victory. At the same time they offered assurances that they would not permit the introduction of conscription for overseas service.

The result of the election, while it gave Mr. Godbout only 53 per cent of the popular vote, nevertheless returned the Liberals to power with a total of 69 members out of a house of 86. The Liberal victory clearly indicated that at least half of the people of the province were willing to place their trust in a Liberal government at Ottawa and their federal French-speaking cabinet ministers, who might be expected to represent their non-conscriptionist views, rather than meet the threat to their well-being inherent in a cabinet in which there would be no French-Canadian representation. From the point of view of the federal government the unexpected rejection of Mr. Duplessis was heralded as an encouraging sign and, at the very least, as a partial endorsement of its war programme.

The echoes of the Quebec election were still reverberating when Mr. King and his government were threatened from a fresh quarter. This time the attack came from Mitchell Hepburn and his Liberal Ontario government. This was a more serious threat still for it was an attack which transcended the natural loyalties of the party. Hepburn alleged that the federal government's war effort was niggardly and ineffective, and a formal resolution censuring it for the manner in which it was prosecuting the war, which Hepburn introduced into the provincial house, passed by a vote of 44 to 10, with the Conservatives supporting it.

Faced on the one hand with the fears of the people of Quebec that the federal government would commit itself to a war effort which might eventually lead to conscription, and, on the other, with a demand from Ontario that it accelerate its efforts, King and his ministry found themselves in a position where it was no longer possible to avoid a showing of hands.

When parliament was called together on January 25 it was to learn that the government had decided to go to the country on the issue of its war effort. The Governor General was asked to open and prorogue parliament all within the space of an hour or so.

King may have had a little difficulty with some of his back-benchers who had arrived in Ottawa thinking they were going to collect a full sessional indemnity, only to discover that parliament was to be dissolved. But five sessions had already been held, and King may have justifiably argued that unless the government went to the country without delay it might not be in a position, within another year or two, to withstand the flood of criticism which might have developed by that time. At all events he managed to persuade the members in caucus that he knew what he was doing.

"Criticism, where it has been constructive," said King, during the subsequent campaign, "has been met by appropriate measures. But other criticisms have developed in recent days, not constructive, but destructive; not designed to further Canada's war effort, but to advance personal ambitions; to spread disunion, and to undermine confidence in an administration whose conduct up to the beginning of the present year received general commendation."

Expressing the view that it was the first duty of any government charged with responsibility in the Dominion to maintain national unity, King declared that he had made this task the supreme endeavour of his public life. The preservation of national unity had been made increasingly difficult as from time to time demands had been made on the government, by one part of the country, for "unconditional declarations of participation" in European conflicts without regard to their nature, and by another part of the country, for no participation in any European wars.

"Once again," said King, "I ask you to consider where Canada would have been at the outbreak of the present war in Europe, if I, or any of my colleagues, had identified himself with either of these extreme attitudes; or if, through unwise and unnecessary declarations in advance of an actual and known condition, we had helped to precipitate an open conflict of opposed opinions?"

Dr. Manion, the Conservative leader, saw Canada confronted with "a grave crisis." The King government, he said, had been responsible for the country's unpreparedness and her "weak" war effort. In rebuttal, King declared that Dr. Manion had held his counsel prior to the war because he had known, as everyone else had known, that the people would not have supported expenditures in peacetime to prepare for active participation in a European war. The government had repeatedly told parliament, he added, that its peacetime military expenditures had been exclusively for the defence of Canada. No other measures would have received the support of parliament.

The other major issue raised by the opposition was its demand for a "national" government. This plea fell on deaf ears. The attractiveness of national government, said King, was more apparent than real and the words "national government" were deliberately used to suggest a sort of patriotic idealism. Actually, he contended, a national government was one which represented the people in parliament. The Liberal government was in the truest sense a national government. Obviously what Dr. Manion meant when he talked of a national government was a union government. A union government was almost certain to mean one of two things: a weak government, or a dictatorial government. Who, asked King, would compose Dr. Manion's "national" or "union" government? Would it include members of the administration which Dr. Manion had so heartily condemned? Would it include Mr. Woodsworth? Would Mr. Blackmore join, and take Social Credit with him? Would Mr. Herridge's New Democracy be born in time? As late as November, 1939, said King, Dr. Manion had expressed the view that an alert and constructively critical opposition was second only in importance to the government. Had he changed his views because he now saw no possibility of the election of a Conservative government?

King was not going to have anything to do with the proposal whatsoever. If the war effort was to be effective then the people of Canada would have to be guided by a government that was "strong, steady, vigorous, patient, provident and experienced." He believed the Liberal party could supply that kind of government.

Later on King was to express the view that he could have won widespread support and popularity for a time had he yielded to the opposition's demand for a coalition.

"I would have been the most popular man in Canada for four or five years, but the coalition would have smashed up and the war effort with it," he declared.

Neither the C.C.F. nor the Social Credit parties had much to say on this issue of a national or union government. In respect to the war effort in general, the C.C.F. favoured limiting Canada's participation to economic aid. The Social Creditors demanded conscription of both wealth and manpower.

The election was held March 26. The Liberal government was returned with the largest majority in the history of the country. It had increased the number of its seats from 180 to 183. It had received a clear mandate to carry on.

At the time Canada entered the war the nation had not yet completely recovered from the depression. In September 1939, about 400,000 Canadian workers were unemployed, and more than 1,000,000 men, women and children were on direct relief.

On the other hand, no attempt had been made to absorb any of the unemployed into the country's permanent armed forces. The total strength of these permanent forces prior to the war amounted to only slightly more than 10,000 men. Canada had a permanent army of 4,500, an air force of 4,000, and a naval nucleus of 1,700. George Drew called the latter Canada's "tin-pot" navy.

The militia, however, constituted a fairly substantial framework upon which an effective fighting machine might be erected. Approximately 90,000 men were enrolled in the militia forces and had been undergoing weekly drills, and some of them had had an annual fortnight in camp. They were not, of course, required to serve outside of Canada.

On September 1, the government had authorized the mobilization of a reserve force. The mobilization was carried out in accordance with plans prepared in peace time, being based, for the most part, on the existing units of the militia. The composition of each division of the force, government officials said, had been carefully worked out in advance, to provide proportional representation, on a basis of population, to every part of the Dominion.

As explained in a previous chapter, early in September it had been decided to mobilize a first division to be used as an expeditionary force, if necessary. In October it was decided to dispatch this 1st division and some ancillary troops overseas. Organization of the division was speeded up and by the end of January, 1940, the 1st Canadian

Division, with the requisite number of ancillary troops, had arrived in Britain. On May 21, 1940, the government authorized mobilization of a second division, for service in Canada or overseas as it might be required. The formation of a number of reserve companies of Home Guards was authorized.

In June the National Resources Mobilization Act, requiring all Canadians to place their persons and property at the disposal of the state, was given effect. A system of national registration was instituted which required all over 16 to register for national service. In its endeavour to ascertain the particular aptitudes of every Canadian the government circulated a lengthy questionnaire in which the citizen was asked among other things whether or not he or she could milk a cow, drive a truck, handle horses, etc. Whether or not the government benefited from the information thus obtained is a moot point. However the registration was high-lighted by the unexpected action taken by Mayor Camillien Houde of Montreal. Believing that this step was the first of a series leading to conscription Mayor Houde called upon the people of his province to refuse to register. He was sent to an internment camp, and although the incident caused considerable commotion for a time, and Mr. King went to some lengths to explain the seriousness of Mr. Houde's "civil disobedience", the incident was soon forgotten amidst the general clamour of more important events. Houde was released from internment in 1944 and was promptly re-elected for a fifth term, although for some time he was to act merely as a figurehead, the actual administration of the city's affairs being under control of the Quebec Municipal Commission.

Compulsory military training for service in Canada,

under the National Resources Mobilization Act, was introduced, and in October, 1940, the first group of men was called up. They were to train for a period of one month. Early in 1941, however, this period was extended to four months, and by June it had been decided that every man who had completed his four months training would remain in the service for the duration.

By the end of December, 1940, Canada's army had a total strength of 177,500, the navy had almost trebled its force and now had 14,872 officers and ratings, while the air force had a total of 36,800.

In the meanwhile, on the industrial front, the country was being organized to meet immediate and future needs. A start had been made on the construction of air training schools. Barracks were springing up all over the Dominion, temporary government buildings were being rushed to completion at Ottawa, dollar-a-year men were flocking into the capital to take up positions with the Wartime Prices and Trade Board, the Department of Munitions and Supply, and in the dozens of government boards, wartime corporations and crown companies which had been set up to control and operate the nation's economic and industrial plant.

The Canadian government, and Canadian business men acting on their own, were having some difficulty in persuading British industry to supply plans and designs for mechanical equipment required by Canadian troops. Canadian industrialists had gone to London to see what they could do but had been disappointed at the few small orders they had received for shells, military clothing, etc. It was evident that Britain had no intention, at this time, of permitting Canada to build an industrial machine for the war effort which conceivably might supplant her own.

However, military and industrial missions continued to

come and go. British military experts, addressing Canadian service clubs, talked of a long war—even a three years' war!

But all the time-tables were soon to be discarded. With the fall of France, in June, the war took on a new and more serious aspect. All hopes of a speedy Allied victory were now dispelled and it was apparent that the Canadian economy would have to be re-established on a more elaborate and substantial foundation. Canada must be developed into the arsenal of the Empire. Every gun, every shell, every single piece of war equipment that could be produced, and every ounce of food that could be grown would now be required if the enemy was to be contained, much less vanquished. It was going to be a long, rough struggle after all. Canadians began to look about and ask themselves what they could do.

Even before Canada had declared war King had taken initial steps to strengthen his cabinet. Hon. J. L. Ralston had returned from private life to take over the finance portfolio, while a little later Hon. Norman McLeod Rogers, Minister of Labour, had been appointed Minister of National Defence. But it was not until July, 1940 that King's real war cabinet finally took shape. By this time Mr. Rogers had lost his life in a plane crash and his portfolio had been taken over by Col. Ralston.

Mr. King's cabinet, as reorganized on July, 1940, was as follows:

Prime Minister, President of the Privy Council, and Secretary of State for External Affairs, Rt. Hon. W. L. Mackenzie King.

Minister of Justice and Attorney General, Rt. Hon. Ernest Lapointe.

Minister of Public Works and Transport, Hon. P. J. A. Cardin.

Minister of National Defence, Hon. J. L. Ralston.

Minister of National Defence for Air, Hon. C. G. Power. (Also Associate Minister of National Defence).

Minister of Pensions and National Health, Hon. Ian Mackenzie.

Minister of Finance, Hon. J. L. Ilsley.

Minister of Fisheries, Hon. J. E. Michaud.

Minister of Munitions and Supply, Hon. C. D. Howe.

Minister of Agriculture and Minister of National War Services, Hon. J. G. Gardiner.

Minister of Labour, Hon. Norman McLarty.

Minister of Trade and Commerce, Hon. J. A. Mac-Kinnon.

Minister of Mines and Resources, Hon. T. A. Crerar.

Secretary of State, Hon. P. F. Casgrain.

Minister of National Revenue, Hon. C. W. Gibson.

Minister of National Defence for Naval Affairs, Hon. A. L. Macdonald.

Postmaster General, Hon. W. P. Mulock.

These, then, were the men in whom Mr. King placed his confidence as he faced the job ahead. For the most part all of the key ministers were to remain in the cabinet until towards the end of the war. A few new faces were to be added, however, and some ministers were to be shuffled from one job to another. In December, 1941, Mr. St. Laurent and Mr. Mitchell entered the cabinet, one as Minister of Justice, the other to succeed Mr. McLarty as Minister of Labour. Joseph Thorson, K.C. assumed the new portfolio of National War Services only to be succeeded shortly by L. R. LaFlèche, former Deputy Minister of National Defence, who, in turn, was later dropped from the cabinet. There were to be a few other new faces from Quebec, but in the main the cabinet membership remained unaltered until the dying days of the war when the conscription issue threatened its existence.

By this time the pattern of the war had begun to reveal itself more clearly. Germany had overrun the Netherlands, France had capitulated, the miracle of Dunkirk was now fading into memory, the full immensity of the threat to the freedom of the entire democratic world was apparent in all its frightening colours. The complacency which many of Britain's political and military leaders had displayed earlier in the war had now completely vanished to be replaced by the feverish activity of a nation preparing to repel a possible invasion. Churchill had offered his people nothing but "blood, toil, tears and sweat," the cry for help had gone out across the waters. Canada, together with the other members of the Commonwealth, had already been forced to alter her original estimate of what would be required in the way of assistance. Canadians were beginning to ask themselves if Canada should not be sending more men.

Mr. King's re-shuffling of his cabinet did not, it is true, meet with the general approval of the official opposition which felt that the cabinet should be more representative of all political groups. In announcing the changes the Prime Minister admitted that he had made overtures to a number of persons outside of parliament, and outside of the Liberal party, but that none of those approached had seen fit to accept his invitation to enter the government.

As an alternative, he now offered the leader of the opposition and several members of the opposition parties the opportunity of serving on the war commmittee of the cabinet in the capacity of associate members. But Mr. Hanson, acting leader of the opposition, interpreted King's offer as a device to saddle the opposition with a share of the government's responsibilities without at the same time giving it any actual directional power. A second suggestion put forward by King that a selected group of opposition members hold regular conferences with the government, at which confidential information could be made available to them, was also rejected on the grounds that it might circumscribe the opposition's prerogative in respect to criticism of government policy and action.

In the administration of the country's war effort, however, members of all political parties were permitted to make their contribution. When the government selected men and women for the key administrative positions in the various new war departments, boards, commissions and crown corporations, party lines were, for the most part, ignored, and an honest effort was made to appoint those who were best qualified.

IV

MANPOWER MUDDLE

EVENTS DURING 1941 and 1942 moved with lightning-like rapidity and force. On December 7, 1941, Japan attacked Pearl Harbour, and four days later Germany and Italy declared war against the United States. These events removed the last remaining restrictions on United States co-operation with the Allies.

With the tide of Japanese conquest sweeping over a thousand miles of sea, and with the fall of Hong Kong and the loss of Canada's expeditionary force, it was now apparent to King that pledges given by all political parties before and during the 1940 election to the effect that conscription for overseas service would not be resorted to in case of war, might, in the future, circumscribe government action in respect to the maintenance of the fighting forces in the field.

In placing the issue before the country in January, 1942, King contended that in the political controversy which had developed and which, he asserted, was not only obscuring the government's war effort but was threatening to impair its effectiveness, attempts were being made to confuse in the public mind a number of separate and distinct questions.

The first question, he said, related to the total effort to meeting total war; the second, to national selective service as a means to such end; and the third, to the application of compulsion without restriction of any kind to conscription for service in the armed forces overseas.

"As respects total effort to meet total war, that is and has been right along the policy of the present administration," King told the House. "As regards national selective service as a method of achieving a total effort, that too is and has been the policy of the government. As respects the use of compulsion in applying the principle of national selective service, that, also, is a part of government policy.

"In the case of compulsion only one definite limitation has been recognized, and that is the limitation of the use of compulsion as a method of raising men for military service overseas."

King then pointed out that in Britain, as in Canada, compulsion was not being used as a method of raising fighting men for the navy and the air force. As compulsion was already being used in Canada to raise men for service in the army at home then the only issue between the government and its opponents narrowed down solely to the question of the application of compulsion in raising men for the army for overseas. Since up to the present the active army had been able to secure the necessary recruits on a voluntary basis, the issue of conscription for overseas service in the army related only to a possible future emergency.

However, he went on, quite apart from the controversy which had arisen, there were now the strongest of reasons why the government should possess complete freedom to act in accordance with its judgment of the needs of the situation.

While the government was of the opinion that neither a general election nor a referendum on the question of conscription was advisable or necessary, it did believe that it should be released from any previous commitments in respect to raising men for military service.

As for the suggestion that the government should proceed in any arbitrary manner and introduce conscription

"WINNIE" TAKES THE SPOTLIGHT

"King was satisfied to get on with the job, let the orchids fall where they might."

without consultation with the people, King believed any such attempt would be thwarted by parliament, and rightly so.

"I do not propose," he declared, "to erect bad faith and the broken pledge into a principle of action.

"I propose at all times to do all in my power to see that the will of the people, not that of my particular section or group or interest, however powerful or vociferous, shall prevail in the government of this country."

Later, in April, when King went on the air to explain why the plebiscite was being held, he stressed the fact that while the government, so far as legal power went, was perfectly free to take any action which the majority in parliament would support, nothing, however, could justify a government in ignoring a specific pledge to the people unless it was clear that the safety of the nation was immediately involved.

The pledge not to impose conscription, he said, had resulted from Canada's experience in the first war. The way in which conscription had been introduced and the manner in which it had been enforced had given rise to bitter resentment. In addition, its military value had been negligible.

Before, and at the commencement of the present war, he declared, the people of Canada had continued to think of the present war in the terms of the last.

"They most certainly did not think of a war in which all the nations of the world would be in danger. Much less did Canadians think of the war as one in which Canada might become the most coveted of all the prizes of war. That, however, is the actual situation today."

He steadfastly maintained that the restriction upon the power of the government had been necessary at the outset to preserve national unity, that it had helped, until recently, to produce the desired result. It had now, however, become a threat to unity and he saw no reason why its removal should be further delayed. He believed its withdrawal would help to overcome a source of "irritation and disunity" within the country. He was satisfied that the army was just as large as it would have been had conscription for overseas service been adopted from the beginning.

On April 27 the people went to the polls to record their answer to the question: "Are you in favour of releasing the government from any obligation arising out of any past commitments restricting the methods of raising men for military service?"

The country replied in the affirmative, and the following July, after long and bitter debate, during which members of the C.C.F. and a small group of French-speaking members argued that removal of the restricting clause would virtually mean the automatic adoption of conscription, the Prime Minister's motion to amend the National Resources Mobilization Act so as to permit adoption of conscription for overseas service passed the House by a vote of 141 to 45.

For a time at least the air had been cleared. Mr. King was proceeding in his usual, slow, cautious, methodical manner. The government now had the power to impose conscription; it could say to Quebec: "We are in a position to impose conscription but, depend upon it, we won't exercise that power unless we have to." Indeed, there were few indications that the government would have to face the issue again during the war. Mr. King had taken a halting step towards meeting the criticism of the opposition; the fears of the anti-conscriptionists had been temporarily allayed; and the country would once again be able to settle down to the work of getting on with the war.

The results of the plebiscite had not been entirely reassuring, however. They indicated a wide division of opinion, and that division was localized in a rather significant if not altogether unexpected manner. While 64 per cent of the people voted in favour of freeing the government's hands, this 64 per cent was anything but evenly distributed over the Dominion. Although Manitoba and British Columbia voted 80 per cent in favour of giving the government complete freedom of action, and Ontario returned a "Yes" vote of 84 per cent, 76 per cent of the electors in Quebec voted "No!" When one considered that the 24 per cent of Quebec electors who voted "Yes" were mostly from constituencies which were pre-eminently English-speaking, then it was apparent that probably well over ninety per cent of the French-speaking electors had voted "No."

It was a clear indication of Quebec's traditional resistance to any form of compulsion that would involve Canada in a European conflict, but, on the other hand, it was not an exact yardstick of the actual extent of Quebec's participation in the war. It was later to be pointed out—not in defence of Quebec's position, but rather in criticism of her effort—that by 1944 only 22 per cent of her male population between the ages of 18 and 45 were in the armed forces, as compared with 37 per cent for the Dominion as a whole.

There were those who argued, many English-speaking Canadians among them, that, considering all the circumstances, this was not at all a bad showing for the people of Quebec. They submitted that in the first place French-speaking Canadians could not be expected to profess any particular sense of blood loyalty to Britain, and that those who did volunteer for service overseas did not have the advantage of the emotional compulsion which stirred the hearts of many of their English-speaking compatriots who felt that they were going to the assistance of the Mother Country. Rather, they argued, the French-speaking volunteers went as the result of a "reasoned" loyalty. It was possible, members of this school of opinion suggested, that many French-speaking Canadians volunteered because of the sentimental ties of language and common heritage which bound them to the people of France. The same sympathetically inclined supporters of Quebec outlook—or what they believed to be Quebec outlook—contended that in the final analysis it would be fairer to suggest that for the most part French-speaking Canadians entered the war because their country was at war and because they were convinced that, fundamentally, the principles for which they were being asked to fight were morally just and sound.

To accept all these rather naive premises, however, would be to ignore completely the actual facts and to assume an attitude of intellectual condescension quite unpalatable to the French-Canadian mind.

If the plebiscite was not a yardstick of Quebec's actual physical participation in the war, it was certainly a definitely-revealing index of Quebec thought. Admittedly there were shades of opinion in the province that ranged all the way from the desire that Canada should play an active part in the war against Germany, to the expressed hope that Germany would defeat Britain and thus free the Dominion once and for all of even the slightest suggestion of British dominance. These were the extremes. In between was that great majority that made up the bulk of those who voted "No" in the plebiscite, and these were openly unenthusiastic in respect to the war. They felt no deep call of duty. They were aware of no good reason why they should leave their own country to fight on foreign soil. They were to maintain this attitude of extreme nationalism throughout the war, an attitude which was accompanied by a studied lack of enthusiasm and, in many cases, evidence of deliberate non-co-operation and even obstructionism.

They made no particular secret of this, for their heart was not in the war. Thousands of young French-Canadians sought and obtained postponements on the flimsiest of excuses and some Liberal members of parliament assisted them, and in the elections of 1945 bragged to their constituents of how many hundreds of thousands of exemptions they had been instrumental in obtaining for them. This is not to say that exemptions were not improperly obtained in other parts of the Dominion, but the number so obtained in Quebec was large, and no social stigma was attached to the act of outwitting the authorities.

In view of this situation one might wonder that the percentage of volunteers from Quebec was as large as it was. Some French-speaking Canadians who hold extreme nationalistic views explain it in the following terms. A very few volunteered because of their sentimental attachment for France; some went because their fathers had served in World War I; many joined up because they were unemployed; a few sought adventure; some liked the army for itself, and when they went into action they fought for the honour of their regiment or "team"; and the majority were volunteers from the N.R.M.A. army who went active because they believed or had been told that conscription would be introduced sooner or later and that they would stand a better chance of being able to choose a branch of the service which appealed to them if they volunteered. Few of them, these same French-Canadian observers contend, volunteered out of any deep sense of loyalty to Britain or to the Commonwealth as a whole.

This opinion is not cited here with the intention of condemning the people of French Canada for their outlook on the war. It is offered merely as an indication of the reasoning some of them applied to the issue of overseas service. In passing, it might be added that plenty of English-speaking Canadians joined up for exactly similar reasons, for adventure, the attractions of army life, to avoid being conscripted, etc. But, on the other hand, the majority of English-speaking Canadians did feel a stirring of their Anglo-Saxon blood. There were those too, who professed no such compulsions but declared they were fighting for Canada alone, against a common enemy.

King had been the idol of the people of Quebec. No one had done so much to extend the independent status of the Dominion. This was an achievement which every nationalist-minded French-Canadian understood and appreciated. Over the years the people of Quebec had come to look upon King as their great emancipator, as the exponent and defender of the Laurier tradition.

But when war came and the people of Quebec found themselves being led, by devious routes, into actual participation in another European conflict their faith in King was rudely shaken. They experienced a deep sense of betrayal. They failed to appreciate that King was offering them at least a half-loaf, that he was holding off the evil day as long as possible. Had King staked his political future on not entering the war, and been defeated, he would have remained the idol of French Canada. Somehow the people of Quebec could not appreciate the fact that King's allegiance was to the people of Canada as a whole. They seemed to feel that they were the objects of his particular if not sole concern. Their disillusionment was great.

Whether the French-speaking Canadians of Quebec

realized it or not, whether they would care to admit it or not, there were other certain material factors which had a definite bearing on the enlistment situation in Quebec. Educational standards in that province had never been as high as in most other provinces of the Dominion, and this was particularly true in respect to technical education. As a result, thousands of French-speaking youths who attempted to join the air force were automatically disqualified because of their lack of technical knowledge. They accepted the circumstance of this rejection with a rather grim feeling of resignation. They felt that the air force was an élite service from which they were being studiously excluded.

Again, Quebec was similarly backward in respect to health standards. The narrow, sunless alleys and back-streets of St. Henri and Griffintown were not conducive to the development of sound and robust bodies. The great, sprawling French-speaking metropolis had more than its share of hollow-chested, undernourished men and women and only a cursory medical examination was necessary to establish the ineligibility of thousands of young men for service in the armed forces.

Still another factor was the tremendous demand for workers by the great industries which were centralized in Montreal where over a third of the population of the province was concentrated. If there were few factories on the prairies and in some other parts of the Dominion the contrary was true of Quebec, and the heavy industries of the province absorbed war-workers by the tens-of-thousands.

These particular conditions did exist in the French-speaking province and could be advanced with considerable justification as important factors contributing to Quebec's appreciably lower enlistment rate. Yet the average French-speaking Canadian will argue that the reason Quebec failed to make a better showing was because she just didn't believe in the war.

But all along the French of Canada suffered from a feeling that they were being placed in the position of an inferior people. They resented the fact that French-Canadians were apparently unable to attain to a post of high military command and pointed to two brigade commanders as the penultimate of achievement in this respect. There had been only one superior French-Canadian officer in the navy and he had been "promoted" to the position of naval attaché. As for the air force, they shrugged their shoulders with Gallic resignation.

That the government was open to criticism in respect to the enforcement of its military and manpower policy in Quebec is a matter of general agreement. One might cite, as an example, the method adopted by the government in setting enlistment quotas. These quotas, instead of being based on population, were based on existing non-permanent active militia units. Thus, those provinces and districts which had developed the militia to the greatest extent before the war were now called upon to produce proportionately more recruits, in relation to population, than districts where militia units had been neglected. Quebec, as a result, might easily meet her quotas with a comparatively small number of enlistments, while British Columbia, where the militia was highly organized, might have difficulty in meeting hers, despite the fact that her enlistments were much greater on a straight population basis. Thus, it was justifiably argued, some districts were being actually penalized as a result of their peacetime patriotism and preparedness.

As the nation's industrial activity steadily increased and the armed forces continued to expand, the tug-of-war between the two for the available supply of manpower began to find expression in rising criticism of the government's whole manpower policy.

Towards the end of 1942 the army was already experiencing some difficulty in filling its enlistment quotas. A very creditable showing had been made to date, however. By December of 1942 the total armed strength of the army was 425,000, that of the navy, 49,000, and that of the air force, 153,705: a grand total of 627,000, of which some 18,000 were members of the various women's auxiliary forces.

A year later the total had risen to 763,204, the largest proportionate increase for the year having been in the navy which had increased its strength by 26,094 to 75,354. The air force had increased its strength by 52,645 to 206,350. The army, on the other hand, had increased by only 56,500 to 481,500. It was obvious that enlistments in the navy and air force and the still rising demand for labour in war industry were contributing to the army's recruiting difficulties.

War employment reached its peak on October 1, 1943, when 1,166,000 or 13.3 per cent of the total population 14 years of age and over, were employed either directly or indirectly on war work.

While much of the criticism of the government's manpower policy was undoubtedly politically inspired, the administration was not undeserving of a vote of censure in respect to the administration of its national selective service regulations. While admittedly the job was not a simple one there had, nevertheless, been considerable confusion at a high level. There was a lack of capable men to administer the regulations, and the failure of some of those in authority to "carry through" in respect to the compulsory provisions of the plan had resulted in a manpower muddle that could not be easily explained away.

Postponements were being granted on political grounds,

and postponements granted to agricultural workers were completely out of line with those granted to workers in other fields of employment. There was a feeling that, in general, the manpower of the nation was not being put to the best and fullest use.

Some justification for these beliefs was forthcoming in November, 1942, when Elliott M. Little, Director of National Selective Service, resigned from his post to be followed, within the space of a few days, by over a dozen men who had occupied key positions in his department.

Mr. Little, in his letter of resignation, charged Minister of Labour Humphrey Mitchell with being chiefly responsible for the "virtual paralysis" of the selection service administration. Mr. Little said that he had found the minister's actions inconsistent with his word, and that there had been obstruction of the director's efforts to obtain control of military call-ups. He asserted that his own efforts to make selective service function effectively had been increasingly frustrated.

"The present situation," said Mr. Little, "is one of ambiguous and divided authority, which has led progressively from confusion to friction and obstructionism. The result has been virtual paralysis in the organization."

Mr. Little's letter was followed a few days later by a demand on the part of the Trades and Labour Congress of Canada for the resignation of the Minister of Labour. In a letter addressed to the Prime Minister the officials of the Trades and Labour Congress asserted that Mr. Mitchell's record was one that inspired little or no confidence on the part of the Dominion's workers.

There were, of course, two sides to the story. There is no doubt that Mr. Little, a sincere and conscientious man who was attempting to do a job for Canada, had suffered from a general feeling of frustration. But while the national selective service regulations had placed a great deal of power in the hands of the Minister of Labour and his Directors of Selective Service, the government's hope had been to use that power only as a last resort. If one can reconcile the use of the two terms, what the government had started out with had been a system of "voluntary compulsion." It had hoped that to some extent the mere existence of its powers to channel and control labour would act as a fulcrum to ease workers into their proper niches. But the caution and indirection exercised in applying the regulations had not always had the desired effect.

The position of the agricultural worker was a case in point. Postponements granted under the heading of "farming" in effect at the end of December, 1944 amounted to 159,927 out of a total of 247,336, or well over half the total number. Obviously farm production was of almost equal importance to industrial production, but whereas the industrial worker had been granted deferment on the understanding that he would be employed throughout the whole 12 months of the year in an essential industrial job, a good many farmers, for some time, were granted postponements merely because they were farmers.

When Humphrey Mitchell took over the Department of Labour in December, 1941, he was faced with the task of reconstructing an entire department to meet the especial needs of the war economy. He made a start by eliminating as much dead-wood as possible and brought in from outside—from the ranks of labour organizations and elsewhere—the men whom he thought could handle the work. Among these men was Elliott Little who had been directing the Wartime Bureau of Technical Personnel and who had been doing a good job. From the first Little demonstrated an unwillingness to take advice and direction from his minister. On more than one occasion he made public announcements without consultation with Mitchell and when the minister took exception to this practice Little felt that he was not receiving the co-operation he was entitled to. Finally, Mitchell, about to leave Canada to discuss manpower problems with Labour Minister Ernest Bevin in London, instructed Little not to make any further press announcements until his return. When Mitchell reached Montreal en route to Britain he picked up the paper to find Little once again making statements to the press. From this moment Little's days with the department were numbered. In addition, Mitchell had advised Little on a number of occasions that he must concentrate on the job of organizing the work of national selective service on a sound and workable basis. This, Mitchell believed, Little failed to do.

The resignation of Mr. Little and his assistants brought the government to a realization of the seriousness of the situation, however. Arthur MacNamara, Deputy Minister of Labour, was appointed acting Director of National Selective Service and attempts were at once made to apply the existing regulations more rigidly and with the purpose in mind of guaranteeing that all who were granted postponements were, in effect, entitled to them. Agricultural workers who had worked in the fields for six months of the year, only to sit around the stove all winter, were now informed that they must accept winter employment in the bush, in the mine, or in the factory. A similar effort was made to reverse the process in respect to seasonal winter workers such as loggers. These were now required to work during the summer months at what suitable employment was available.

The establishment in 1941 of a national employment service under the Unemployment Insurance Act was a step which soon began to pay dividends in respect to the effective placement of workers, and by 1943 the regulations had been amended to provide for the freezing of high-priority workers in their jobs. The employees, in return, were protected against improper dismissal by employers. The freezing of wages was another step which, in conjunction with price control, had beneficial effects which carried through into the post-war years and contributed to the economic stability of the Dominion.

In comparison with the United States, Canada had a much more effectively-controlled labour force. In the States, employees could move from one job to another, seeking higher pay or other advantages, to the detriment of the industries in which they were employed. This situation was largely overcome in Canada.

Undoubtedly the government had contributed to its own difficulties by its policy of immobilizing in Canada a large army of physically fit men who had been called up under the National Resources Mobilization Act for service in Canada and its territorial waters. By the end of 1944 a total of 153,115 men had been enrolled under the N.R.M.A., but of these 48,256, or more than 31 per cent, had volunteered for general service. It is true that the N.R.M.A. army constituted a training ground for potential volunteers for the overseas army, but it also drained off a great pool of industrial manpower. The effective strength of the N.R.M.A. army in November 1944 was approximately 60,000 of which 42,000 were considered suitable for infantry service. Opposition to the government's policy of keeping these men immobilized in Canada on the grounds that they might be required for the defence of the country—at that time a very remote possibility—grew stronger with the passing of time.

True, efforts were made to "encourage" as many as possible of these N.R.M.A. men to volunteer for general service overseas, and these efforts led to abuses of a most deplorable nature. Let it be said at once that the measures taken by some officers who were responsible for getting their units up to strength were neither even tacitly authorized or knowingly condoned by the military or governmental authorities at the top level.

But many officers, faced with the problem of finding recruits to bring their units up to full strength felt justified in taking unusual measures to obtain these recruits. Men in the N.R.M.A. army were subjected to humiliating lectures in the belief that they would be shamed into volunteering. Taking another approach, some officers hinted that those who volunteered for overseas service would receive extra leave, would be relieved of unpleasant camp duties, would be given preferred treatment of one kind or another. Conversely, those who failed to step forward could expect few favours. To the contrary, they could expect more than their rightful share of rough camp work. Such tactics may have induced some N.R.M.A. men to volunteer. But for the most part those who volunteered went willingly enough, convinced that the need was now imperative and that the moment for decision had arrived; or because they believed conscription was imminent.

But despite lack of Quebec support, government mistakes, the natural period of trial and error in many fields of industry, Canada was forging ahead, surprising not only herself, but the world at large. Industrially, she accomplished in five years what it would have taken her 25 years to do under normal conditions. Taxes were high, there was rationing of many items which people had come to accept as a matter of course, and the stress and strain of a nation at war was having its effect on the individual. But Canada was now the second greatest exporting nation of the world. She was producing not only the food to feed Britain, but tanks, guns, planes, ships and other essential sinews of war for herself and the Allied nations.

V

THE DAGGER UNSHEATHED

THE FIRST CONTINGENT of the Canadian 1st Division had landed in Britain in December, 1939. By January, 1943, Canada had an army in Britain consisting of two army corps: one corps of three infantry divisions, the other of two armoured divisions. Together with ancillary troops, the armed forces overseas numbered over 190,000 men. In Canada there were 210,000 men on active service, with some thousands more enrolled in the reserve army.

Despite the fact that the main body of Canadian troops had not yet come to grips with the foe, Canadians had participated prominently in a number of hot engagements. In August and September, 1941, there had been the expedition to Spitzbergen. Then in December of the same year Canada's ill-fated expedition to Hong Kong had resulted in the loss of 2,000 men killed or taken prisoner. On August 19, 1942, Canadians stormed up the beaches of Dieppe to feel out the enemy defences of the Atlantic Wall and to divert enemy attention from the impending invasion of North Africa. For ten hours the men of the Canadian 2nd Division maintained their foothold, at length withdrawing. Of the 5,000 Canadians who landed 3,350 were killed, wounded or taken prisoner.

But for the main body of Canadian troops in Britain the prolonged period of inactivity had been a real hardship.

"Some of the Canadian soldiers who were first to cross the ocean," noted the London *Times,* "have now been on duty for more than three years in the British Isles. If they have been condemned to inaction it has been . . . by no

QUEBEC CONFERENCE, 1943

"King was instrumental in harmonizing
the views of Churchill and Roosevelt."

Canadian design, but by the considered strategic plan of the United Nations."

Referring to the disposition of the Canadians, King declared: "It has not been easy for them to watch the forces of the other nations of the British Commonwealth engaged in battles they were not able to share.

"Since June, 1940, they have stood at the very point where they would be the first to be hurled into a counter-stroke against an invader. They know that at any moment they may be called upon to cross the English Channel or to fight on any other front. The Commander-in-Chief, General McNaughton, has sought to make the Canadian army in Britain, for its size, the best trained and equipped, the most highly integrated and effective striking force in the world."

But this period of inaction told on the Canadian troops and had its effect on their morale. They felt that they were losing face, that, perhaps, for political reasons they were being kept out of the fighting.

In 1941 when Prime Minister King was in Britain he visited the Canadian troops at Aldershot and was booed. It is true that the incident was magnified in the press out of all true proportion, and was seized upon by the opposition as a means of presenting King in an unfavourable light, but it did indicate the general dissatisfaction among the troops at their enforced idleness.

King was surprised and somewhat hurt by the demonstation which was led by a small group of Toronto Scottish. The men had been on manoeuvres, the day was a wet one, and when King arrived to inspect them they were tired, cold and restive. When they learned that they would have to listen to a speech they forgot their manners.

King took the booing in good part, and with a smile

went on with his speech. Then, because the men realized that, after all, King was their Prime Minister, that he had flown overseas in a draughty bomber to visit them, that he was getting on in years, and was making an important war contribution himself, they relented. As he left the field they gave him a rousing cheer.

But the story proved embarrassing to King at home for it was made to appear that the troops overseas had lost confidence in their Prime Minister, and their government. The fact that Sir Sam Hughes, Canada's Minister of National Defence in World War I, and Sir Robert Borden, when he was Prime Minister, had both been accorded similar treatment from overseas troops, had been forgotten by most people.

Unfortunately, too, the first Canadian Press flash of the incident arrived in Canada just in time to make the Saturday afternoon papers. By the time the whole story reached Canada—including the fact that the troops had cheered King when he left the field—and it could be seen in its complete perspective, the afternoon papers had gone to press. The whole story appeared in the Monday morning papers, but the explanation of the incident never caught up with the original version.

Later, King was to point out that the British press had entirely ignored the incident, not thinking it worthy of notice. As a matter of fact, even the notoriously anti-Liberal Toronto *Globe and Mail* did not carry the first story, its overseas correspondent apparently attaching no particular significance to the scattered round of booing. But the *Globe and Mail* correspondent soon received an admonitary wire from his editor asking him why he had failed to play up the incident. Later the *Globe and Mail* made the most of it.

McNaughton's Army—his "dagger pointed at the heart

of Berlin"—was to remain inactive for some time yet, and it was not until June 10, 1943, that continuous Canadian army activity on the continent of Europe began with the invasion of Sicily. In this operation the 1st Division and the 1st Armoured Brigade were given a vital position in the line of battle. On September 3, with the invasion of Italy, the Canadians swarmed ashore as part of the attacking force. By late fall more Canadians had reached Italy and the 1st Canadian Corps was organized to fight under Canadian command as part of the British Eighth Army.

The Canadians were "in it" at last, a fact which was soon grimly attested to by the long lists of casualties which began to reach Canada.

There is reason to assume that the gradual breaking up of the Canadian army was accomplished with the full knowledge and support of the government. The belief was growing that the maintenance of a distinct Canadian army, with all the necessary manpower to service it and provide necessary replacements, was beyond the ability of a nation of 12 million people which, at the same time, was attempting to further a most ambitious industrial programme. It was becoming more and more apparent that Canada could not maintain, let alone accelerate, her industrial output and at the same time service a distinct Canadian army.

Back in Britain, General McNaughton was wondering what had happened to his army. It had been his hope and dream to see it go into action against the enemy as a complete, self-contained fighting unit. He had planned to retain practically the entire army in England for the invasion of Europe through northern France. No doubt he had counted on commanding it in the field. Now it was being broken up, its forces scattered, its effectiveness as a highly-mechanized and armoured shock formation seriously imperilled.

While there is reason to believe that King was in full sympathy with McNaughton's desire to keep the army intact, it is also reasonable to assume that King was aware of the necessity for breaking it up. In Canada there was a growing clamour for more action and a fear on the part of many that the war might suddenly terminate without Canadians having borne their fair share of the fighting. National pride demanded that Canada show her metal.

Thus, in April, 1943, King himself hinted at the possibility that the Canadian army might be split up as the result of decisions reached at a higher level than that of the Canadian government itself.

"If Canadian formations have not been broken up for service in other theatres," he explained, "this has been due entirely to the considered judgment and advice of those concerned with the strategical direction of the war. It has not been because of any restrictions imposed by the government of Canada. War strategy must be planned as a whole. With respect to the operations of Canadian troops, our government, since the outbreak of the war, has taken but one position. It is that Canadian forces, in whole or in part, should be used where and when they can make the best contribution to the winning of the war."

But the dispatching of Canadian troops to Sicily and Italy had been decided upon by the Canadian headquarters staff and the government in defiance of McNaughton's wishes.

It soon became apparent, however, that the Canadians were to become permanently integrated into the Eighth Army and that McNaughton's plan for a distinct Canadian army had been, at least for the time being, relegated to the background.

McNaughton became bitter and morose. "Every time

I'm away from headquarters for a few days," he told a war correspondent attached to his headquarters, "they take something away from me."

McNaughton must be given great credit for his leadership in building up the Canadian forces from the earliest days of the war. McNaughton loved "his boys" and that affection and esteem was returned tenfold by the men. He had wanted to lead them into battle. Instead he was seeing them split up and placed under other commanders, and he was powerless to do anything about it.

On the other side of the ledger—the government and headquarters side—the argument was advanced that McNaughton was being unduly difficult, that he was demanding from the cabinet a steadily increasing degree of jurisdiction and responsibility and that Col. Ralston was finding it more and more difficult to dovetail the Canadian military war effort with that of the Allied command. Certainly Ralston had differed with McNaughton's view that it was not necessary to get the men into battle for "blooding" and general front-line experience.

When in December, 1943, the news of McNaughton's resignation reached the troops there was a feeling that someone had let them down. Some of the resentment the men felt was directed towards Ralston and, a great deal of it, towards King.

As for McNaughton's resignation, it is not a pretty story. McNaughton was compelled to resign, not on account of ill health (this was so much nonsense) but because he and the government and his own headquarters officers had reached the point where co-operation had become practically impossible. McNaughton's letter of resignation, in which he cited ill-health as the reason for his desiring to be relieved of his command of the Canadian army was, in effect, dictated by the authorities at Ottawa. McNaughton, knowing that he was outnumbered, merely sat down and signed his name to a letter of resignation giving reasons which he knew were false. It is significant that from the day of his retirement up to the present moment McNaughton has not experienced a day's illness, despite the fact that he has been working steadily at a job which demands the utmost in physical and mental fitness.

His resignation was a device to save the face of the Canadian headquarters staff at Ottawa, of Col. Ralston, and of the government.

What part the Prime Minister played in this battle of personalities, this tug-of-war between McNaughton on the one side and Ralston and his powerful headquarters group, and the cabinet, on the other, is hard to say.

But King must have been opposed to the demand for McNaughton's removal. Certainly he was to lose no time in demonstrating his personal confidence in McNaughton's ability.

In addition, there had been other more sinister and unfriendly forces at work. McNaughton had made enemies in the British war office, persons who resented his tremendous popularity in the United Kingdom and with his own troops, and who accepted with a poor grace the favourable publicity Canada's popular commander was receiving. There is nothing to indicate that the British war office was directly responsible for McNaughton's removal, however. Had the war office desired to "immobilize" him all it had to do was refuse to give him major assignments. But the influence of individual members of the British war cabinet no doubt had its effect in weakening McNaughton's position with his own people.

By June, 1944, the Canadian forces were of such sufficient strength and effectiveness in respect to training that

the 3rd Canadian Division formed part of the Allied landing forces in Normandy. Other Canadian forces followed,
and by August the 1st Canadian Army was in action in
France. It consisted of the 2nd, 3rd and 4th Divisions, and
the 2nd Armoured Brigade.

While the Canadian army had been waiting to get into
action on a major scale, the navy and the air force had not
been idle.

From the hour, six days before war began, that Canada's
first convoy steamed out to sea, the R.C.N. had been making
history. By the end of the European war her 254 escort ships
were to have escorted a total of 23,343 merchant ships
carrying 181,643,180 tons of cargo to the United Kingdom,
including the war's largest convoy of 167 ships carrying
over 1,000,000 tons. Following Pearl Harbour, Canada's
part of the Atlantic convoy never fell below 40 per cent and
was often as high as 48 per cent. After the summer of 1944
until the collapse of Germany the R.C.N. was to provide
more than 80 per cent of close convoy escort.

At the end of March, 1945, the R.C.N. was to boast a
total of 939 ships, of which 373 were combat vessels. These
ships had sunk or helped to sink 68 surface vessels, damaged
41 others and captured two. In addition they had sunk 23
enemy submarines and had been credited with another
eight "possibles."

Losses during the European phase of the war included
24 warships, with casualties of 2,300.

In 1943 the war had been brought very close to King
when he had received news of the death at sea of his
nephew, Surgeon Lieut. W. L. M. King, R.C.N.V.R.

Surgeon Lieut. King, was one of the late Macdougall
King's twin sons. Like his father, he had followed the
medical profession, and he was on duty on the Destroyer
St. Croix when it was torpedoed.

As for the R.C.A.F. it had given a magnificent account of itself. The peak of efficiency of the British Commonwealth Air Training Plan was reached in the spring of 1944. By the time the plan was brought to a close on March 31, 1945, a total of 131,553 aircrew personnel had been trained and graduated, and of these some 72,835 were R.C.A.F. The total number of R.C.A.F. squadrons overseas in the Spring of 1945 was 47, of which approximately one-third were heavy bomber units equipped with Lancaster or Halifax aircraft and operating in the R.C.A.F. Group of Bomber Command.

Some idea of the part which the R.C.A.F. played in the war can be gathered from the fact that in 1944 alone R.C.A.F. squadrons flew a total of 99,367 operational sorties and dropped 86,216 tons of bombs. As a result of these operations 605 enemy aircraft were destroyed, 31 probably destroyed and 212 damaged.

For the magnificent work he accomplished as Minister of National Defence for Air, Hon. C. G. Power won the undisputed right of a permanent place in the Canadian pantheon.

This, however, is not the place to speak of the magnificent courage and accomplishments of Canada's armed forces. Statistics are cold things at best, and they have been offered here merely for the purposes of the record.

Now that the Canadian forces were engaged in battle on a number of fronts and casualties began to mount, the need for additional infantry reinforcements became more and more apparent. Difficulty was being experienced in finding the trained volunteer soldiers to fill the gaps in the ranks overseas and there was a resurgence of the demand that conscription be invoked without further delay and that trained men from the N.R.M.A. army be made available for overseas.

So critical, indeed, had the situation become, all of a
sudden, that holding units in Britain found themselves
scraping the bottom of the barrel. Officers in these holding
units could not produce the reinforcements needed. Cooks,
batmen, tradesmen—everyone who could possibly be spared—
were gathered together and rushed to the front. Unfortunately many of these men were insufficiently trained. Some
reached the front without having received instruction in the
use of essential·arms. When some of these men wrote to
their members of parliament in Canada and explained that
they were in France but had never thrown a Mills bomb in
practice or handled a Bren gun, the opposition made the
most of the information.

Most serious of all, perhaps, was the fact that men who
had been wounded in France or Italy, and who had been
recuperating in Britain, found that immediately they were
returned to their holding unit they were at once dispatched
to the front again. This caused intense bitterness among
the veterans, and sentiment against the government and the
"zombie" army increased.

Another source of dissatisfaction among the men in
Britain was the fact that in order to reinforce the infantry
units it became necessary to transfer officers and NCO's
from the artillery and some other service units. While the
officers and NCO's involved had received some basic
infantry training they felt that their particular training in
the artillery and service units did not adequately fit them
for service with the infantry. They had been developed as
part of McNaughton's mechanized army and now they
were being asked to lead infantry attacks. They knew, too,
that they had only a fifty-fifty chance of coming out alive if
they served with infantry units, while on the other hand the
number of artillery officers lost to date had been comparatively small.

Meanwhile, Canada's hard-pressed infantry units were coming out of battle badly mauled only to find that no replacements had arrived. Feelings ran high and a spirit of criticism and apprehension spread rapidly throughout the army. This soon found expression in demands from the front that the N.R.M.A. army be sent overseas. The blame was laid squarely at the door of the government, and Mr. King as the head of that government, came in for a full share of personal abuse.

In Britain, members of the other Commonwealth forces, and Americans who had been conscripted for service under draft laws which had been in effect since early in the war, were puzzled at Canada's conscription policy. From early in the war Canadians had had to sit with red faces and listen to Lord Haw Haw proclaim the news that Canada "boasted" two armies—"one in England, fighting to get home; another in Canada, fighting to stay there!"

Despite the continuous demands in the House by individual opposition members for the adoption of conscription, the Conservatives had never been able to obtain support in caucus of a party demand in this connection. But there were powerful influences at work, and not all of them were completely patriotic in their motives. One section of the Conservative party, looking towards a return to power, believed that if there was one issue upon which the government could be defeated that issue was conscription. If they could force the government into an untenable position much ground might be gained. In addition, there were those reactionary elements in the country who were opposed to the government's announced social security programme and they believed that the one practical way to circumvent the introduction of further social security legislation was to defeat the government. This would naturally mean the postponement of the programme for an indefinite and, they hoped, a protracted period.

In June, Hon. John Bracken, the Progressive Conservative leader, was virtually forced into the position of having to demand conscription for overseas service. Bracken's approach to the manpower problem had been that while there must be proper direction of manpower, conscription should never be resorted to. He was motivated by his belief that maximum industrial production in Canada depended primarily on national unity.

But continual pressure was being exerted upon Bracken by certain members of his own party and by the powerful conscriptionist group from Toronto which included Hon. George Drew and the Toronto *Globe and Mail*. Bracken's telephone in Ottawa was ringing constantly as the conscriptionists in Toronto sought to beat down his resistance and effect his conversion.

Suddenly, on June 19, at Guelph, the Hon. C. P. McTague, K.C. then National Chairman of the Progressive Conservative Party, addressing his own nomination meeting, came out flatly for conscription.

"National honour demands," he declared, "that without an hour's delay the necessary order-in-council should be passed making these reinforcements available . . . We stand four-square with the Canadian Legion on this policy."

Bracken was sitting on the platform. He had not yet spoken and there is reason to believe that he had not seen a copy of McTague's speech until an hour or so before the meeting.

Pushed and prodded by this powerful minority group within his own party, there was little else that Bracken could do. He rose to his feet and, in effect, uttered the words: "Me, too!"

From then on the Conservatives at Ottawa continued to demand conscription. But they were unhappy in the role they were playing. They had a lion by the tail and they were afraid to let go.

But it was not Bracken who put the party on record in the House. This duty was delegated to Gordon Graydon, the member for Peel. On July 11 Graydon rose and said:

"I now call upon the government to pass immediately the order in council making the home defence army available for service anywhere and demand that the mobilization call-up be applied equally to the end that equality of service shall be achieved in all parts of Canada."

VI

THE ISSUE FACED

In all his long and sometimes uneasy political career no greater nor more perplexing problem had ever faced King than the question of conscription for overseas service.

It was, in principle, the same problem that had confronted Borden in the dying days of World War I when the government went to the country on the issue. But this time the stakes were infinitely higher, and King knew that if he were to play out his hand successfully he would have to call upon every last ounce of skill and ingenuity and statecraft at his command.

From first to last he was to be subjected to severe criticism for his failure to give a definite undertaking as to future plans, but his refusal to commit his government to hasty anticipatory action and his unyielding determination to make sure that the will of the people and the supremacy of parliament should be upheld cannot be questioned. By adopting a studied policy of compromise, delay and calculated diversion he was successful in preventing the development of a national crisis which, in the early days of the war, might easily have had a most devastating effect on the nation's war effort.

It is true that the adoption and implementation of this policy had been a constant source of embarrassment to the government, and King had to defend it month in and month out. But the preservation of national unity was, indubitably, the basic and fundamental prerequisite to a successful war effort and King was persuaded that unity could be maintained only by keeping the contentious question of conscription as far in the background as possible.

There was yet another aspect of the situation which King believed possessed international implications of the first order. He was convinced that any evidence of disunity in Canada would be eagerly seized upon by the enemy's propaganda agencies to indicate to the world at large that at least one member of the British Commonwealth of Nations was not entirely wholehearted in its support of Britain and the Empire. Such evidence of disunity as might result from ill-considered action might similarly provide ammunition for the isolationist forces in the United States. This latter consideration, he felt, was an important if not too-widely understood and appreciated one, and he saw it as having a possible direct bearing on the future of American participation in the war. For all these reasons King hoped to avoid any unpleasantness at home which might provide encouragement and satisfaction to the enemy.

In addition, King was looking towards the distant future and the effect which any unhealthy manifestation of wartime domestic wrangling would have on the fundamental and continuing question of national concord. Canada might still be able to make an important war contribution even though open dissension developed during the war, but the disruptive effect of such discord, he believed, would have its repercussions for generations to come. At all costs, trouble at home must be avoided.

In order to attain his goal King had to fight an uphill battle against forces which sought to make political capital out of every convenient issue. While King sought to reassure and calm the public mind, pleading for a cool, reasoned war effort, the official opposition, and the conscriptionist forces generally, made their chief appeal to the unsettled emotions of the Canadian people and in so doing contributed in no small measure to the government's difficulties.

In the end, the conscription issue was to precipitate a cabinet crisis which might easily have necessitated King's resignation and brought about an election at a time when it was still essential that there be no dimunition in the national war effort.

From the earliest days in the history of the Dominion the preservation of unity between the French-speaking and English-speaking people of the country has been the nation's greatest domestic problem. It was the one upon which the great Conservative leader, Macdonald, won a place in the history books of Canada. It was the one to which Laurier devoted the best of his talents and leadership. It is the one which must never be taken lightly, and the time may never come when it can be dismissed as unimportant.

"No other man could so have inspired Canadians with confidence in their country as he did; none other so held in check the fighting elements, so smoothed away or toned to a note of unity the inharmonious characters of the Canadian national life. . . ."

This was not written of King, nor yet of Laurier, but of Sir John A. Macdonald, by the British press, after his death. The passage highlights the great Canadian problem of the past, the great political and national problem of the present and of the future.

"The Canada Sir John knew," declared one English journal, in paying tribute to his memory, "in the first days of his political life was a bundle of jealous provinces, and with Upper and Lower Canada united in a bond of political wedlock in which there was neither peace nor advancement. He has left a strong Dominion, with Confederation not only an accomplished fact, but an accomplished success."

"Whatever is to be the future of Canada," observed another British editor, on the same occasion, "she can at any rate never again fall to pieces, while every year that passes will strengthen her cohesion. In short, Sir John Macdonald found a number of scattered colonies and left a nation. The work of nation-making is one of the features of the close of this century, and will, no doubt, be a chief occupation of the next."

Never again fall to pieces? Little could the writer of these reassuring words dream of the travail through which the world was to pass during the early years of that "next" century, nor of the compulsions of loyalty and national pride which were to bring Canada quickly to Britain's side. But the effort was to strain mightily the bonds which bound Quebec and the rest of the Canadian provinces together.

It is true they held, though they were taxed to the breaking-point. French-speaking Canadians did volunteer and fight at Britain's side during the first war despite the fact that when the volunteer army was being recruited it could hardly be expected that French-speaking Canadians would experience the same strong upsurge of emotion that brought the masses of English-speaking Canadians to the colours.

There is no question but that Canada played an important and heroic role in World War I, but in contrast to the part played by the other larger Allied countries her contribution had been a relatively minor one. The situation in respect to the present war, however, was completely different. Canada from the outset had committed herself

A CHAMPION COMES HOME

Barbara Ann Scott is welcomed by Prime Minister King
and Mayor Stanley Lewis of Ottawa.

to an all-out industrial effort that was to strain her manpower resources to the limit. In addition she had girded herself to raise, equip and maintain a modern army, navy and air force. On top of this she had shouldered the major share of the great Commonwealth Air Training Plan.

Indeed, this time Canada was playing the role of a major world power. She was contributing not only the men for her three armed services, but the men and women required by the many auxiliary services essential to the successful operation of a huge military, naval and air machine. In addition, she was attempting to utilize every ounce of her industrial, agricultural and economic potential. It was quite clear that any serious disruption on the home front could have been just as disastrous in its end result as actual reverses on the field of battle.

Very early in the war, King, speaking in caucus, warned of the danger of Canada spreading her manpower too thin. King visualized, correctly, as it so happened, the tremendous industrial expansion which the Dominion was to witness during the first few years of the war, and for this reason, from the very outset, he was opposed to Canada committing herself to a military programme which would drain essential industrial manpower from the bench and the lathe. Canada should send a well-equipped army, yes! maintain an air force, and a navy. But she should not embark impetuously upon a programme which she could not hope to complete. A proper balance between military and industrial power should and must be maintained.

That an honest effort was made to utilize the nation's manpower where it would have the most telling effect is a matter of public record. Mistakes were made, of course, and the advisability of Canada maintaining such a large army for home defence is a matter that will always be open to debate. But, on the other hand, if the Japanese had managed to gain a foothold on Canadian soil Canada's home defence army might have served a more useful purpose. It might even have proved to be numerically inadequate.

"Conscription," said King, speaking in the House in 1940, "might have served to meet a certain clamour of the hour, but in the long run it would have made for disunity in Canada.

"Instead of aiding Great Britain, as we are doing today, with our forces in the air and at sea, with munitions, with ships and other equipment, we would have placed upon a beleaguered island an added burden of feeding numbers of men not required at the present time."

King's famous "not necessarily conscription but conscription if necessary" was seized upon by his detractors as a masterpiece of rhetorical fence-sitting. But it was, in effect, a concise and exact statement of his conscription policy.

Perhaps King erred in his judgment as to when the "necessary" moment had arrived. When at last the pinch did come, and it appeared that the only way in which Canada would be able to obtain reinforcements for her units in the field was by invoking conscription for overseas service, King held back. His continued postponement aroused the impatience and indignation, in particular, of those who, serving with the Canadian forces in the field, saw the practical results of the lack of reinforcements late in the war. But the stakes were still high, and King hoped that with a little luck he could still finesse the country out of its difficulties.

As the pressure to apply conscription became almost overwhelming and Ralston, upon his return from the front in October, demanded positive assurances from King that conscription would be invoked as of a definite date, should a last appeal for volunteers fail to produce the necessary reinforcements, some of King's cabinet colleagues grew increasingly restive. Most of them listened to King and held their own counsel, but there was a growing feeling among them that perhaps King was going too far, that the time for procrastination and indecision had passed, and that the issue should be resolved without further delay.

It was a time to try the quality of King's personal courage and test the confidence of those whom he led. He felt that a strong current of opposition to his policy of "watchful waiting" was building up among his colleagues. Contrary to popular belief at the time, however, this feeling was for the most part implied rather than expressed. Macdonald was the one member of the cabinet who from the first had openly supported Ralston. As for Ilsley, it was apparent that he believed conscription should be invoked at once, but at the same time he refused to make a clear-cut issue of the question, and there was no suggestion that when the moment of final decision arrived he would be prepared to desert King. Gibson would have been glad to see King give way to Ralston but, again, he was not prepared to challenge openly King's decision, whatever it might be.

As for Howe, he may have felt that the time for further postponement had passed, but he was ready to support his leader.

Mitchell, Mulock, McLarty and St. Laurent may have had momentary, recurrent doubts as to which course should be followed, but their allegiance to King never wavered.

When it came to MacKinnon and Mackenzie, their allegiance to King was of a very special kind. Someone has suggested that it was akin to the hot, burning loyalty of two clansmen to their chieftain. In this hour of testing they offered a proud, unquestioning fealty.

Power's position, of course, had been made known long before. He had made very definite promises to his people in Quebec that he would not remain in the cabinet if conscription were invoked.

As for the majority of the French-speaking members of the cabinet, they were either directly opposed to conscription or were discreetly waiting to see which way King veered. Most of them, in the final analysis, were ready to support him.

Gardiner, whose own son had volunteered in the air force and who had died on active service, was definitely opposed to conscription, had even threatened to join the C.C.F. if the government attempted to introduce it.

The few members of the cabinet who were clamouring for conscription, led by Ralston and Macdonald, were exerting considerable pressure. Towards the end Mulock and Crerar swung over to their side and were strong in their demands for conscription.

No doubt the French-Canadian members of the cabinet took their cue from St. Laurent. The latter was disposed to the acceptance of King's views and, indeed, at a later date was to confess to the House that up till the evening of November 22 he had sincerely believed that the voluntary system would produce the desired number of reinforcements.

The point had been reached where it looked as if King was going to be "damned if he did, and damned if he didn't!"

The pressure from within the cabinet—elusive, hidden, uncertain as much of it was—was greatly exceeded by the pressure being exerted from without, by the official opposition, which was joined in its demands for conscription by the Social Credit party the leader of which, John Blackmore, had lost a son overseas in 1943, and by a wide section of the press.

The C.C.F., with its constant clamour for the conscription of wealth as well as manpower, was not, however, demanding conscription for overseas service.

That King managed to weather the cabinet crisis is undoubtedly a tribute to his tremendous powers of determination and leadership. He held his colleagues in line until the crisis had passed. He refused to meet Ralston's "conditions", informed Ralston that he had found a man who was ready to take over the defence portfolio, whereupon Ralston tendered his resignation.

Again King's "middle-of-the-road" tactics had triumphed. With Ralston taking a place to the extreme right and Power a place to the extreme left, King walked straight down the middle of the road and got what he wanted.

So far as the cabinet as a whole was concerned, when its members learned that McNaughton had agreed to take over, they were elated. There was an immediate easing of the tension under which they had been working. They felt that King had again demonstrated his ability to save the government at a time when it was in imminent danger of collapse.

This successful handling of a situation which was fraught with the gravest consequences must ever stand as the crowning achievement of King's career. By maintaining a sensitive but none the less firm and effectual control over his colleagues he made possible the continuance of a united and effective war effort. He prevented the reopening of old wounds which had resulted from the imposition of conscription in World War I, and the inflicting of new ones. Failure to do so might have thrust the cause of national unity back beyond Confederation, or even further.

King's success in this instance was the full-flowering of the ideal which had been cherished by Laurier and Macdonald and which he had nurtured diligently throughout the years—the ideal of unifying Canada's conflicting nationalities, of extinguishing prejudices, and of welding all together in a strong, a great, and a united nation.

Nor should the importance of the feat be underestimated. To people outside Canada King's handling of the situation was a masterly stroke of statecraft. A highly-placed British public servant, discussing King's actions, privately expressed the belief that it was the zenith of King's career.

"It was," declared this skilled and independent observer, "a magnificent achievement, and a remarkable demonstration of King's talent for leadership and his ability to reconcile conflicting elements. Perhaps I cannot agree with all the methods he took to achieve his end; but who else in Canada could have handled such a delicate and potentially explosive situation in such an admirable manner? And who could have been found to replace King had that contingency developed?"

Even many members of the opposition admit that King disposed of the situation with skill, courage, and adroitness. One member of the C.C.F. party who represents a large labour riding and who is diametrically opposed to King on most major issues gives King unqualified credit for his successful handling of the conscription problem. Indeed, in every corner of the House one may find those who are convinced that only King could have brought Canada through the war years without serious trouble at home.

Opening the debate on the reinforcement issue in

November, 1944, King chose Laurier's words to express his own position:

"If there is anything to which I have devoted my political life," he told the House, quoting Sir Wilfrid's actual words, "it is to try and promote unity, harmony and amity between the diverse elements of this country. My friends may desert me, they can remove their confidence from me, they can withdraw the trust they have placed in my hands, but never shall I deviate from that line of policy. Whatever may be the consequences, whether loss of prestige, loss of popularity, or loss of power, I feel I am in the right, and I know that a time will come when every man will render me full justice on that score."

That was King's line. It set the key-note of his long and detailed exposition of the situation. It was the olive branch extended to Quebec. In effect, King told the French-speaking people of Canada that the situation had reached the point where he was prepared to stake his political future, and the future of the government and the Liberal party, on their understanding and acceptance of the government's actions. He had held out as long as he could. He had exhausted every alternative. The time had come when he could do no more.

The debate on the reinforcement issue—it took place on a motion by King "that this House will aid the government in its policy of maintaining a vigorous war effort,"—occupied the attention of parliament from November 27 to December 7, when the government was sustained by a two-to-one majority. It was a signal victory for King for he had made the issue the occasion for a straight vote of confidence in the government.

Just before the vote was taken King reviewed the events leading up to the situation as it then stood.

Recalling the results of conscription in the first war he

235

admitted that like others of his party he had taken the position that if Canada were to participate in another war he would not support, but would oppose, conscription for overseas service.

After the outbreak of war, he explained, in the general elections of 1940, he along with other party leaders had taken the position that conscription for overseas service should not be resorted to. But as the war continued and Japan joined with Germany, it had become increasingly apparent that the pledges given not to resort to conscription might, at some time, prevent the government of the country from taking a step which might become necessary to maintain the fighting forces in the field.

It had been in anticipation of such a policy that a plebiscite had been taken in April, 1942. This plebiscite, he argued, had released the government and all parties in the House from all pledges respecting conscription, and had given to all complete freedom, from that time forward, to take whatever course in their judgment was necessary and advisable.

Subsequently Bill 80 had been introduced to amend the National Resources Mobilization Act so as to permit, if necessary, the use of conscription for overseas service.

"The issue of conscription for overseas service was settled once Bill 80 became law," he reminded the House.

But, he added, he had given an undertaking that the power conferred by Bill 80 would not be used until it became "necessary and advisable."

"That was two and a half years ago," he concluded. "Canada is indeed fortunate that the need has not arisen until this late date in the war. The need having arisen, by ensuring against any possible lack of reinforcements, I feel that today I am keeping faith with the House of Commons, with the people of Canada, and with the fighting men in Canada's army overseas."

This, as previously pointed out, was not the opinion of all the men in the front lines, nor of many members of the opposition. They held that if King was "keeping faith" he was doing so rather late in the day.

But perhaps King realized what far too many people failed to appreciate at the time—the paramount importance of preserving unity at home. Would it have benefited Canada in the long run had she helped win the war in Europe only to find that the cause of unity had been lost at home? When King was called to face up to the conscription issue the war was being won, the end was almost in sight. Indeed, information possessed by members of the cabinet, but not by the public, pointed to the possibility of victory within a very few months. There were those who thought that King jeopardized the lives of Canadian soldiers by placing them in the position where they might suffer heavier than ordinary casualties as a result of the lack of adequate reinforcements. This would probably have been the case had unexpected reverses been suffered by the Allies, or had the war dragged on much longer. Perhaps King did stake the lives of men at the front against the possibility of riots and bloodshed at home. But had early adoption of conscription split Quebec away from the rest of Canada not only would the war effort have suffered but the work of the Fathers of Confederation might easily have been largely invalidated.

While King's handling of the problem may have been politically sound, and all his actions motivated by the highest principles, the means he employed to achieve his ends—his delaying tactics, his refusal to accept Ralston's advice, his eleventh-hour conversion—have in them the seeds of hot and bitter controversy.

The people of Quebec, however, realized that King had done everything possible to prevent the adoption of a policy which, to them, was distasteful. Anything short of this genuine effort at compliance might have resulted in acute bitterness and mistrust. With Quebec having voted over 70 per cent against conscription any action which might be interpreted as completely disregarding Quebec's feelings could have permanently alienated the support of that province.

It is interesting to speculate to what extent purely domestic and, perhaps, personal political considerations influenced the decision of individual members of the cabinet. It is reported that no minister openly expressed himself in council in respect to this aspect of the matter. Assuming that King fought his entire battle on the principle of maintaining national unity, and that the future of the Liberal party, inasmuch as it might be imperilled by whatever decision was reached, was never openly considered in cabinet, still the implications inherent in the question were no doubt apparent to every minister.

They all must have realized that King's decision, whatever it might be, could upset disastrously their own political plans. Should they stand by King and brave the storm, or should they seek shelter on their own account? No doubt every individual member of the cabinet weighed and reweighed the possible results of these alternatives and fought the thing out in the secret recesses of his own mind; and to that extent their personal motives may have influenced their individual actions. It would appear that faith in their leader out-weighed any fears they may have entertained as to the correctness of the course he was taking.

"Had Ralston proved just a little less unbending in his attitude," one cabinet minister observed, "perhaps he could have stayed on. King gave him every opportunity to stay, but he would not retreat one inch from the position which he had taken upon his return from his inspection of the army overseas."

Undoubtedly this particular period can be epitomized as a tragedy of bad guesses. To begin with, Ralston first misjudged the situation when he told the House earlier in the year that he did not believe N.R.M.A. men would be required overseas. Subsequently he discovered his mistake, and when he attempted to correct it, and his recommendations were not accepted, he felt that his position had become untenable. King, himself, failed to take into account all the circumstances, known and unknown, when he called in McNaughton and accepted the latter's plan for the procurement of additional volunteers. McNaughton, in turn, over-estimated his own ability to obtain the necessary reinforcements by volunteer methods. He over-estimated the extent of his own personal influence with the public and the degree of co-operation he might expect from his headquarters staff. What happened is history. The volunteers were not forthcoming.

But to the very last King remained convinced that McNaughton could have accomplished the task had he enjoyed the wholehearted support of the headquarters staff. When McNaughton met with headquarters officers to discuss his forthcoming recruiting campaign his appeal to them resulted in anything but a hearty evocation of enthusiasm. Anything but an optimistic attitude prevailed among the D.O.C.'s when McNaughton called them together on November 14. They frankly were not disposed to believe that the job could be done and they indicated their indisposition to translate McNaughton's plans into action by their defeatist attitude. The drive for volunteer reinforcements was doomed from the start.

McNaughton was sworn in as Minister of National

Defence early on the morning of November 2, Ralston's resignation having been accepted the previous night.

At a hastily called press conference later in the morning King explained that Ralston had resigned because he had "felt it his duty to maintain a certain position he had held right along."

King then presented McNaughton whom, he explained, had agreed to take over the portfolio.

"I have," McNaughton told the press, "undertaken this task in order to serve Canada, and for no other purpose, and to assure that the army overseas receives support in the fullest measure needed."

That McNaughton was entirely sincere in his belief that he could, during the course of the next few weeks, obtain the necessary recruits, can hardly be doubted. When he launched his first big appeal at Arnprior a few days later he appeared quite confident of the success of his plan. But the appeal failed to arouse the enthusiasm of members of the N.R.M.A. army who formed the largest pool of available manpower.

Actually, there existed in the Canadian general staff at the time a condition bordering on actual mutiny. High ranking officers were refusing to accept orders from the government. King was acutely aware of this situation and it caused him more than passing concern.

The failure of headquarters officers to support McNaughton in his drive for volunteers was a concrete example of the obstructionism and obstinacy being displayed by the general staff. Those in charge of recruiting, pointing to previous unsuccessful recruiting campaigns they had taken part in, told their friends McNaughton's plan was ridiculous and could not be carried out.

At the time, King levelled no charge against members

of the headquarters staff. To do so would have revealed the precariousness of the government's position in respect to the conscription issue. But, speaking in the House on November 27 in support of his own motion asking for an expression of confidence in the government's war effort, King said that he believed, with all his heart, that the appeal for volunteers would have succeeded if the government had had the support of members of the opposition, of their following, and of their press. He charged an "organized" opposition to the voluntary enlistment plan.

Ralston was extremely bitter about the matter of his resignation which, in effect, had come about by King's refusal to meet his terms. He would have naturally preferred to stay on and see the job through to completion, but he would not budge from the position he had taken and King was just as determined and unflinching in his stand that the time for conscription had not yet arrived.

Undoubtedly Ralston felt that he was being offered up to Quebec as the sacrificial lamb. During those first few hours out of office, when events were developing with bewildering speed and suddenness, he was understandably cynical.

An officer from headquarters staff who was with Ralston the morning McNaughton was presented to the press relates one of those little ironical stories which now and then enliven the otherwise sombre pages of the official record. Ralston, who had tendered his resignation the night before, had dropped up to his office in the Woods Building to tidy up a few papers. He was explaining to some of his subordinates that McNaughton would soon be up to the office to take over and that he hoped they would give him every co-operation, when he happened to walk over to the window.

The window provides an excellent view of the main door of the East Block. Suddenly Ralston's gaze riveted on two figures coming out of the distant building. It was King and McNaughton!

"Look," exclaimed Ralston, unable to suppress a smile of grim humour, "if you want to see a man being led up the garden path, there you are!"

Newspapermen who were covering The Hill during those hectic weeks of cabinet crisis will never forget the atmosphere of suspense and speculation which hung over the East Block. Throughout the day and long into the night members of the cabinet gathered, officially, around the council table under the watchful eye of the Prime Minister, or by themselves, in little groups of two or three, in nooks and corners where they hoped they could talk without being observed or importuned by news-hungry reporters.

All sorts of stories, some with a basis in fact, others the product of inventive or purely mischievous minds, were going the rounds. Everyone was certain, of course, that King was having difficulty with some members of his cabinet, but the exact extent of the defection could merely be guessed at or, at the best, ascertained only in part. There was talk of the entire cabinet walking out, of King resigning—the possibilities seemed endless. Adding to King's cabinet difficulties was the insistent and unceasing demand of the press as a whole that he declare himself, and without further delay, on the vexing issue.

It was well known that Angus Macdonald was supporting Ralston, and it was assumed that if Ralston went Macdonald would follow. Both were trailed by the press. Neither would commit himself. On one occasion when newsmen followed them to Ralston's office in the Woods

Building the two ministers, weary and distraught from long hours of fruitless thought and discussion, outwitted their unwelcome callers by leaving the building via a fire escape at the rear.

Another minister much sought after at the time was Mr. Power. The Air Minister, keeping his pledge to the people of Quebec, was to resign from the cabinet when conscription was finally adopted.

As for Macdonald, Ralston had begged him to remain to see conscription through the House. Macdonald did stay on to "finish the job," but when election time came around he did not choose to run.

Never before in all his political career did King burn so much of the midnight oil as he did during the seven days just prior to Ralston's resignation. Day after day he sat there in council listening to Ralston and Macdonald demanding an end to the delay, wondering just how many of his colleagues he could depend on when the moment came for a show of hands, trying to feel out and assess the electric undercurrents of thought which, while intense and vibrant with meaning, were yet intangible and elusive imponderables.

King's position might have been rendered somewhat less difficult had a few of the strong men in the cabinet been a trifle more articulate. He must have felt, at times, that some of them were demonstrating a sudden disposition to place the bulk of the responsibility upon his shoulders, that they were "putting him on the spot." He encountered considerable difficulty in obtaining from them a clear-cut and unequivocal expression of opinion, one way or the other.

Those final cabinet meetings were tense with excitement and suppressed drama. It was said one could almost feel the drag of deep, compulsive tides of personal doubt and indecision, the powerful under-tow of conflicting emotions. There was no raising of the voice on King's part, no desk-thumpings, no recriminations or threats, no resort to emotionalism or didactic rhetoric. King made his points quietly, logically, conclusively. Then, one by one, the ministers were asked to declare themselves. The results were inconclusive and unsatisfactory. The pace began to tell. King began to doubt his ability to retain control.

"After seven days," one minister declared, "King was beaten. He was on the verge of giving up."

It may have seemed so to those who sat on either side of King around the council table. But he had not yet exhausted his patience nor his resources. In between cabinet meetings he sought out individual ministers, the men who had been with him longest, and argued the case with them, one by one.

It was clear, at this stage, that if he persisted in maintaining his position he would lose Ralston, possibly Macdonald. How many others might bolt it was impossible to say.

Ralston was pressing. He was using the stick. Not once, but twice, thrice, and four times he reminded King that he had tendered his resignation on a previous occasion. He clearly intimated that if they could not resolve their differences then King could take action on this previous resignation.

This resignation dated back to 1942, following the plebiscite. At that time Ralston wanted to proceed at once with conscription, on the basis of the favourable plebiscite result. King had demurred, whereupon Ralston had written out his resignation and handed it to the Prime Minister.

"Nonsense," King told him at the time, "I won't accept it."

KING AND TRUMAN AT MONTEBELLO, QUE.

"King was pleased when he came in for
a little limelight now and then."

"You can keep it, then," Ralston said, and went back to his job as minister.

But now Ralston was holding the resignation, like a cudgel, over King's head.

At one point King addressed himself directly to the little group in the cabinet who had been pressing for conscription. "Are any of you gentlemen prepared to take over and form a government which can carry on under conscription?" he demanded. Then he addressed himself, in turn, to each of the three or four members of the cabinet who had been clamouring for conscription. "Would you be prepared to form a government?" he asked. And then, from one to the other, "Would you? . . . Would you?"

Most of them met King's eye squarely. No doubt a few mental convolutions were indulged in. But none of them was prepared to accept the responsibility King faced them with. Not one of them would accept the invitation to form another government.

It was around this time that King asked Ralston if he would step aside if another man could be procured who would undertake to carry on the Department of National Defence and continue with the government's present recruiting policy. Ralston said that if another man could be found to do the job he would be ready to step aside. For some time King had had McNaughton in mind, but he had not yet brought his name forward nor had it been suggested by any other member of the cabinet.

The night prior to the fateful cabinet meeting which resulted in the acceptance of Ralston's resignation King telephoned Ian Mackenzie at the latter's home. He had, during the day, been in touch with other ministers, seeking their opinions, weighing them one against the other, doing everything possible to reach a final conclusion.

It was close to midnight when Mackenzie got out of bed

to answer the call. Rubbing the sleep out of his eyes he advised King to hold on. He promised to send King a detailed memorandum covering his views on the problem early next morning. This midnight conference over the telephone was indicative of the stress and strain under which every member of the cabinet was carrying on.

A number of ministers have described the long cabinet meeting which took place next day, and which climaxed the week's discussions as "tremendously dramatic."

That evening, as council was ending, King acted. After having listened to his ministers arguing their points all day he suddenly bundled his papers together and crammed them into his brief-case.

He recalled that he had asked Ralston if he would step aside if another man could be obtained to do the job. He explained that he had asked General McNaughton if he would be willing to take over the defence portfolio and if he could give his assurance that he could obtain the necessary reinforcements by voluntary methods. These assurances had been forthcoming, he added. Under the circumstances he was accepting Col. Ralston's resignation.

The sudden injection of McNaughton's name came as a distinct surprise to all members of the cabinet, and, in particular, to Ralston. McNaughton's name had not been mentioned in council in connection with the problem and King had not discussed McNaughton's availability with Ralston personally.

At this juncture, Ralston, who was sitting next to King, turned and shook hands with him. Then with a little sigh, which seemed to be as much one of relief as of resignation, he walked around the table shaking hands with most of his colleagues.

Someone has written that when Ralston rose to leave

Macdonald started to follow him. Actually this did not happen. Macdonald remained in his seat. He had already given Ralston his word that in the event of the latter's resignation he would stay with the job until conscription was well under way.

Ralston tendered his written resignation the following morning.

King's critics were quick to pounce upon the cabinet disagreement as an excuse to question again the wisdom of the government policies. King was charged also with having "dismissed" Ralston, and it was said that he used Ralston's 1942 resignation as a means of relieving himself of his Minister of Defence. The facts of the case are that Ralston had agreed to resign if King could find someone who was ready to carry on in his place. King had found such a person, and Ralston had fulfilled his promise to resign.

Actually, King might have followed a course which would have placed Ralston in a much less favourable light. He might have laid a greater degree of responsibility for the development of the reinforcement problem on Ralston's shoulders. King maintained that when Ralston returned from Italy in October the situation as then outlined by the Defence Minister came as "a shock" to the members of the cabinet. And Ralston, himself, admitted in the House that when he visited the battle areas and checked on the situation he, too, had been "shocked." Yet, Ralston also admitted that in August he had received a telegram to the effect that there was a serious shortage in the strength of the infantry units, and that he had failed to bring this message to the attention of the cabinet until a later date. He had "simply initialed the telegram and handed it back to the chief of the general staff."

"As a matter of fact," Ralston told the House, "if I had known as much then as I know now I would have realized that this meant it would be unlikely that the pools would be built up, although if it had come to my mind at all I would have thought that the men who were being trained in England would be coming in again in three weeks, and that this was simply a situation to be tided over at that time."

Ralston made much in the House of the fact that the reinforcement situation had "shocked" him when he visited the front late in September. Perhaps King was justified in feeling that his Defence Minister should have been closer to the situation than his admission that conditions at the front had "shocked" him indicated.

King declared that the severance of his relations between Colonel Ralston and himself had been "one of the most painful experiences" of his life. No man in Canada, he added, would question the sincerity of Colonel Ralston's motives, his personal integrity, and his disinterested patriotism. "No man in Canada have given more selfless and devoted service to our country throughout the war," said King. Their disagreement had been on a straight matter of policy, each at the time holding separate and incompatible views in respect to the method to be employed in obtaining the necessary reinforcements.

VII

BITS AND PIECES

In all his public utterances King exercised an unusual degree of caution. He made no appeal to emotion. He placed the plain facts before his listeners and then followed up their presentation with a statement of well-reasoned conclusions. Certainly this practice did not lend any Churchillian robustness or piquant flavour to his public addresses, his radio talks, his guardedly worded press statements. Here were no marching words, no purple passages, no soaring flights of full-winged oratory.

No matter how desperately they tried to inject a little colour and punch into King's speeches, his assistants found themselves up against the stone wall of King's passion for moderation and under-statement.

For some time Leonard Brockington, K.C., was on King's staff. After war broke out King decided that it would be an excellent thing to have a man of Brockington's widely-known cultural attainments and patriotic outlook working close to him. He thought that if Brockington would keep abreast of the general situation and prepare a weekly synopsis of events which he might use as a guide when addressing the House or making other speeches he would have more time for state matters. It was King's hope, actually, that Brockington would become interested in the task of writing the history of the war, and to this end King placed much official information at his disposal.

But Brockington did not seem particularly interested in such an arduous chore. He wanted to write articles or make speeches, and he rebelled at the thought of being tied down to routine tasks. Brockington had no peer in all Canada as a persuasive and heart-warming speaker, and when he prepared anything for King he thought King should accept it without question. But King had never been able to deliver a speech which someone else had written for him. He might accept ideas and even phraseology, at times, but usually when he had finished with a speech someone had prepared for him it bore little similarity to the original version.

Brockington's inability to get his speeches past King without countless deletions, additions and corrections of one kind or another was a mortification to his soul. At last, one day, he put the matter squarely up to the Prime Minister.

"My purple passages," he complained, "you keep cutting them out. I like them. I think they are good. Why won't you use them?"

"Ah," said King, "the one thing you forget, Brockington, is that the public remembers purple passages!"

Truly, to a greater degree than did any of his contemporaries, King realized that opponents sometimes have the disconcerting habit of recalling some "brilliant" bit of rhetorical indiscretness and turning it to their own advantage.

Brockington eventually became disillusioned and frustrated. He began cynically to describe himself as the "Welsh Harpist who plays pleasant music to Mr. King's words." Brockington and King had both more than a trace of the prima donna in their make-ups and it was only a matter of time before Brockington found himself occupying a place of comparative unimportance. King might have made much more effective use of his talents as a propagandist; instead he hid Brockington's light under a bushel basket.

But King had gone into the war quietly and calmly and with a full knowledge of the seriousness of the situation. He assumed no heroic stance, unfurled no golden banner, raised no shining sword. Nor, from the heights of authority, did he thunder any trumpet-tongued call to arms. He was obsessed from the first with the belief that this would be a long, hard struggle and he would have no part of any theatrical drumming-up of public sentiment. It was a time for a cool head and a firm hand. King had both.

"It's the result that counts, not the figure you cut while you are getting there," he told friends. "Any man in this position could have made a big show in wartime, but it would have been wrong. Other people were really suffering. I was doing what I felt I should be doing. And I could not go around the country . . . My work was here."

It may have worried King, at times, to be called colourless, and unfair criticism often aroused his impatience, but he kept his gaze riveted to the goal ahead.

After the war he was to refer to this long period of self-discipline.

"All during the war," he told the House, "I was very conscious of the fact that much of my real self was being repressed, and necessarily so, because of an unwillingness to say a word or do anything which might, however great the provocation, occasion the least strife or increase opposition between parties in this House and in the country.

"During the period of the war I often wished I could let loose on some hon. gentlemen opposite, but at the time I realized I was the leader of a party government and that there were other parties in the House, so that much I should like to have said in answer to what seemed to me most unfair criticism of the administration, I felt I should refrain from saying, and endure in silence.

"Repression is not good for anyone, particularly in the matter of speaking one's own mind. I confess that not infrequently I felt a bit ashamed of myself sitting here and listening without retort to some of the very unfair and unjust criticisms which were made from time to time. But if it helped to get through that period as well as we did, then it was all to the good."

Asked why he did not reply to public statements made by political opponents, King once heatedly replied:

"I don't feel I need to be rushing around advertising myself, or bellowing nostrums. This shouting from the housetops, this yelling across from one nation to another, this propaganda, this clamour—it has killed reason, it has buried thought. It has produced the unrest of today. It has brought about the war. I'll never lend myself to it, if I never get a day further in public life."

The deeply religious side of King's nature was to find expression in many of his wartime speeches. There was never any doubt in his mind as to who was the actual enemy. It was not Germany, it was not Japan, it was not the individual—it was the Spirit of Darkness, the Spirit of Evil, the very anti-Christ himself.

"We are fighting the forces of evil. Nothing could be truer than that," he declared when speaking on the defence of common liberties in New York, late in 1942. "We shall have missed altogether the inner meaning of the present world conflict if we see in it merely a struggle for material gain, a lust for power, even a greed so unlimited as to be satisfied only with world domination . . . The Nazi purpose is something infinitely more sinister and dangerous . . . It is ours to keep inviolate the majesty of the human spirit. It is ours to defend the fortress of man's soul!"

These were not the words, surely, of the politician, nor even of the professional statesman. They were from the pulpit, the grim and burning exhortations of the religious crusader. Neither Churchill nor Roosevelt would have sermonized like this, but coming from the lips of King the Preacher they seemed fitting enough.

King's address on "A New World Order," delivered in Toronto, in 1941, on the occasion of his welcome to Wendell Willkie, was, in effect, merely a pastoral comment on the brotherhood of man.

"A new heaven and a new earth—are not these, in very truth, what we seek today?" asked King. "A heaven to which men, and women and little children no longer will look in fear, but where they may gaze again in silent worship, and in thankfulness for the benediction of the sun and the rain; an earth no longer scarred by warfare and torn by greed, but where the lowly and the humble of all races may work in ways of pleasantness, and walk in paths of peace."

King could even find it in himself to preach to the people of Canada on the subject of temperance. In December, 1942, when he announced new restrictions on the sale of liquor, he delivered a little lesson which might have come direct from the lips of a Sunday School superintendent.

"Few would venture to deny the advantages of temperance in increasing the efficiency of a nation at war," he said. "Yet many hesitate to advocate its benefits and to set the necessary example. As we all know, many persons, young and old, accept stimulants merely because they think it is expected of them. They do not wish to occasion embarrassment to others by refusing to take what is offered to them by way of hospitality.

"To most sensitive natures it requires much more courage not to yield to some social habit, or fashion, or custom, than it does to face physical danger and peril. A change of attitude in some things at a time of war might even be made to constitute a new code of honour.

"We must," he warned, a few paragraphs later, "put on the whole armour of God!"

Because King felt that he could not morally ask others to make a sacrifice unless he himself was also prepared to do so, he abstained from all intoxicating beverages throughout the war.

Early in the war, in 1941 to be exact, King's little dog, Pat, died. It was a very real loss to King as Pat had been his constant companion for some 17 years.

A year or two later some friends presented King with another dog, Pat II. Like Pat I it was an Irish terrier, but whereas its predecessor, perhaps on account of age and training had been a quiet, sedate sort of dog, Pat II was a bit of a wag. He was a few years old when he came to King and already his personality was fairly well developed. He had been taught to do a number of tricks and King used to derive considerable amusement from putting him through his paces.

A visitor to Laurier House, meeting Pat II for the first time, inquired if he had taken the place of Pat I in King's affections.

King patted the little terrier in a kindly manner and then answered, pretty solemnly, that no dog could ever do that. Then he explained that Pat II was an "army dog with military manners."

He said "Salute!" and Pat sat up and held out his paw in the "shake-hands" way. Then, at command, he leaped over King's foot and flopped down on his belly (Get into the trenches!) Crowning trick was "Find the enemy!" From some place or other, apparently his pocket, King pro-

duced a cookie. Putting the dog out in the hall he closed
the door and placed a morsel of the cookie on the top of a
chair back. Then he let the dog into the room again and
told him to find the enemy.

The dog sniffed around the room, quickly located the
cookie and retrieved it in a couple of seconds. This pleased
King very much.

The personal side of King's life had become almost
completely subordinated to the demands of office during
the war years, but on the other hand the sacrifices that were
being made by thousands of Canadians awakened a new
understanding and sympathy within the Prime Minister's
heart. Daily he sought to interest himself in what was
happening to his friends. In a hundred and one little ways
he demonstrated this interest and understanding.

When Grattan O'Leary, who had said harsher things
about King than most Conservative editors, received word
that his son was reported missing, King, then attending the
First Quebec Conference, took time out to long-distance
O'Leary and personally express his sympathy. When
O'Leary's second son was reported missing King was in
England and cabled his condolences.

When Ernest Hansell, Social Credit member for Mac-
Leod, lost a son overseas King happened to be out of the
city. Upon his return he sent for Hansell and had a long
chat with him which Hansell later declared comforted him
greatly.

On one occasion, when Paul Martin's young son was
having a birthday party and King learned that Martin
would be unable to attend owing to a speaking engagement,
King took time off to substitute and thus ensure the party's
success.

And when Mr. Gardiner lost his wife King looked after

the hundred-and-one little details that must be attended to at such a time.

When the House prorogued on January 31, 1945, the Governor General's Speech made reference to the legislation which had been enacted during the session and indicated the policy which the government intended to pursue during the years of peace which now seemed close at hand. Three new departments had been set up to administer the various acts designed to facilitate the reconversion of the country's resources from wartime to peacetime tasks. These were the Department of Veterans Affairs, The Department of Reconstruction, and the Department of National Health and Welfare.

Already 200,000 veterans had been re-established in civil life, and the War Service Grants Act and the Veterans Insurance Act, passed during the session, rounded out a comprehensive programme for the welfare of war veterans. The Department of Reconstruction was engaged in preparations for the speedy reconversion of war industries to peace-time needs and the Department of National Health and Welfare was already making plans for important extensions of health and welfare work.

Arrangements were being made for the registration of children in anticipation of the payment on July 1 of the first family allowances. The government reiterated its intention of supporting a scheme of nation-wide health insurance and a scheme of contributory old-age pensions.

The spring and summer months were ones of intense activity for King. In the early months of the year the Allied drive continued with increasing force and intensity and on May 7 Germany surrendered unconditionally. By mid-summer troop movements from Europe and the United Kingdom were in full swing and Canada's fighting men were pouring back home.

The war in the Pacific still had to be faced, however, and government policy in this connection was to precipitate still another controversy. It had been decided that Canada's contribution to the armed services of the United Nations in the Pacific war would consist wholly of volunteers and it was indicated that veterans of the European war who wished to volunteer for service in the Pacific would be given priority in their return from Europe. At the same time an additional inducement of thirty days leave and increased pay and bonuses were offered to veterans who desired to volunteer for Pacific duty.

Immediately the cry arose that those who had served in Europe had done their share, that they should not be asked to volunteer for the Pacific but that the government should use N.R.M.A. soldiers who were still in Canada but whom the government had now released from all obligation.

"The government," observed the Vancouver *Province*, "has already announced that the draft is over. So there will be no conscription for the Pacific war. Only volunteers will be taken. There is, no doubt, an element of unfairness in asking men who have borne the brunt of war in Europe to volunteer for further service in the Pacific while men who have seen no service at all wear the Canadian uniform. But there is not much that anyone can do about it."

Even less charitable towards Mr. King and his government was the Calgary *Herald*. On May 12 it said: "With many thousands of draftees still living comfortably off the public taxpayer and entitled to all the rehabilitation benefits available to the fighting man, this is another example of the King government's weak-kneed attitude on the whole manpower and conscription issue. It is still a case of leaving all the fighting to the volunteer and protecting the zombies, and on the eve of a federal election it should win

Mackenzie King some grateful support in the province of Quebec."

"Meanwhile," declared the Toronto *Globe and Mail,* "the government has released from all obligation 42,000 physically fit draftee troops who have sat out the war in the shelter of political cowardice . . . When Prime Minister King first announced his policy it seemed a pretty shabby welcome home in spite of the embroidery. Now that the details and the pressure are revealed 'shabby' is a charitable word for it."

However, only a small advanced party of Canadian troops, most of them officers, ever left Canada for Pacific duty and these got only as far as Kentucky where they were to be trained. Of the thirty thousand men Canada had planned to send to the Pacific under the command of Major General Bert M. Hoffmeister the great bulk of them did not leave their Canadian training camps.

The atomic bomb had done its work and by the end of August the war was over.

During April King had gone to San Francisco to attend the opening of the United Nations conference on a world security organization, heading a multi-party Canadian delegation. Before the conference completed its work, however, he left to begin his election campaign. He covered the Dominion from coast to coast, made some 10 nation-wide radio broadcasts, addressed many meetings and spent three days in his own constituency of Prince Albert.

The election on June 11 resulted in a Liberal victory and it was a serious blow to the hopes of the Progressive Conservative Party which had believed that under the leadership of Mr. Bracken it might be returned to power. But outside of Ontario the Progressive Conservatives had obtained only 19 seats.

Mr. King himself suffered a personal defeat in Prince Albert. He was given an opening in Glengarry but was forced to run against an Independent. Here, however, he won hands-down without making a speech or appearing in the constituency.

Probably one of the bitterest and most stubbornly sustained political controversies which arose during the war was that which revolved around the dispatching of a Canadian contingent to Hong Kong, in October, 1941. The force was sent at the request of the British government and it was later disclosed that not only were some of the men not fully trained, but owing to an unforeseen and uncontrollable circumstance the ship which was carrying much of their equipment failed to reach Hong Kong.

The controversy became widespread in January, 1942, when Col. Drew charged that untrained men had been attached to the force. In February the Duff Commission was appointed to inquire into the circumstances surrounding the situation and Col. Drew was named opposition counsel. When the Duff report discredited the charges made against the government and found that the expedition was "well trained and well equipped" Drew declared that the secrecy surrounding the investigation had effectively concealed the official blunders which he alleged had been made.

A charge laid against Drew under the Defence of Canada Regulations was never proceeded with and in July Drew wrote the Prime Minister asserting that the Duff report had distorted the evidence given before the commission. Mr. King refused to make this letter public on the grounds that it violated the secrecy of the commission.

The "secrecy" explanation evoked cynical comments from many critics of the government; but it is a fact that the Canadian government, because of its punctilious observance of such diplomatic and state confidences, stands higher in the esteem of the British government than, perhaps, any other member of the Commonwealth.

"Findings of the commission," said Drew's letter at one point, "are directly contrary to the statements in textbook after textbook introduced at the inquiry."

Although Mr. King refused to make the letter public, it was circulated, and portions of it were published in the press. In February, 1949, Drew again demanded that it be tabled and upon Prime Minister St. Laurent's refusal to do so Drew handed copies of the letter to the newspapers.

Perhaps the government, throughout, went out of its way to represent the findings of the Duff Commission as the verdict of a court and, as such, sacrosanct and above criticism. The net result was a growing demand for the abandonment of the practice of appointing members of the judiciary for such purposes.

Although the Hong Kong matter plagued the government off and on throughout the entire course of the war, providing as it did an ever-available subject for opposition criticism, it was not until 1948 that the controversy again assumed major proportions.

In January of that year, however, Maj.-General G. M. Maltby, former British Commander at Hong Kong said that while the 17-day defence of the outpost had been a worthwhile gamble, the Winnipeg Grenadiers and the Royal Rifles of Canada had arrived "inadequately trained for modern war" under the conditions then existing in the Island Colony.

This led to further opposition demands for the tabling of the Duff Commission evidence and the Drew letter. Finally, in March, the evidence, consisting of about one million words, was tabled in the House together with a

oto by Canadian Army

EISENHOWER VISITS CANADA

"The war was over and King was experiencing
a sudden easing of the burden."

number of last-minute messages which had passed between the British and Canadian governments. The tabling of the documents revealed little or nothing that was not already common property.

Undoubtedly the Hong Kong episode is one that will afford material for political pot-boiling over the years; but it was magnified out of all true proportion by the opposition and the Tory press.

Mainly, the criticism of the government's actions centred, first, on its decision to send the troops in answer to an appeal from Britain; and, second, on the manner in which the troops had been trained and equipped.

It was suggested that the government should not have been so impetuous in meeting the demand for assistance from Britain, in view of the extent to which available troops had been trained. But it is obvious that the Canadian government, while it may have believed that hostilities in the Pacific would ultimately develop, also believed that it was sending garrison troops and that their training could be completed at Hong Kong. The government did not think it was sending a task force, nor, apparently, did it have any information at its disposal at the time, either from the British government or the United States authorities, that an attack by Japan was imminent. Indeed, when one considers that the United States was caught completely unprepared at Pearl Harbour the difficulties faced by the Canadian government in assessing the possibilities of early war in the Pacific were manifestly great.

In fact the telegram received by the Canadian authorities from the British government three days after the Canadian force sailed contained no hint of the probability of early hostilities, but rather dwelt on the psychological value which the arrival of the troops would have:

"We are very grateful to you for dispatching your contingent to Hong Kong at such short notice," the telegram stated. "We fully realize the difficulties of mobilization and distance which have had to be overcome. The moral effect of their arrival in November will be much greater than it would have been two months later."

Thus, apparently, the British government itself had no thought of an early attack.

"I have no doubt that the course taken by the government was the only course open to them in the circumstances," Sir Lyman reported.

Whether or not the government erred, one must take into consideration the effect which negative action would have had on the Canadian public following the fall of Hong Kong. There is reason to assume that the opposition would have attempted to pillory the government for having failed to meet Britain's request for men.

Towards the end of the debate on the Hong Kong episode King became increasingly resentful of the insinuation that he was trying to hide something and that the Chief Justice's integrity should be in any way questioned.

"I don't know what they hope to achieve by this sort of thing," King confided in private. "If the people of Canada prefer to take the word of Mr. Drew in preference to that of the Chief Justice of Canada, then I have nothing more to say."

Another problem which caused the government considerable concern during the war was the matter of desertions from the N.R.M.A. army, and the criticism which was levelled at the administration for its failure to check the exodus. Actually, while desertions did occur on a fairly substantial scale it was not an entirely unexpected nor an unprecedented problem. Following conscription in World War I there were plenty of desertions in Canada and they were not confined to any single province. Many conscripts only waited for the first opportunity to go AWOL, and in many instances it was deemed necessary to place heavy guards about Canadian training centres. The same thing was to happen in World War II, and when the government was later criticized for granting amnesty to these deserters it was merely adopting a policy which had been established following World War I. Nor did the official opposition oppose, in any collective manner, the granting of amnesties.

Still another point which the opposition belaboured was the sending of the 13th Infantry Brigade to Kiska in the Aleutian Islands in the summer of 1943. It was argued that this was sending troops outside of Canada and that in sending N.R.M.A. men to Kiska the government was guilty of gross inconsistency in its policy. By no stretch of the imagination, it was argued, could service in Kiska be considered as being within the required orbit of "Canada and Canadian territorial waters." The government had, in effect, introduced a limited conscription in an underhand way.

PART THREE

I

CLOAK AND DAGGER

THE WAR WAS over, but not all of Mr. King's worries. One gray, blustery afternoon, late in the fall of 1945, Igor Gouzenko, a cipher clerk employed by the Russian Embassy, slipped out of the building and made his way hurriedly up Laurier Avenue, his overcoat buttoned tightly about him as if for protection against the raw, penetrating wind. But it was not the weather young Mr. Gouzenko was thinking about. Tucked under the folds of his overcoat were a score of documents which, at the risk of his life, he had removed surreptitiously from filing cabinets in the Embassy's secret radio room. In succession, within the space of the next twenty-four hours or so, Gouzenko took the papers to an Ottawa newspaper office, the Department of Justice, the city magistrate's office, and, finally, after his apartment had been twice raided and ransacked by members of a Russian strong-arm squad, to the Royal Canadian Mounted Police.

Gouzenko's story was that the documents proved the existence of a widespread espionage system, the tentacles of which extended into various government departments and actually held within their coils, as a Russian agent, a member of parliament, one Fred Rose, the Labour Progressive member for Cartier.

On February 15, 1946, Mr. King announced to parliament that information of undoubted authenticity had reached the Canadian government which established that there had been disclosures of secret and confidential information, directly or indirectly, to unauthorized persons, including some members of the staff of a foreign mission at Ottawa, to the prejudice of the safety and interests of Canada. This was followed by the appointment of a Royal Commission consisting of Mr. Justice R. Taschereau and Mr. Justice R. L. Kellock of the Supreme Court of Canada to hear evidence and report thereon.

The story of the Russian spy probe is now an old and rather thread-bare tale, but, at the time, it caught the imagination of the Canadian people and provided them with a little of that kind of excitement which they had been missing since the end of the war. The fact that tools of the Russian government had been found "boring from within" in the very East Block itself, that a member of the House of Commons was implicated, and that possibly important secrets in connection with the atomic bomb had been revealed to a foreign power provided the ingredients for a first-rate melodrama.

One would have thought that in taking swift and effective measures to apprehend all those who were working against the interests of the nation the government would have received the universal and unqualified support and approbation of the country.

But soon, the action taken by Mr. King and his cabinet was being criticized on the grounds that the government had used "star chamber" methods in obtaining "the facts." The opposition was later to question the government's action in seizing without warrant and holding incommunicado a number of those involved or suspected of being involved.

Since the beginning of time the innocent have invariably suffered as a result of the misdeeds of the guilty; and perhaps in their efforts to secure evidence and prevent the escape from the country of those suspected of conspiracy the government employed methods which under normal circumstances would not have been resorted to. Police methods in general, the right of *habeas corpus,* and the right of an accused to be represented by counsel from the moment of his arrest are matters upon which there is not always a unanimity of opinion when the safety of the state is involved.

At any rate, King's action was forthright and positive. He "nipped in the bud" an espionage system which one day might have assumed most formidable proportions.

That the activities of the spy-ring had actually permeated right into the House of Commons itself seemed ample justification for swift, sure remedial action.

"I think it was said that perhaps I should have smothered up this business altogether, that it was bound to have serious implications and it might have very serious consequences," King told the House on March 19. "May I say, Mr. Speaker, I have done what I thought was right, and I have yet to find that taking the course which is right is doing other than the course which will prove the best in the end."

King had not moved without giving the matter a great deal of thought and consideration, however, nor until he had consulted both London and Washington and the other party leaders in Canada. In September, 1945, he had taken the matter up with Truman and had then proceeded overseas to see Mr. Attlee.

Canada had always been a little behind most other countries in its stand against Communism, but King's action brought the issue right out into the open.

Following the spy inquiry King redoubled his efforts to reveal Communism to the people of Canada in all its venomous and malignant ugliness.

It was significant that his last words to the National

Liberal Convention in 1948 constituted a ringing indictment of Communism, which he described as "the greatest menace of our times."

"Communism," King told the convention, "is the most subtle of all evils, because its appeal is made in the name of freedom, and it marches under the banners of Freedom. Its appeal is to the masses, whom it promises to deliver from their chains. It speaks in the name of enlarged opportunity and increased security. It is, in reality, none of these. The immediate purpose of Communism is the complete control of the individual in the name of the state. Its ultimate aim is world domination. Beneath its mask are concealed the secret police, slave labour, and the concentration camp."

The fact that agents of a foreign power had had the impudence to operate openly under the shadow of the Parliament Buildings literally took King's breath away.

Discussing the première of *The Iron Curtain*, Hollywood's version of Igor Gouzenko's dramatic story, King, referring to the activities of the Russians, declared: "To think of the audacity of those people . . . ordering those incinerators, and operating them. . . ."

His voice trailed off and he shook his head in amazed bewilderment.

Today, with the threat of Communism hanging over the world, the people of French Canada who looked askance at King throughout the war, are beginning to see him in a somewhat different light. Even some ardent nationalists are wondering if a country like Russia would permit a small nation like Canada to go her way unmolested. They are beginning to think that perhaps Canada's way lies with the way of Britain and of the United States, with the way of Atlantic Union, and they are beginning to feel that Mr. King's concept of a great union of free and independent nations, bound together by a mutuality of interests and inspired by common intellectual and spiritual ideals may be, in the final analysis, the only practical solution to their problems.

During the summer of 1946 King attended the Paris Peace Conference. It provided him with an opportunity to make a number of side trips. He wanted to see occupied Germany, and he made separate journeys to Berlin and Nuremberg. He visited Dieppe for the fourth anniversary of the 2nd Division raid, August 19, and made a tour of the Normandy beaches.

On the German trip, King and his party made the flight from Paris, directly to Berlin, flying over the Ruhr en route and landing at Gatow Airfield in the British section of the city. Those who accompanied him found him serious and preoccupied. He appeared to be feeling the burden of his responsibilities very greatly. The performance of the Russians at the conference, which had been held for the purpose of establishing peace treaties with Italy, Finland and Germany's Balkan satellites, had disturbed King and he was deeply concerned about future international relations. King had been well briefed on the Russian situation by Dana Wilgress, the Canadian ambassador to Russia, and the picture as King saw it was not without its ominous shadows.

On the trip King kept referring back to his youth. He persistently dodged political discussions with the newsmen who were along but he was ready to talk about his youth, and in particular about his early student days in Berlin.

During the few days that he was in Berlin King was taken on a tour of the ruined city, and one of his major interests was to find the house where he had lived while pursuing his post-graduate studies. Finally, in a pile of ruins off the Tiergarten, about half a mile from the Brandenberg Tor, he located a rubble-piled street and a shattered house which he thought was the one he sought.

His companions noticed a wistful look creep over his face as he surveyed the ruins. It was apparent that he was thinking back upon the carefree days he had spent in the vicinity, perhaps of sunny afternoons along Unter Den Linden, boating expeditions on the Spree, aimless wanderings in the cool, blue shadows of the early evening. So intense was King's preoccupation with the scene that some of his companions began to think that the old house must have some connection with a romantic episode of his early years.

Certainly it was obvious that his interest in finding the place was based on something more than just a desire to see an old, familiar landmark. But, at the time, King never hinted at what was going on within his mind and his companions could only give their fancy free rein in their attempt to read between the lines.

Actually, there was no lingering memory of any long-lost romance in King's thoughts. He was merely letting his mind slip back into the past in an attempt to recapture a little of the high beauty, the peace, and the contentment that had once given life and meaning to the old house. He recalled, to himself, the day when as a student he had first walked up the steps and knocked on the door, to be welcomed by one Anton Weber, and his wife and family. Weber was an artist of some standing who had painted the portraits of many members of the old German nobility, including those of Kaiser Wilhelm, other members of the royal family, and Hindenburg.

The family had been unusually kind to King during his stay in Berlin and he had never forgotten the fine, Christian, home-like atmosphere of the Weber home.

King ended up by asking that his picture be taken on the site of the old house. A young army officer, a member of the Canadian Berlin mission, had been snapping pictures during the course of the drive around the city and King's companions beckoned to him to take a picture of the Prime Minister. As luck would have it, the officer had just run out of film. He was quite at a loss as to what he should do. There was the Prime Minister striking a pose in front of the heap of rubble and here he was without any film, having used it up on what King would probably consider far less important subjects. Completely flustered, he decided to go through the motions of taking a picture, hoping that King would never ask to see a print. With King posing in the midst of the ruin, the officer raised his camera, squinted through the sights, and clicked the shutter just as if the camera had been fully loaded.

Then, very indiscreetly, as it turned out, the photographer later boasted to his friends of how he had fooled the Prime Minister. The story was too good to keep to himself and, apparently, some of those in whom he confided were of a like opinion. The story went the rounds and eventually reached King's ears.

Then the fat was in the fire. King was genuinely exasperated that the photographer had not only failed to get the picture but had then gone around bragging about his smartness. King reported the incident to General Pope, the head of the mission. Pope immediately wanted to dismiss the officer, but King said that he did not want to see such action taken. He did think, however, that the officer should be reprimanded. In the end, the matter was straightened out. The indiscreet photographer stayed on, but he was in disgrace for months afterwards.

During the party's visit to the Reich's chancellery King

was taken down into the bunker where Hitler and Eva Braun are reputed to have died in the last hours of Berlin.

It was a dingy, dirty concrete bunker, deep in the earth, and as King walked from room to room, through the dank filth on the floor, he suddenly spat out: "Rats, vermin! Like rats and vermin they came into this hole to die!"

It was an explosive statement and it surprised King's companions. His face was grim when he spat out the words.

A few minutes before King's party left Gatow Airfield for Nuremberg some Russians on the other side of the airfield, where their zone extended, began practising mortar fire. Suddenly, around the plane, the air was filled with whining chunks of shrapnel. One chunk of steel was picked up within 50 feet of the plane. King arrived a few minutes after the firing had stopped. He did not seem particularly concerned and when asked by a newspaperman if it would be all right to write the story he replied: "Why, certainly!"

In Nuremberg King visited the cell block where the top Nazi prisoners, Goering and company, were being held in custody. The court was in session at the time and the only accused in his cell was Rudolph Hess. He had not been feeling well and had been excused from appearing in court.

King peered through the small opening in the guarded door and took a look at Hess who was sitting at the end of his bed. Hess looked up at King who had put on his pince-nez glasses to have a better look. The prisoner's face remained perfectly blank. At that time Hess was playing a successful game of pretending he was insane.

For a few minutes afterwards King remained silent as he walked down the corridor between the cells. Then he said to one of the party: "I wonder if he recognized me?"

The same lack of recognition showed on Goering's face when King passed close to him in the courtroom. Goering always sat right-front-corner of the group of accused, closest to the spectator-press section.

King looked intently at the now greatly chastened head of the once powerful Luftwaffe, and Goering, wearing smoked glasses, returned the look with a baleful stare. Again, King wondered if this arch-criminal had recognized him. He thought Goering had. To his companions King recalled that he had last seen Goering and Hess when he had visited Berlin before the war.

At Dieppe, King was shown around the town and escorted along the beaches. He visited the cemetery on the hill behind the town where over 800 Canadians are buried.

"He was very moved about the whole thing," recalled one of his friends who was present, "and his sentiment about the Canadian army, its exploits and its sacrifices, were even more apparent when he visited Normandy later."

For two days King toured the Normandy battlefield around Caen, Falaise and Bayeux. He was tremendously impressed and pleased at the reaction of the French people to his presence.

His energy seemed endless. A good many in his party, including the newspapermen, were done in following him about. On the last night of the Normandy trip King and his party had eaten two huge Norman meals, with all sorts of wine and cider. They were just finishing up the second big meal when King learned that he was expected at another town. He insisted, despite the fact that it was then around 10.30 o'clock, that this unexpected appointment be kept. And when he arrived at the town, after a long and tiring ride, he insisted on eating some more food so that the townsfolk would not be disappointed.

Most of the party were completely exhausted as a result of the day's activities, but King took it all in his stride and seemed to enjoy every moment of it.

II

MEN ABOUT KING

KING COULD NOT have accomplished all he did without the help, advice, and loyalty of the personal assistants who stood beside him throughout the years.

He possessed a genius for picking able assistants, and all of them, in one way or another, contributed to his success. He has admitted this fact time and again.

"I have learned," he once said, during the war, "to realize that one man's powers are limited, that others are working as hard as myself. I have learned how to share burdens."

Most of the men who worked for King went to his side in the first instance because they felt that it would be a privilege to work with him. This was certainly true in the case of Fred McGregor, a student in political science who admired King's great grasp of the subject. Similarly, the late Norman McLeod Rogers, and J. W. "Jack" Pickersgill, served King because they were interested in working close to a great public figure.

The majority, once they were on the job, found that working for King was no sinecure but that to the contrary it was an apprenticeship that left them little if any time for their own private and domestic affairs. Office hours were strict, and a man was on call at any hour of the day or night. During the war many of King's secretaries were accustomed to work three nights a week, sometimes five.

Over the years a small army of secretaries and other assistants crossed the threshold of King's office, stayed for a time, then passed out by another door, usually to a better job. A few like John S. Nicol, King's confidential messenger, Edouard Handy, his confidential secretary, and Jack Lay, his chauffeur, were able to stand the pace. Nicol, when he retired on superannuation in the fall of 1948, had been in King's employ for almost thirty years. Handy and Lay at that time had both exceeded ten years' service.

It was no secret around the East Block that after a man had spent a few years with King he was ready for a good, long rest. King himself realized this. He set a strenuous pace and he knew that his assistants had to work hard to keep up with him. But usually the rewards were worthwhile.

When Clare Moyer became assistant private secretary to King in 1922, Fred McGregor, the chief secretary at that time, was close to a nervous breakdown. He had been with King from 1909 to 1911, had worked with him during the writing of *Industry and Humanity* during World War I, and had become his chief secretary following King's re-election in 1921. He and King worked together smoothly and effectively. It was not that he was finding King particularly hard to work for now, but he had become over-tired, run-down, and nervous.

One morning he walked into King's office carrying a stack of letters, records, and other work. As he entered the room King glanced up and made some thoughtless remark. It was nothing serious, and probably under different circumstances McGregor would have paid little if any attention to it; but on this particular occasion it was like setting a match to a stick of dynamite. For a moment McGregor stood there looking blankly at his chief, then, with a sudden whoop, he threw the pile of papers high into the air and without another word left the room. It was six months before the East Block saw McGregor again. Then one morning he walked in and took his place as if nothing had ever happened.

In the meanwhile, however, realizing that McGregor needed a holiday, King arranged to send him on an errand to Britain. Sir William Peterson, the big British shipping magnate who had come out to Canada to discuss shipping contracts with the government, had dropped dead on the steps of the Chateau Laurier. McGregor was appointed to accompany his body back to London.

McGregor always thought that King's action in sending him to Britain to forget his troubles for a while had been a very thoughtful gesture. He returned much benefited by the sea voyage. A year later King appointed him Registrar of the Combines Investigation Act, a post which he still holds, now with the title of Commissioner.

The government service is liberally dotted with King's former secretaries. Arnold D. P. Heeney, Under-Secretary of State for External Affairs, was King's secretary for some time, then, later, Clerk of the Privy Council and Secretary to the Cabinet. Heeney's background, like that of most of the young men whom King selected to work at his side, combines high scholastic attainment and experience in professional life and public affairs. Heeney, a Rhodes Scholar, taught school, practised law and was president of the Montreal Junior Board of Trade before coming to Ottawa.

Walter Turnbull, now Deputy Postmaster General, was "loaned" to King by the Post Office Department in 1936 and became his chief secretary in 1941. Turnbull, who had unusual ability as an office administrator, remained throughout the war years.

Clare Moyer, who is the son of Mrs. Sylvester Moyer who taught King in public school in Berlin, offered his

"MONTY" HAS TEA AT LAURIER HOUSE

"Easy and graceful hospitality . . ."

services to the Prime Minister in 1922. He stayed with King until 1927 at which time he left to set up his own law practice in Ottawa. In 1938 King appointed Moyer Clerk of the Senate.

Howard Measures, who was King's first Laurier House secretary, became Chief of Protocol, with the rank of Counsellor, in the Department of External Affairs. An authority on the sometimes baffling subject of protocol, Measures has published a book of standard reference entitled *Forms of Address*.

H. R. L. Henry, who served as secretary at the same time as McGregor, Moyer and Measures, has been Registrar of the Exchequer Court for some years. Edward Pickering, now with the Robert Simpson Company in Regina, was also on the staff at that time as a secretary.

Ralph Campney, now in private business in British Columbia, is a former secretary who was rewarded with the position of Chairman of the National Harbours Board, a post which he held for many years.

During the war years part of the secretarial load was borne by Dr. James Gibson, King's secretarial assistant in the office of External Affairs, and Perigrine Acland, who was appointed to do a number of special jobs.

Gibson, a Rhodes Scholar who had taught economics at the University of British Columbia, was interested in a career in the diplomatic service. He wrote a civil service examination and joined the Department of External Affairs. But instead of finding a permanent place in the foreign office he found himself seconded to King's personal staff. Shortly after the war he left to teach economics at Ottawa's Carleton College.

"Perry" Acland, with a long and distinguished career as an educator and advertising expert behind him, left the faculty of Groton School to come to King during the war. He may have had some sentimental reason for accepting a post with King because he is the son of the late F. A. Acland whom King brought down to Ottawa from the old Toronto *Globe* to become Secretary and then Deputy Minister of the Department of Labour. Later F. A. Acland became King's Printer. "Perry" Acland returned to the advertising business in 1948.

The late Norman McLeod Rogers, who before his death in 1940 was regarded by many as King's political heir, was another young Canadian who wanted a career in the public service. A veteran of World War I, a university teacher, a Rhodes Scholar, a practising lawyer, he wrote to King asking if there was not some place in the government service where he could be of use. He became secretary to King in the latter's capacity as President of the Privy Council, but King was so impressed by his ability that he persuaded him to enter politics. Elected to the House of Commons in 1935, he was appointed Minister of National Defence in 1939. Rogers became one of King's most trusted ministers and, indeed, King's affection for the young man was close to that of a father's love for his son. When Rogers died in the wreckage of the National Defence Department plane in which he was travelling on official business, King's grief was deep and personal.

Pickersgill was another Rhodes Scholar. He had taught history at United College in Manitoba from the time he left Oxford in 1929 until he joined the Department of External Affairs in 1937. When he tried a civil service examination he came out first and was duly enrolled as a third secretary. But, again, King wasn't overlooking an opportunity to strengthen his own staff. Almost at once he seconded Pickersgill. He was to become one of King's most trusted advisers, a key man in the government service.

But of all the men who were close to King in a secretarial capacity, the one who probably had the best opportunity to fathom his innermost thoughts and feelings, his likes and dislikes, his foibles and his inconsistencies, was Edouard Handy, his confidential secretary. Handy, despite his English name, is French-Canadian. He speaks with only a slight accent, however, and he can take shorthand in either French or English. He is the exception that proves the rule: the only one of King's close assistants who cannot boast an impressive college record. At the same time Handy was the only one of King's assistants who possessed secretarial training, being a graduate of an Ottawa business college.

Handy entered the government service as a bilingual clerk-stenographer in the decoding room of External Affairs. When King returned to office in 1935 the late Dr. O. D. Skelton remembered Handy as a "discreet" and capable employee and drafted him for the Prime Minister's office. He remained with King until the end.

There is no doubt that King was always an exacting man to work for, and yet he had no use for yes-men. He was inclined to treat them with contempt, and, in time, to cast them into outer darkness so far as any real affection or genuine respect was concerned.

He could, and would, apologize to a subordinate if he felt he had overstepped the bounds of gentlemanly conduct.

King's all-consuming interest in his own work and the tremendous backlog of physical and mental energy he possessed led him to assume that others should be able to keep pace with him. He seemed blind to the possibility that his assistants might have obligations and responsibilities outside of office hours.

He has been known to tell a man to take the week-end off and have a good holiday, and then, almost in the same breath, load him up with enough urgent work to keep him at his desk for the rest of the week.

But the majority of King's secretaries were made of good stuff. They entered King's service because they were eager to work close to "the man at the top." They were not looking for easy jobs. King looked after them in most liberal fashion and saw most of them established in highly remunerative positions.

It may be true, however, that looking back over their years with King, some of them may have wondered how they had managed to stand up under the load as long as they had.

On the other hand they all have something good to say about King, and most of them are ready to make excuses for his driving ways and his occasional thoughtlessness.

"In actual fact," one of his former secretaries declared, "King is pretty much the reverse of what he's supposed to be.

"He is supposed to be a cold, aloof, humourless person without friends, spending his time spinning political webs, possessing a peculiar gift of political astuteness not equalled by any other public figure.

"But actually he has a great capacity for friendliness and charm. He is indiscreet to a fault, and when he gets into a chat with someone and becomes interested he is likely to be quite carried away by an exchange of confidences. It is perhaps because of this natural weakness of his to talk too much when he becomes interested that he deliberately shuts himself away from temptation.

"King was inclined to be a better loser than a winner.

Sometimes after a triumph he was inclined to remember that he was a great man, and expect his staff to treat him accordingly; whereas after a reverse, while he might do some casting about for a scape-goat, he was also inclined to look for a kind word from his friends and advisers."

Once, when a newspaperman rang the home of one of King's secretaries on a Saturday afternoon hoping to find him in, the man's wife dolefully observed: "Surely you didn't expect to find my husband here on a Saturday afternoon; he hasn't had a Saturday afternoon off in three years!"

Perhaps a slight exaggeration, but none the less an indication of the unceasing demands King always made on the time and effort of those about him.

Many years ago, when Francis Giddens, then one of his secretaries, wanted to get away early one evening in order to attend a hockey game in which his son Bob was starring, King was taken aback. Giddens got to the game, but it was beyond King why anyone should want to sit in a hockey rink when there was work to be done.

III

MR. WAIT-AND-SEE

KING WAS ACCUSED on countless occasions of forgetting, or neglecting, once in office, many of the high plans for social betterment which he indicated as desirable reforms in *Industry and Humanity* and which he later brought forward at the Liberal Convention in 1919 in his famous resolution on industrial relations.

That resolution advocated that "in so far as may be practicable, having regard for Canada's financial position, an adequate system of insurance against unemployment, sickness, dependence in old age, and other disability, which would include old-age pensions, widows' pensions, and maternity benefits, should be instituted by the federal government in conjunction with the governments of the several provinces; and that on matters pertaining to industrial and social legislation an effort should be made to overcome any question of jurisdiction between the Dominion and the provinces by effective co-operation between the several provinces."

But King did nothing, contend some of his critics, except introduce a "niggardly" system of old-age pensions and a "fairly adequate" system of unemployment insurance. His "Baby Bonus", while being accepted with alacrity by the "have not" provinces, brought screams of anguish from Ontario which argued, none too logically, that it was already paying 47 per cent of all national taxes and was now going to be "milked" to assist in the acceleration of the birthrate of the other provinces, notably that of Quebec.

King's plan for a system of contributory old-age pensions, while still in the blueprint stage, is a step in the right direction, but it cannot be implemented effectively, it would appear, until Ontario and Quebec are ready to sign tax agreements on the dotted line.

It is true that, close on the heels of the announcement of his retirement, King took a hesitant step towards the introduction of a national health insurance plan.

This was in the form of grants amounting to $30,000,000 annually for hospital construction, treatment, and surveys in all provinces for the purpose of setting up a detailed plan for health insurance which will cost, if and when introduced in its entirety, an estimated $250,000,000 a year.

King's critics have consistently charged that he has yielded to popular pressure only when that pressure was strong and sure. This cannot always be considered a fault. King is convinced that one cannot legislate a nation into Utopia, cannot force reforms upon the people until the national economy is capable of supporting them. This seems like good common sense.

"I can tell you in my heart I am pretty radical," King said when addressing a meeting in Vancouver, in September, 1935. "I will not promise things, however, unless I know my party will back me to the limit and enable me to carry them out."

Again he said: "The ship of state is not a steam-driven vessel which you can drive straight through to its destination. It is a sailing vessel. Often you must tack and veer and run out the storms, so long as you always keep in mind the port where you are going."

In the little office which King used to occupy just across the corridor from the Government lobby there used to be a little model of a full-rigged sailing ship. It stood on the mantle-piece, in a glass case. No doubt King kept it there as a reminder that it is sometimes good seamanship to run before the storm.

Certainly, in order to introduce a good many of the social reforms which he fathered, King had to "tack and veer" and sometimes ride out the storms. But he never forgot his port of destination.

At a press conference in San Francisco, in 1945, it was suggested to him that his avowed intention of waiting for the right moment before discussing Canada's amendments was a policy of "wait-and-see."

"No," said King. "We have things in mind, but there is a season for all things. The more experience I gain in public life the more and more I realize it is the greatest mistake to take too decided a position at the outset. Too rigid a position creates opposition. It is better to get our point without saying anything."

Speaking to the people of his native Kitchener in September, 1947, King warned them against becoming too enthusiastic over promises of extreme action in respect to social advancement. He was directing his words towards the policies of the Co-operative Commonwealth Federation.

"Today, as a means of ensuring a wider measure of equality of opportunity, and of social security, the state is taking the necessary steps to secure a national minimum standard of living and human well-being for all," he asserted.

"This is being done a step at a time, as the need for state action becomes apparent. There has been no attempt to change a social order, which we have developed along lines which have served us well over the years, and which experience has shown makes for progress.

"In a closing word, let me warn you to beware of change just for the sake of change; or what, in national affairs, is even more dangerous, against accepting at its face value any untried Utopia, or any proclaimed panacea for social ills, real or imaginary.

"Make certain before you act upon them that conclusions drawn from conditions as they exist in other parts of the world follow logically from conditions as we know them to be in our country."

King firmly believes that in Canada there has been no trend towards dictatorship or Imperialism, that the whole trend has been away from both. Canada has become increasingly democratic, he believes.

"Is not our way of life, our Canadian way of life, based as it is on freedom, on initiative, on opportunity, on tolerance, on co-operation and on good-will, deserving of a further trial before we risk our happiness and prosperity by taking something that is new and untried?" he asks.

Patience had undoubtedly been one of King's strongest and most dominant traits. He has always known the value of waiting until, to use one of his own stock phrases, the "opportune time" has arrived. This ability to "sit it out" has provoked the accusation of over-caution. But King has made it pay. His Buddha-like attitude has been at once the despair of his opponents and the secret delight of his supporters.

King was no doubt familiar early in life with Pitt's famous dictum in respect to qualifications for statesmanship. When asked what were the three most essential requisites Pitt replied: "Patience, first; the second, patience; the third, patience!"

"Patience," said King, when discussing the subject, "comes with experience. It is one of the fruits—you learn patience. I have always sympathized with younger men's desires for quick reforms. As a young man I was impulsive."

When King became Minister of Labour he was surprised at the slow, deliberate and sometimes apparently unconcerned manner in which cabinet dealt with some matters. He thought cabinet should reach decisions quickly, act without delay. He thought there was too much levity at some meetings. He was impatient then, had not learned that it is sometimes a good thing to sleep over one's problems. In later years he was to confess that his youthful enthusiasm for immediate action had been all wrong.

Someone has said that politically King is a man who all his life has hidden his meaning behind large phrases and involved rhetorical intricacies. There were times, no doubt, when King was deliberately vague and obscure, but usually he sought to convey to the House and the country exactly what was in his mind. Unfortunately, too often, in his efforts to achieve clarity, to be exact, to leave no chink in his arguments which would permit his opponents to misinterpret or misrepresent and distort his words, he wellnigh smothered his meaning beneath an avalanche of repetitive, explanatory words and phrases.

When King went into the House to present government policy he felt that he had to justify and rationalize every step which he had either already taken or proposed to take. With an eye to the future, he carefully built up the record, word by word, sentence by sentence, quoting precedent and authority and furnishing an arsenal of argument to drive home each separate point, no matter how trivial that point might seem at the time.

But because he took this trouble to present his case so thoroughly and in such detail he avoided many of the embarrassing situations in which less astute and methodical politicians sometimes found themselves.

The care which he exercised in marshalling his facts, his exceeding attention to detail, often annoyed and tantalized his opponents. It is difficult to strike an adversary in a vital spot when he offers no convenient opening, and King seldom let his guard down.

But, as has been pointed out, King could be tantalizingly vague when it suited his purposes. Following one of his statements in the House in connection with his resignation as Liberal leader, someone observed: "He took two thousand words to say what Calvin Coolidge said in six!"

If ambiguity and evasiveness were amongst his most useful political tools, perhaps their use resulted from over-caution which in turn stemmed from bitter experience.

In 1924, when the demand for an election became more and more insistent with the passing of the months, King hedged and talked his way around the subject.

"I have said that I will not, if I can prevent it, have parliament run beyond its constitutional term," he declared, "and I have said that I would not, if I could avoid it, bring on an election while the war is on."

King operated mainly on the principle that the fewer definite promises one makes the less trouble one gets into. That is why so many of his statements could be interpreted in different ways.

Such ambiguous statements provided King with convenient fire-exits in case of emergency. These were always left unbolted and they opened freely on well-oiled hinges.

There were those who said that King, while attempting to convey the impression that he was following a master line, actually was a political opportunist who merely capitalized on whatever propitious situation happened to develop. This assumption was probably based on the fact that King found out early in his career that, despite the copy books, a straight line is not necessarily the shortest distance between two given points. He found that some-times one can make greater progress following a quiet side-road than travelling a crowded highway.

King followed a master line, but when he found his way blocked he could waltz, form-fours, side-step, back-track and run in circles, if need be, but always he ended up a few steps ahead of where he had started.

His entire conscription policy, for instance, had been a master line which he followed step by step, from the moment he implemented the National Resources Mobiliza-tion Act, thereby introducing conscription in its mildest form, to the moment he signed the order-in-council authorizing the conscription for overseas service of mem-bers of the N.R.M.A. army.

Senator Ian Mackenzie, who during the war years was probably as much in King's confidence as any of his ministers, recalls that throughout the entire period King was always calm, no matter what the emergency, that he never once betrayed a sign of nerves. King, himself, explains this calmness in the face of crises: "Experience teaches. At the first international conference I attended I did not understand. One learns there is a world of dif-ference in looking at a job from the top instead of from the bottom."

King has never ceased to learn. "Politics," he told a friend, "is a great school. You are learning all the time."

IV

GENTLEMEN OF THE PRESS

LISTENING TO ONE of King's interminable speeches in the House, an effort rendered dull and lifeless by the repeated use of "if's" and but's" and other qualifying and precautionary words and phrases, a bored and disillusioned correspondent turned to one of his more experienced colleagues and shook his head in despair.

The older man smiled sympathetically. Then he observed: "You may think that what Willie is saying is pretty puerile stuff and that he doesn't know what he is doing. Don't be misled. King knows what the score is. He is not trying to impress the House. He is speaking for the benefit of the electors in some back constituency and they'll see copies of Hansard, never fear. King is quite content to lose arguments in the House so long as he can depend upon the electors' votes when he needs them."

In his relations with the press as a whole King was always satisfied to follow the same general principle. He didn't mind so much what the newspapers had to say about him in between elections so long as he could gather in the votes when election day rolled around.

King seldom railed against the press and usually took his medicine like a man. Certainly he never courted favour with individual newspaper men and he claimed he never paid any attention to the press in estimating public opinion, that he knew instinctively what the people wanted and how they were thinking.

Once, to his friend Lord Beaverbrook, he asserted: "I pay no attention whatever to the press."

In his personal relations with newspaper men King was always slightly on the defensive. He had a peculiar little habit, when approached by reporters outside his office or in one of the corridors, of backing slowly away like a bashful crustacean, at the same time nodding his head affably in disarming fashion and occasionally glancing over his shoulder for a convenient door to place between himself and his questioner.

This bashfulness was not merely a pretence. King was actually afraid of the press in its physical embodiment, afraid that he might be tricked into saying something that he shouldn't. He was afraid of himself. He did not take easily to being put through his paces by a group of energetic, prying, uninhibited newspaper men, and he shied like an unbroken colt at the unexpected and embarrassing questions which reporters sometimes fired at him. King liked to mull over a problem before reaching a final decision. That is why he preferred to make his infrequent press conferences short, formal affairs at which he did most of the talking. He usually managed to confine discussion to the specific matters he had in mind and in respect to which he was completely informed.

Unlike the free and easy conferences held by President Roosevelt during the war, King's press gatherings were dull, uninteresting and uninspiring. He seldom took the press into his confidence, or provided them with "background" material. Any such off-the-record information was supplied at the weekly external affairs press conferences conducted by Lester B. Pearson, Hume Wrong or Norman Robertson.

King's conferences followed a definite, undeviating pattern. After being kept waiting in an outer office for from fifteen minutes to half an hour the correspondents were ushered into King's East Block office. He would bid them be seated, express his regret at being unable to meet them more often, read a few notes from a scrap of paper before him and then sit back signalling that the conference was at an end. Of course, these attempts at peremptory dismissal seldom proved immediately effective, and there were always a few questions asked. But King had a most tantalizing method of disposing of them. He retired into his shell, and before one realized what was happening King was bowing the correspondents out of his office.

Like most normal people King was pleased when he came in for a little limelight now and then, but unlike a good many others who find themselves in the public eye and who are ready to go to extremes in courting publicity, he usually sought to avoid the spotlight. He never in his life struck a theatrical pose for the benefit of the public.

When he was pushed into the centre of things, however, and found himself one of the main performers he was no shrinking violet. If he scorned the tin-flute pipings of everyday publicity he was not adverse to the Wagnerian overtures of great occasions.

King could be the soul of courtesy when meeting individual members of the Fourth Estate. This was invariably so if one managed to obtain an interview at Laurier House. In the privacy of his study he would relax and expand. He might not impart any important news or reveal any state secrets but he would talk at length on questions of general interest and be as helpful as he could without over-stepping the bounds of caution.

Correspondents always waited for King outside the doors of the Liberal caucus room. Usually he had little to say. His stock answer was to the effect that the caucus had been "very satisfactory." It didn't matter if the reporters had caught the muffled sound of upraised voices or had observed other interesting signs of internal dissension, King's answer was always the same, and his smile was always sphinx-like and satisfied.

On one occasion when a group of reporters button-holed King following a meeting of caucus he gave his usual answer. It had been a most satisfactory meeting and a number of problems had been discussed.

"Such as . . . ?" ventured one of his questioners, hopefully.

King grinned his Mona Lisa smile.

"Such as none of your business!" he chuckled.

Senator Charles Bishop was one newspaper man who always had ready access to King's office. Bishop was parliamentary reporter for the Ottawa *Citizen* away back in 1900 when King was appointed Deputy Minister of Labour. He was one of the few newspaper men whom King addressed by his Christian name. For years "Charlie" was the dean of the Press Gallery, and for years he was known familiarly to his colleagues as "The Senator." Every time King called a press conference Bishop's colleagues would suggest to him that at last King was going to appoint him to the Senate. King knew all about this, of course, for it was not only his friends in the Gallery who gave Bishop the title of Senator. Members of parliament and others who had been around The Hill for a long time all used the term. So, when, at long last, King did actually appoint Bishop to the Upper Chamber, it was no great surprise. In no way could Bishop's appointment be construed as a reward for "services rendered." He had always reported the news in an objective and non-partisan manner. But he had covered King's convention triumph in 1919 and had been around ever since. The sentimental Mr. King was merely remembering in a tangible way another old associate.

When on the occasion of his seventy-first birthday, the Parliamentary Press Gallery elected him an honorary life member, King was tremendously pleased.

Another man who could always get in to see King was the late "Tom" Blacklock. Blacklock always wrote for papers with definite Tory leanings, but he had a great respect for King. Once, upon returning from an interview with King, he remarked: "I may be a rabid Tory, but you can get more out of that man King than out of any Tory in this country."

King always respected a man who showed gumption and enterprise. Once, on the eve of King's departure for the 1926 Imperial Conference, Fred Mears of *The Gazette* who had been trying unsuccessfully all day to reach the Prime Minister received a call to his office. When Mears arrived King unbuttoned his vest, put his feet up on his desk, and began to chat about the forthcoming conference. Suddenly he picked up a long cable from the British Prime Minister and read it to Mears.

"That sounds like the agenda for the conference," hazarded Mears. "I suppose you know it hasn't been published yet."

"I suppose it hasn't," admitted King, "but, if you want to, go ahead and use it."

Mears scooped the world on the story.

One thing did get under King's skin, however, and that was when a newspaper went out of its way to place an improper interpretation on his words, or otherwise attempt to pervert the truth.

"It seems to me," he said on one occasion, during the war, "that the two cardinal sins in public life are detraction and perversion of the truth. The man in public life, the journalist or the citizen who attempts to get ahead by belittling the other fellow's reputation, by smearing and slandering another's character, is doing a great disservice to us all. And the man who perverts the truth to his own use, who misquotes statements and misrepresents policies and views—he too is harmful to the state.

"These men spread hatred and mistrust. They stir up class and national strife. The war in Europe is of their making, and in a lesser field we have them right here. Belittlement and dishonesty are cardinal sins."

At home or abroad King never attempted to capitalize on his position, or make the headlines. Sometimes this attitude proved most annoying to the foreign press who felt that King as Prime Minister of Canada should be able to provide copy with more punch to it. This was particularly true in the States where newspaper men were conditioned to Roosevelt's regular, newsy conferences. The Man in the White House knew how to get the widest possible publicity when he wanted it.

After one of King's visits to Roosevelt at the White House, a Washington correspondent summed up his colleagues' reactions to King's characteristic reticence with the following doleful chant:

> William Lyon Mackenzie King,
> He never says a gosh-darned thing!
> But what he reads of himself in the press
> Will make his face turn red, I guess!

King was always satisfied to get on with the job, let the orchids fall where they might.

Aside from the press, King had other direct contacts with the public. Any man who becomes Prime Minister of his country soon has a heavy mailbag. In King's case, due to the fact that he remained in office for so many years and also because he was an inveterate letter-writer his mail assumed staggering proportions.

During the war King received an average of 1,000 letters a week, and on special occasions such as the celebration of his birthday, Christmas and the New Year personal letters, telegrams and gifts completely snowed under his staff of secretaries. On his seventy-third birthday he received over 1,000 messages of congratulation.

To handle this tremendous volume of correspondence a very efficient staff of correspondence clerks was required. King tried to make it a rule that all letters should be answered immediately—within 24 hours if at all possible. If a complete answer could not go out within this time then an interim answer must be sent.

Sir William Mulock had laid down this rule in the Department of Labour years before and King had always remembered it.

"Nothing annoys people more," King would tell his staff, "than not knowing whether their letter has arrived."

Of the 1,000 or so letters that arrived each week perhaps only a hundred found their way to King's desk. It was one of the skills of the correspondence clerks to be able to sort out the important from the unimportant, the departmental from the personal. A typical morning's mail might include at least one invitation to speak somewhere in Canada and, especially during the war, these were usually refused. The procedure was to send the request into King with a draft reply by one of his aides declining the invitation.

There might be one or more requests for some sort of a "message." Some might be granted, others refused. During the war hundreds of such requests were received. These, too, would go to King's desk with draft answers attached.

Seldom, however, did the draft letter go out unaltered. King was always extremely careful of everything, however seemingly unimportant, which bore his signature. Quite often even routine letters would come back to the wearied

295

staff with whole sentences crossed out and King's corrections scribbled on the margin in his barely decipherable handwriting.

The only letters that were ever ignored by the correspondence staff were letters from cranks, campaign letters, circulars, and so on.

The mail always covered an unusual amount of territory—pleas for jobs, favours, permits, priorities. Usually, too, there was a fair amount of unsolicited advice. Mr. King should do this. Mr. King ought to do that. Such letters never reached King's desk unless the writer was someone known to him or a person of some importance.

But the bulk of the mail was answered within the 24-hour deadline, about ninety per cent of the letters being signed by one of his secretaries. A weekly correspondence chart went in to King indicating what people were writing to him about. The number of letters received and their general topics were noted on the report.

Among King's regular correspondents was one middle-aged lady who lived in a small eastern town and who wrote to him over a period of many years. Her letters were the kind which Frank Sinatra or Ronald Coleman might get from their bobby-sox admirers.

Occasionally King received a letter threatening him with the wrath of God or even personal injury. Early in the war a number of such threatening letters came to him at Laurier House. But he paid little attention to them; he was too busy with other things.

He recalls that the first threatening letter he ever received arrived in 1922, shortly after Lady Laurier had willed him Laurier House. He received a letter informing him that the sender intended to blow up the house. He turned it over to the local police and forgot about it.

A few nights later as he was entering the house he caught sight of a shrouded figure half-concealed on one of the side verandahs. Approaching the figure cautiously he demanded: "Who are you, and what do you want?"

The figure detached itself from the shadows: "Who are YOU and what do YOU want?" it demanded.

It turned out that the stranger was a city constable in plainclothes who had been assigned to watch the premises.

During the war the Royal Canadian Mounted Police provided a guard at Laurier House. This was not on account of the threatening letters but because King kept a duplicate set of state files and despatches at home. Thus a number of R.C.M.P. officers, working in eight-hour shifts, remained on duty twenty-four hours a day. They were removed some time after King retired as Prime Minister and after all important official documents had been transferred to the East Block.

When one considers the tremendous effort involved in providing protection for the President of the United States, who always has at least one secret service agent at his elbow, and who never appears in public without a flying squad of White House protective officers acting as a human screen against the bombs or bullets of possible assassins, then the relatively indifferent manner in which the lives of Canadian Prime Ministers are protected seems worthy of passing comment.

Perhaps, some day, a Canadian Prime Minister will fall victim to an unexpected attack; in which event his successors will probably be placed under the same sort of protective custody as are the Presidents of the republic to our south.

But for some reason or other, whether it is a matter of climate, a lack of emotional intenseness on the part of the people in respect to politics, or a mere oversight on the part of fate, no Canadian leader's life has ever been seriously threatened. The United States, on the other hand, has lost three presidents at the hands of assassins—Lincoln, Garfield and McKinley. An abortive attempt was made some years ago on the life of President Franklin D. Roosevelt, resulting in the death of Mayor Cermak, of Chicago. But the only political assassination which has occurred in Canada was the death by shooting of D'Arcy McGee. This was a result of the Fenian troubles, and McGee's death was more the product of Irish political factors than of national ones.

Occasionally King received a letter or a gift which was intended as a reflection on the policies of his government. Thus during the fall of 1946 he received a flour-sack diaper from a housewife who wrote that she could not afford to send either clothes or money to Europe's needy but that she could donate this item, a duplicate of what her own children were wearing.

Another unusual letter came from a school teacher in a little town in Quebec. After explaining that she had always voted for Mr. King, and was urging everyone else to do likewise, she asked for a picture of the Prime Minister for her school room. Then, as an afterthought, she mentioned a few other things she would like, including a dressing-gown, matching slippers, and some candy for her pupils. King never saw the letter, which was turned over to the Film Board. They sent the woman a picture of King and later billed her 35 cents, the usual nominal charge for a picture to be used in a school or other government building.

Among the greetings which King received on his last birthday were thirty messages from persons whose birthdays fall on the same day and who write faithfully each year.

Sometimes the letters increased suddenly to a flood,

especially when King made the mistake of saying something which displeased a certain section of the country or a particular political or ethnic group. Thus when an American periodical reported that King "has little fondness for French Canadians as such" the East Block was deluged with a flood of letters from French-speaking Canadians who wanted to know if this statement was a true reflection of King's views. King answered these letters by pointing out that the opinion expressed was that of the magazine in question but that he believed that the editor had meant to say French-Canadians did not have specially favoured position with him.

V

THE SHADOW KNOWS

IT HAS BEEN said that Washington is a place where every whisper is heard in the White House.

The same was true of Ottawa when King was Prime Minister: there was little that went on in parliamentary or departmental circles which did not eventually reach Laurier House and King's private ear.

How did this news, important, and sometimes unimportant, reach King? Did he maintain a sort of private Gestapo? How did he keep abreast of what his ministers and back-benchers were thinking and doing outside of parliament?

Probably King alone can answer these questions. But certainly he always knew what was going on. His sources of information were numerous and reliable,

A Prime Minister has excellent reasons for knowing at all times just what his followers are putting their minds to. If King kept abreast of the affairs of those about him he did so because he believed that, as Prime Minister, he was under a definite obligation to the people of Canada to provide every possible guarantee that their affairs were being administered by men of ability and unimpeachable integrity. For his own sake, and for the sake of the party, he knew it was wisest to entrust the administration of government to men whose family life, for instance, was above reproach, to men whose habits of sobriety and punctiliousness in respect to personal financial affairs marked them as eminently fitted for positions of trust and responsibility.

Even as the bank manager is interested in the spending habits of his cashier, and the railway executive in the sobriety of the company's locomotive engineers, so King believed that he should satisfy himself that he had sound, capable trustworthy men about him.

Just how King's grapeline telegraph operated, of course, is a matter for conjecture. Certainly he had exclusive sources of information at his disposal—within his own cabinet, among his backbenchers, in key posts scattered throughout the government service.

Amazingly enough, sometimes information of value even trickled through concerning the activities of opposition parties. Forewarned is forearmed, and in politics such information, if not directly sought, is certainly welcomed if and when obtained. In politics, as in other fields of human endeavour, there are those who for reasons known only to themselves, perhaps to advance their own selfish personal interests, perhaps to sabotage the career of one of their own political confrères, are not above selling out to the opposition. To give due credit to the members of all political groups in Canada this seldom occurs. But there have been exceptions to the rule. Members of one of King's cabinets used to benefit from information they received from a member of the opposition who kept them posted on what went on in his party caucuses. Naturally they did not hold this individual in very high esteem, and they could not decide whether he was merely stupid or whether he was disgruntled with the personal treatment he had received from his party and was taking this method of venting his displeasure. But for a time the cabinet knew well in advance practically every tactical move the opposition planned.

Cabinet ministers and others knew all about the existence of the news-gathering agency which made possible

King's highly-developed system of political prescience, and there is no doubt that it had a salutary effect upon their actions. One is apt to be more circumspect when he has reason to believe that his actions are under surveillance.

As one old and experienced member of parliament observed to a newly-elected Liberal member when the latter first came to Ottawa: "If you want to get ahead, my boy, watch your step. If you go out on a bender, travel with fast women, or otherwise stray from the straight-and-narrow path, depend upon it, King will know all about it next morning, and he will make a little mental note of it."

When it came to filling cabinet vacancies, or appointing parliamentary assistants, or choosing men for important jobs at home or abroad, King was usually in the position of being able to make his selection on the basis of personal knowledge.

One saw the zeal and rectitude of young men like Abbott and Martin and Chevrier, to mention but a few at random, rewarded by a cabinet portfolio. One saw men of talent and integrity like Ilsley rewarded for years of gruelling work by appointment to less onerous posts, by elevation to the Senate, or by promotion to senior cabinet positions, according to the circumstances involved and the personal desires of the appointees themselves. Eager young parliamentarians like George McIlraith, Robert McCubbin, Leslie Mutch, Robert Winters, and many others, found that taking the game of politics seriously had its reward in positions of increased importance and responsibility.

To give King credit, he did not draw the line too sharply. Time and again he made exceptions to the general rules of conduct he required of those who worked with him and shared his responsibilities. This was particularly so when unusual qualifications, personal charm, and political awareness far outweighed minor shortcomings. There is no real bigotry in King's make-up, despite the fact that there is more than a trace of John Bunyan in his character.

But toeing the mark did pay off. When King began concentrating on an appointment he gave the problem all his attention. He has stated on numerous occasions that he felt a very definite sense of responsibility in respect to cabinet appointments. The same thing held true when he made an appointment to the Senate or when he chose an ambassador or a minister. He was ever jealous of Canada's position abroad and would have it ably represented in foreign capitals. He would not have Canada's foreign service merely a happy hunting ground for worn-out politicians or party workers. There may have been exceptions, of course, when purely political and party considerations proved the overruling factor, and even Prime Ministers must sometimes give way under extreme pressure. But on the whole King fought for the appointment of fully-qualified individuals, and time and again he refused to jeopardize the safety of the state by the appointment, under pressure, of persons he believed were not properly qualified.

It goes without saying, then, that King found it impossible to satisfy everyone when it came to handing out rewards. The streets of the Capital and of every other city in the Dominion, perhaps, are daily trodden by former parliamentarians and party workers who feel that they have been shoddily treated because no political plum has dropped in their lap. Most of them can advance most plausible arguments to support their contention that they should have been treated more generously. But, if the truth were known, King has probably just as many convincing arguments to support his action in not appointing them to the Senate, the Civil Service, or to membership on some board or commission.

Mention of the Civil Service brings to mind the fact that King is credited with having done more for the merit system than any other Prime Minister. He saw to it that positions of senior rank were filled by men on the job, that civil servants were protected against the appointment, over their heads, of "outsiders" and "Johnny-come-latelies" who, while they may have had some claim on the government or the party, were not entitled to supersede civil servants who had given a lifetime of service to their departments.

It has been said that in order to keep his cabinet in line King applied the principle of "divide and rule." There may be a modicum of truth in this, although it would seem to be an over-simplification of King's genius for leadership. King was always able to maintain control of his cabinet by the sheer force of personality and will-power and his ability to reason things through to their logical end. In addition he believed in keeping his ministers happy. Yielding a little here, giving way a little there, King found that this was an excellent way to build up the confidence and loyalty of his ministers. Then, when a major crisis threatened he could usually depend on the undivided support of those about him.

"King was always the voice of reason," one of his cabinet ministers said. "He never bellowed or blustered in council, but he could beat you down with the cold, clear logic of his reasoning."

King's habit was to sit at council and listen to every minister say his piece in turn. Then, and only then, did he begin to talk. He would sum up the situation, meet argument with argument, and finally lay down the course which he believed should be taken.

Usually by the time he was through he had persuaded his colleagues that his way was the right way, and unanimity resulted.

"King," said another of his colleagues, "had a genius for delegating authority; but if you didn't deliver you were out."

King placed tremendous emphasis on the importance of the party caucus. There, everyone was given an opportunity to talk, and usually took advantage of it. In contrast, Bennett absolutely dominated party caucuses and only those cabinet ministers whom he called upon felt free to express their views. As for the back-benchers, they might just as well have been sitting back at home in their constituencies, for all the chance they got to express themselves. This control from the top did a lot of harm to the Conservative party and one of Bracken's first steps when he took over the leadership was to set up a shadow cabinet and delegate authority to his most capable followers.

Liberal caucuses under King were always presided over by a back-bencher; back-benchers were encouraged to talk, and full freedom of expression was permitted. King usually wound up the caucus with a short, succinct speech in which he left nothing to the imagination. As a result, his caucuses, while sometimes lively and even stormy affairs, had a stimulating and altogether healthy influence on the party membership.

Referring to the Liberal government of 1935, when he had the largest following in history, up to that time, King expressed his views on the efficacy of free expression of opinion within the party.

Pointing out that as a result of by-elections his following at dissolution was actually greater than at the beginning, King said:

"That, I suggest, is evidence of that unity which we seek for the country. These men were not all of one mind. They included men of conservative ideas and some of very radical thought. Some were monetary reformers, some protectionists, some for low tariff, some, like Mr. Deachman, for absolute free trade.

"I always encouraged them to express their views freely. I put a tremendous emphasis on the party caucus, let them influence the judgment of each other—to get the party meaning.

"Thus they saw clearly that extreme men could not get their own way. I did not lay down the law; they simply laid the law down to each other. Often, after a hammer-and-tongs argument, I might say: 'Gentlemen, I see as usual we're all united!' and then followed agreement."

King was fortunate in the men he chose for cabinet posts throughout the years. The only important shuffle he was forced to make, outside of changes necessitated by the death, illness or retirement of a minister, was the one occasioned by the resignations resulting from the conscription issue. It was his habit to keep ministers in their posts year after year. This was often criticized on the grounds that ministers became stale on their jobs. In Britain the practice has been to shift ministers from one department to another to strengthen the ministry.

King's judgment in selecting cabinet ministers was splendid in the main, but it was not always infallible and on occasion the need arose for shifting or even dropping ministers who had failed to measure up.

Early in the war King moved McLarty from the Post Office to the portfolio of Labour but soon discovered that McLarty was not the man he wanted. Realizing that the manpower problem was to be one of the biggest, if not the biggest problem to be dealt with, King decided that he must have a minister who was thoroughly conversant with labour problems. Accordingly he brought in Humphrey Mitchell, a man who had worked his way up through the ranks of labour. Mitchell proved himself and justified King's selection.

Among ministers who were holding portfolios early in the war, but who seemed to be unable to deliver were Thorson and LaFlèche. LaFlèche, appointed Minister of National War Services in 1942, was sent to Greece as Canadian Ambassador. Thorson, for whom King had high hopes and whom he had appointed Minister of War Services in 1941, resigned a little more than a year later to become President of the Exchequer Court of Canada. They could not stand the pace.

Throughout the war King was fortunate that he could rely on stalwart men like Ilsley, Howe, Gardiner, Macdonald, Power, Ralston and St. Laurent. In a pinch such men can be shifted around to strengthen the government, and a number of them were. King lost his three defence ministers towards the end, but they had done their job, and done it well. Such men as McKinnon, Gibson, Fournier, Glen and Jean, although not outstanding in debate in the House, proved themselves capable and level-headed administrators throughout the war years.

King's choice of men to carry through into the post-war years would seem to have been fairly sound with men like Chevrier, Abbott, Martin, Claxton and McCann making more than an average good showing.

King's ministers did not always behave as well as he would have liked them to, and at times he had his share of embarrassment, when one or two members of the cabinet, fond of the flowing bowl, were absent from their desks for reasons which the public would not, as a whole, have accepted as valid. But in most instances, too, these same individuals possessed peculiar capabilities and personal qualities which far out-weighed their shortcomings, and their wartime record was outstanding.

Perhaps it was because King always tried to be loyal to his ministers, despite any backslidings on their part, that they, in turn, were loyal to him when loyalty counted most.

Thus one found a former cabinet minister who had been "promoted" to the Senate and who was still smarting under the indignity of having been relieved of his portfolio still giving "The Chief" his unhesitating and unquestioning loyalty:

"He has always been my leader; right or wrong, he has always been my leader. . . . Velvet and steel, velvet and steel! That is King. He is a great man and a great leader!"

This from a man who was now "safe for life" in the Senate and who could say what he chose about his former chief without fear of effective reprisals.

Over the years King picked many great men for his cabinet and forwarded their careers. Robb, Dandurand, Lapointe, Rogers, Dunning, Ralston, Power, Cardin, Howe, Ilsley, St. Laurent, Gardiner, Mitchell—to mention only a few—all rode the crest of King's power and benefited either in their public or their private life.

Of his wartime cabinet and top government officials, King more than once expressed his appreciation. "Had I known at the beginning of the war I should lose such men from around me," he said on one occasion, referring to the death of Skelton, Lapointe, Rogers, Dandurand and others, "I doubt if I could have carried on."

Again: "All the members of the cabinet have pulled their full weight in the boat!"

HOME FOR A VISIT

"It was good to see all those happy faces."

Someone once asked King what principles directed him in choosing a cabinet.

"Integrity, of course, is essential," he replied. "But what I most look for is a sign that a man is anxious to do something for his fellow men, that he is interested in public service or in the job of doing a job. If he has not this zeal or enthusiasm the future is not encouraging. You have to be careful, too, that a man's enthusiasm is not for personal advancement.

"Given some assurance as to their spirit and good faith, it is then a matter of integrity, of good judgment and common sense. Oh, yes, it is a combination of many things. And in picking a cabinet this is doubly so. A cabinet should combine many attributes: training, skill, experience, enthusiasm, a strong moral sense, vigour, courage and tolerance. It is a group of people who supplement each other—but still the first question must be 'does he want to work for his fellow men?'"

It is interesting to note just how King's mind worked in making some of his cabinet appointments. For instance, many people were quite surprised when he appointed Dr. J. J. McCann to the post of Minister of National Revenue. McCann had been prominently mentioned for the portfolio of National Health, but it seemed that a lawyer, or a man trained in economics, would have been the logical choice for the Revenue Department. Certainly it seemed rather strange that King should choose a medical man.

But King knew what many others did not know, that McCann had been largely repsonsible for putting a well-known trust company back on its feet; that he had interested himself most successfully in a number of other business enterprises; and that he had a sound business sense.

"Why do you want a man like me for the job?" McCann asked King when he was called over to the East Block to discuss the appointment. "I'm a doctor, not a lawyer or an economist."

"Because I want a man with good common business sense who is capable of doing a tough job," said King. "I think you're that kind of a man."

Usually when King sent for a man with the idea of inviting him into the cabinet the object of his attentions came a-running. But this was not always the case and King was not always able to get the man he wanted, particularly if he sought him outside of parliament. Once King was kept waiting some 12 hours by one of his followers whom he had decided to promote to cabinet rank.

Early in his career Humphrey Mitchell had made it a rule never to allow anything to interfere with his Sundays at home. He did no business over the telephone on that day nor saw anyone on a business matter, but devoted the entire day to his family.

Thus one Sunday, early in the war, when the telephone in the Mitchell home rang it found the family gathered comfortably around the fireplace. Mr. Mitchell's young son answered the telephone.

"There is a Mr. King on the telephone and he wants to talk with you, Daddy," reported the lad.

"King? King?" mused Mitchell to himself, "Whom do I know by that name who would be calling me on Sunday?"

When he went to the telephone he was surprised to find it was the Prime Minister. Mr. King said he would like to see him down at Laurier House that very afternoon.

"I'm sorry," said Mitchell, probably more through force of habit than anything else, "but I never go out on Sunday, Mr. King."

"Well," said King, after a slight pause, "will you drop around to Laurier House tomorrow at nine?"

Mitchell "dropped around" the next morning and that night was Canada's new Minister of Labour.

Intellectually and physically King always dominated his cabinet. When he entered the council chamber small-talk ceased on the instant and members of the cabinet automatically straightened up in their chairs. King seemed to possess the initial advantage of expecting and receiving respect. He seldom joked with his ministers and when, occasionally, he did attempt a sally his colleagues had to think twice before deciding whether or not King was, indeed, trying to be funny.

Because King disliked tobacco smoke, ministers made a habit of knocking out their pipes and snuffing out their cigars and cigarettes when he entered the room.

But once settled in his chair King relaxed, addressed his ministers as "Humphrey", "Clarence", or "Chubby", and listened attentively while each said his piece.

"I never saw a man with such an even temper," one of his cabinet colleagues remarked towards the end of the war. "He is as bright mentally as when he was forty. He is the most considerate man I ever met. He respects the opinions of his ministers at all times, and I have yet to see him lose his temper."

But opinions varied.

"King may have had dinner with you at your home the night before," said another minister, "but when he meets you in council the next day it is as Prime Minister and not as a personal friend. You can expect no favours, you can make no mistakes. King can accept your hospitality one day and be perfectly ruthless with you the next."

"Don't let anyone tell you that King can't be tough," said one man who had been in the cabinet for many years.

"He knows how to wield the big stick when necessity arises."

King could always out-sit his colleagues. It was said that he sometimes adopted a deliberate policy of prolonging cabinet meetings until every one of his opponents was worn down to the point of exhaustion and ready to throw in the sponge. It is true that he would sometimes spend hours discussing relatively unimportant matters, leaving major problems to the end of the meeting. Finally, when the members of the cabinet were weary and spent, and weak from hunger, King would place the contentious question before them. Virtually starved into submission and acquiescence the dissenting ministers would give way and King would make his point.

But King would laugh at the suggestion that such tactics were part of a preconceived plan of attack. Actually, at times, he became so absorbed in the subject under discussion that everything else was forgotten. His powers of concentration were such that when he was directing his attention to a certain problem a curtain in his mind came down shutting out everything else.

And, of course, Mr. King had no one at home waiting to hear from him.

VI

THE YEARS TAKE THEIR TOLL

IN MID-WINTER, 1947, King was in his seventy-third year, and he was beginning to show his age. The war years had taken their toll, and to a greater extent than even he himself realized. He had managed to stand up to the tremendous demands that had been made upon his physical and mental powers throughout the war, but the pressure had been cumulative in its effects and the wearing-down process had been none the less real because it had been slow and imperceptible in its action.

There had been days during the war when King returned to Laurier House spent and exhausted after long, trying hours in cabinet or the House. Sometimes he was too preoccupied with the gravity of the problems confronting his government and the nation, and the even more serious crises facing the democratic world as a whole, to settle down to eat a proper meal. He got into the habit of rushing home at noon and snatching a sandwich from the sideboard, washing it down with a cup or two of coffee. Then he would plunge into work again with a ceaseless, driving energy which appalled and exhausted his colleagues.

The pace, however, had begun to tell, and when he returned from Britain in 1946 he was steeped in gloom, an evidence of mental as well as physical fatigue.

"Looking beneath the surface," he said, at that time, "one could not but feel deeply the tremendous burden mankind seems to have placed upon its shoulders in the recent past, and could not but wonder what will happen to

313

human society if soon we do not find some way of effecting peace and goodwill among the nations of the world. . . ."

This condition of mild depression became more acute as the year progressed. By fall King was not only more deeply depressed at the state of world affairs, but he began to feel that attempts were being made by those around him to hurry him into making decisions. The press was full of speculative stories touching upon his possible retirement, the selection of a successor, and the state of his health.

In External Affairs he resented pressure from civil servants to get vacancies filled. Certain officials were pressing to have overseas appointments approved. King was worried by this unseemly desire for haste in the appointing of diplomatic representatives. There was no reason, he believed, why Canada should rush in and appoint consular representatives to every little nation in the world.

In particular the rash of speculation as to who would be the next Liberal leader did not sit well. At a press conference he made it abundantly clear he would be the leader for still another session, and no question about it. Asked if there was a possibility of appointing a deputy Prime Minister, King bridled: "Oh, I'll see what I can do myself for a while," he said, shortly.

He reminded reporters that all he had said about his possible retirement was that he would not run in another general election.

"Don't forget," he said pointedly, "this Parliament lasts until 1950."

King had weathered the storm; now in the comparative calm of the aftermath, the load of responsibility he had unflinchingly borne, the unceasing pressure of work, the political uncertainties at home and abroad, were taking their inevitable toll.

"If you would know," King had once told a colleague,

"the word of all words in public life is endurance. That is the greatest quality in politics—to endure with patience . . . to endure unto the end!"

King had been patient, and he had endured; but the handwriting was on the wall for all to read. He was feeling the weight of the years. The old resilience, if not gone, was certainly not so apparent. The time had come to think about the future and, as well, to give attention to the present.

In December King divested himself of the portfolio he had carried so long. He resigned as Minister of External Affairs and appointed Mr. St. Laurent in his stead.

He had long been anxious to divorce the portfolios of Prime Minister and Minister of External Affairs. During the war, he explained, that had been impossible, but the opportune moment had now arrived.

"Now I'm hoping that being relieved of it I'll be able to stay a longer time in public life than I otherwise would," he said. "Already I feel considerably younger."

At the press conference at which he announced his resignation as Secretary of State for External Affairs he was reserved, quiet, reminiscent, much like the parent who finds that the time has come to delegate some of the duties of the household to his son. He had a word or two of advice and guidance for those who might follow in his steps.

"These international conferences are becoming a greater problem. They last so long, take people away so much . . . We'll get through this difficult period . . . It takes a little time, a little time. I think the main thing today is an attitude of goodwill . . . I become increasingly a believer— I won't say in postponing things—in letting things mature. There's too much of this sudden business . . ."

There was a hint in King's words that he was feeling that events were rushing onwards at a furious pace.

At the end of the year King's physical condition was reported as "perfect" but early in the New Year he had casually consulted one of his own ministers, Dr. McCann, about a nervous pain in his left shoulder. McCann suggested an electrocardiograph reading and at the same time advised Mr. King that it would do no harm if he were to consult a heart specialist. Dr. Campbell Laidlaw was consulted. Apparently there was nothing in Mr. King's condition to cause alarm, however, and after the check-up he went about his duties much as usual.

On the night of February 12 King attended the Governor General's diplomatic ball. He had a slight cold, but it was not worrying him unduly. In fact he felt so fit that he danced throughout the evening and it was two o'clock in the morning when he left Rideau Hall for Laurier House. That was on a Wednesday. By the following Monday his cold had grown worse and Dr. F. W. Mohr, who was then attending him, ordered him to bed. He was soon running a high temperature.

Faced with his first serious illness in years, it is just possible that King recalled with a little start of apprehension the particular circumstances surrounding the sudden death of one of his ancestors—his great grandfather, one Daniel Mackenzie. Daniel came to his death as the result of a cold contracted at a dancing party. That had been in 1795, at which time his son, William Lyon Mackenzie, was only three weeks old.

It was not long before word of King's illness had spread. Telegraph keys rattled the news from Halifax to Vancouver, from London to Canberra.

"Mr. King," the majority of the reports ran, "is critically ill. There is a possibility . . . !"

But Mr. King was to live up to his reputation for

indestructibility. Dosed with penicillin, he rallied quickly and within a few days was out of danger. Soon he was up again and joking about his condition. He recalled another occasion when someone, hearing he was ill, sent him a telegraph expressing sympathy. King, not as ill as had been reported, sent back an answering wire. It said, simply: "Purely Tory propaganda!"

This time it had been a close call. Despite the fact that he came back with characteristic bounce and buoyancy and was soon well enough to leave for a holiday in the Southern States, it had given him pause for thought, and he was glad to get away for a time to a milder climate and enjoy a complete release from the immediate responsibilities of office.

Not since 1938, when he went to the West Indies with the late Dr. Skelton, for a three-week bask in the sun, had he taken a real holiday.

There is no doubt that the excellent health King enjoyed throughout the years was directly attributable, in large measure, to the almost Spartan mode of living which he had adopted as a young man. Temperance in all things had been his guide to good health. He made it a rigid practice not to overeat, overdrink, or overwork. There were times, of course, when he experienced some difficulty in keeping his working day down to a maximum of 10 hours, and this had been particularly so during the war years.

As a rule, during his years in office, he rose at eight, started his working day at nine, retired around eleven.

It has always been his contention that no man can do justice to the job he holds unless he is in first class physical condition.

When Gordon Graydon, the Progressive Conservative member for Peel, took over the House leadership of the party while the Conservatives were casting about for a permanent leader, King took him aside in a fatherly way and gave him some kindly advice.

"This is a tough business," he told Graydon. "You've got to watch your health. See no one after eleven o'clock at night—no one! Take all the rest you can."

While King's rigid adherence to the maxim of "early to bed and early to rise," has formed the keystone to his general rules of conduct in respect to health, his forbearance along other lines has been an important factor in his continuing physical and mental well-being.

Possessed of no mean temper, he schooled himself throughout the years to keep it in close check. There was less possibility of a rise in blood-pressure if one took things calmly, he believed.

As the years slipped by King not only held to his fundamental rules of health but very wisely tightened them up as necessity demanded. He gave up too-strenuous forms of exercise—horseback riding, long-distance hiking, chopping wood on his Kingsmere wood-lot. But even in his early fifties he used to scorn the elevators in the House of Commons, running up and down four flights of stairs from the Commons Chamber to his office, then on the fourth floor. But the time came, at last, when his only exercise consisted of a brisk walk from Laurier House to the Commons and occasional rambles over the hills of Kingsmere.

King never learned to smoke. He had an aversion to the use of tobacco in any form. Once, when he was visiting the war graves in France after World War I, an officer handed him a cigarette and for some reason or other, perhaps to be sociable, King took it and lit up.

"He handled that cigarette as if it was a firecracker," someone who observed the incident reported.

On King's seventieth birthday Bruce Hutchison had written: "Mr. King still retains more physical energy and more intellectual force than the youngest member of his cabinet. In a cabinet jaded by four years of war the Prime Minister is the only man who seems stronger than he was when the war started. He is the toughest man in Canadian politics, a fact which is hidden from most of the public by his apparent diffidence of manner . . ."

Indeed, King carried the burden of war more lightly than most of his colleagues. Younger men in his cabinet bent or broke under the load. In 1944, Mr. Ilsley, then weighted down with the tremendous responsibilities of Minister of Finance, was forced to take time off in order to avoid a complete breakdown. Mr. Howe began to look his age, and even the ever-youthful Mr. Power was away through illness. Later, Mr. Mackenzie found himself under a physician's care, while Mr. Glen, having escaped during the war, suffered a serious illness soon afterwards. Mr. McLarty had passed away in the midst of the war. Mr. Cardin's death was undoubtedly hastened by the intensity of his wartime contribution, while Col. Ralston had returned to the practice of his profession for only a comparatively short time when he, too, died. With a very few exceptions the members of the cabinet came out of the ordeal bearing unmistakable traces of the tremendous pressure under which they had carried on during the war.

VII

BILLY GOES HOME

In September, 1947, King returned to Kitchener after the lapse of some years and, step by step, revisited the scenes of his childhood.

He lost no time in going out to "Woodside". He found it greatly altered, for it had, indeed, fallen on evil days. It had passed through a succession of hands and during the depression it had housed a number of relief families. Overcrowding and neglect and vandalism had left their mark, and although the present occupants had done their best to keep the few downstairs rooms in which they lived in a decent state of cleanliness and repair, the house as a whole was falling slowly but surely into decay.

When King announced his intention of paying a visit to Kitchener, interested parties went out to "Woodside" to see if something could not be done to make the place fairly presentable. The house had become the property of Louis Breithaupt, the sitting member of Parliament for North Waterloo, and Mr. Breithaupt and members of the local Liberal association had discussed plans for the establishment of a memorial fund for the purpose of restoring the house and setting it aside as a national landmark. They found that for the present, short of complete rehabilitation, there was little they could do. Nearly every window in the house was broken, the once-beautiful grounds were overgrown with brush, rubbish littered the lawns and flower-beds. All they could do was organize a general clean-up of the grounds, replace the broken window-panes, sweep out the deserted rooms.

The sight of the old house standing there in the middle of the little wood, so desolate and down-at-heel, must have brought a sudden pang of emptiness and regret to the heart of the homecoming Prime Minister. In vain he must have sought to picture it as it had once looked. Like the boy who had once romped with his brother and sisters, playing hide-and-seek in the tangle of the wood, the house, too, had grown old.

Whatever King thought as he stood there with a few of his old friends about him, contemplating the crazy handiwork of time, he was soon to experience one of the most pleasant and moving moments of his life, a moment of sheer happiness which was to sweep away, as if with a single stroke, the dust and litter of the years, and which was to invest the old house with some of the glory of its happier days.

Out of the house and up the path came a little, fair-haired, blue-eyed girl, six-year-old Marilyn Kilbasco, the daughter of the Polish couple who for some nine years had occupied a few of the rooms on the ground floor and who now called "Woodside" their home.

Marilyn was wearing her best Sunday dress. A bright ribbon tied her hair and in one tiny hand she grasped a single flower. It was for the Prime Minister. In carefully rehearsed phrases she welcomed him back to "Woodside". As she stood on tip-toe to place the flower in King's button-hole he leaned down and returned her infectious smile. Then the child reached up and planted a damp but firm kiss on King's cheek.

King had a wonderful time from then on. He wandered all over the estate, poking his way into out-of-the-way corners, surveying the house from every conceivable angle, groping back into the dim corridors of his memory to recall a-thousand-and-one incidents of his boyhood. He took rosy-cheeked Mrs. Kilbasco by the arm and begged her to show him "the old spring." He followed her into the Kilbasco living room which had once been his father's library and sat down and gazed about him attempting to refurnish it with the images of the past.

He groped his way up the creaking stairway to the room in which he had slept as a boy. He slid back the window and looked out. Where was the tulip tree that had once stood outside the window? He could not find it, for it had grown out of all recognition. He opened a cupboard door and looked inside as if half expecting to find some familiar object. Out in the hall again, he gazed raptly about him. Here was his brother's room, and here the room his sisters had shared. Here, at the front of the house, was the room in which his parents had slept. Little by little, memories came flooding back. It might all have been yesterday. The aged floor creaked beneath his tread and he glanced down and noted that the original boards, though warped and worn, were still sound.

One can only experience vicariously the bewildering whirlpool of emotions which must have raced through King's heart as he wandered through those empty, silent chambers. He must have been profoundly moved as he climbed the once stately stairway to find the fine old bannisters now rickety and unsafe, and held in place by only a few broken. rungs. He must have noticed the sagging ceilings and the patches of plaster falling away from the laths. He must have marked the broken windows (the committee had failed to replace a few of them) and the overlying film of dust and grime which had collected over the years. This was the house in which during the most formative period of his life he had been provided with the fine, solid home background that had meant so much to him throughout the years. What tremendous changes time had wrought!

It must have seemed strange to him that fully half a century after he had left "Woodside" to begin his fight against the evils of unfair labour conditions, poverty and fear, that he should return to find that poverty—not hunger, perhaps, nor cold nor lack of clothing, even, but poverty nevertheless—had entrenched itself in a corner of "Woodside."

The day set aside for King's official welcome turned out fine and warm. As he took his place on the steps of the City Hall and looked about he remarked at the many changes which had occurred since the day he had first left town, back in his 'teens.

True, here and there in the crowd, he picked out a familiar face; and since his arrival the friends and acquaintances of his youth had been coming forward and making themselves known. But for the most part King was looking upon a new generation of townspeople.

It was good to see all these happy faces before him; good, also, to hear no single heckling note, no catcalls, no sign or sound to remind him that he was a politician.

This was HIS day, and he intended to enjoy it to the full, every last minute of it.

He glanced up at the big banner that covered the facade of the building. "Welcome Home, Bill!" it read.

He liked that homey, personal touch. Perhaps, after all, he had been wrong in his belief that a leader and a Prime Minister should efface himself as much as possible, should hold himself aloof from the crowd. Perhaps . . .

The holiday spirit of the occasion entered into his blood. He was guilty of a hundred puns and as many bad jokes as he did his best to unbend and be "just plain Bill King."

"I was born just a stone's throw from here—if you have a strong throwing arm," he told the crowd.

"I understand there is some kind of tabernacle there now," he observed. "That may have been the influence of my early days."

When an eleven-year-old school girl came forward in plaid skirt and jacket, King smiled and asked: "How about a kiss?" He got one on his tanned cheek.

"Again, sir," pleaded photographers who had missed this unrehearsed human interest shot.

Shown a 25-year-old portrait of himself in the City Hall, King laughed: "I don't look any better than I do now," he admitted.

If Mr. King enjoyed himself, the townsfolk did too, particularly the youngsters, many of whom were seeing their Prime Minister in the flesh for the first time.

At a picnic in Waterloo Park a crowd of 4,000, mostly children, passed before the canopied stand while a well-meaning functionary kept repeating: "Now then, if you'd had a good look at him move along and let somebody else have a look."

King had a difficult time keeping a straight face.

Speaking to one gathering, King recalled that he always thought of Kitchener every twenty-fourth of May. It had always been a big day for him because when he was a boy it was on that day that he was allowed to shed his winter underwear!

Welcomed by Dr. T. M. Robinson, of St. Jacobs, he was informed by the 88-year-old physician that the latter had assisted at the birth of some 4,020 babies.

"Good gracious," said King, "that's terrible!!" Then he caught himself. "That is to say, it's wonderful," he corrected.

A POSIE FOR THE PRIME MINISTER

"You looked so pretty in your little Highland costume."

At Floradale, 80-year-old Joseph Ott waited on the porch of his home for King to pass. When the Prime Minister stopped to shake the old man's hand Ott recalled that he had made King's first morning coat, just after his election to parliament in 1908.

"I also made you a sack coat when you were a student," he added.

King was so pleased with everything that he was heedless of the time, the state of the weather, or when he had last eaten.

Addressing the school children at Elmira, he told them it would be a pity if they had to return to their classes and he suggested that the teacher give them the day off.

"Isn't that just typical of a Scotsman born in Kitchener," sighed Mayor C. E. Gibson, with a grin. "It's five to four now!"

VIII

THE KILBASCO LETTERS

WHEN LITTLE Marilyn Kilbasco placed a flower in King's button-hole the Prime Minister "fell in love." Ensued an exchange of letters and gifts. King was to keep the child in his mind for the rest of his life. Upon his return to Ottawa he sat down and wrote:

"My Dear Little Friend: I hope you have not forgotten the way you greeted me so sweetly on the morning of my recent visit to 'Woodside.' I shall never forget the welcome given me by your mother and yourself; and later by the other members of your family.

"It was a great experience for me to visit the home of my boyhood. I am particularly pleased to see how much improved it was in appearance from my visit of some years ago. I know that it is due to the care and attention which your mother and father have given to the home and grounds in the years that 'Woodside' has been your home.

"Will you please tell your mother how much I appreciate her kindness in allowing my friends, as well as myself, to see through the house; also the pleasure it gave me to have her come to the garden and point out the location of the old tulip tree and other parts of the grounds which I recall from earliest years, but which have greatly changed meanwhile.

"You looked so pretty in your little Highland costume on the day of my visit. In case you may not have seen the photograph of you presenting me with a flower, I am enclosing one herewith. I am enclosing a little remembrance with which I should be pleased if your mother would secure you a ribbon, or other little remembrance which you might keep as a souvenir of my visit.

"Under separate cover I am sending your mother a picture of 'Woodside' as it was when I lived there as a boy, and which will let you see how the grounds looked at that time.

"The white horse in the picture is 'Billy' whom everyone knew when our family lived at 'Woodside.' In the picture you will see my mother and myself; also my two sisters in their riding habits, and one of my sister's friends, Miss Bowman, who was making a painting of the house when the picture was taken.

"May it bring you all some of the happiness which memories of 'Woodside' will always have for me.
Yours sincerely,
W. L. Mackenzie King."

And then, a few days later, King wrote again, this time to Mrs. Kilbasco:

"Dear Mrs. Kilbasco: I am enclosing a picture of 'Woodside' which was taken in my boyhood days. I should be pleased if you would accept it as a slight souvenir of the visit I paid, along with Mr. Breithaupt and others, to 'Woodside' at the time of my recent visit to North Waterloo.

"I shall always remember your kindness to myself and the other members of the party in allowing us to see through the house and in helping me to discover the old tulip tree. It was kind of you to have everything so neat and attractive at the time of our visit. Your thoughtfulness has added to the many memories I have carried away from the visit to my old home.

"I have sent a separate letter to Marilyn which I hope she

327

will safely receive. I shall never forget how pretty she looked on the morning of our visit, or the sweet welcome she gave me in fastening the little flower in my buttonhole.

"I meant to speak to you of the words 'Home Sweet Home' which I saw had been placed in an opening in one of the trees. Someone told me that they thought they had been placed there by some member of your family. If so, I should like to express very warmly my appreciation of this kind thought.

"Please let this letter bring every good wish to Mr. Kilbasco and yourself and all the members of your family. Continue to take good care of 'Woodside' while you are living there.

"Wishing you all a happy Thanksgiving,
                              Yours sincerely,
                                        W. L. Mackenzie King."

Just before Christmas King received word that Marilyn's father had died suddenly. He was deeply touched by the tragedy that had befallen the little girl who had so won his heart.

"My Dear Marilyn," he wrote. "Nothing in many years has touched my heart more deeply than the word that came in your letter of a day or two ago. I am indeed pained to know that your dear father has been taken away, and that so suddenly and unexpectedly. I think I know just how sad you feel, also your dear mother and your brothers and sisters, and I feel for you all more deeply than my words can begin to express.

"You must try, notwithstanding your great loss, to make Christmas Day at 'Woodside' just as bright and cheerful as you can. You may be sure that God did not send into the world the little Child born on that day, so many centuries ago, to let us see from his life what God himself was like as a father, without having a very loving heart.

"While we cannot see God we have the story of the life of the little Christmas Child to let us know what He is like.

"So I am perfectly sure that your dear father, while taken away from you, has been taken to Heaven where God Himself is, and that though you cannot see your dear father, he can see you, and that his spirit will be watching over you and your mother and brothers and sisters at all times.

"When I was a little boy at 'Woodside' I found all this very difficult to comprehend but as I have grown older I have come to believe it more strongly every year, and I might say almost every day.

"So don't think of your father as gone, when you say your prayers ask him, as well as God, to watch over you, and to continue to care for you, and your mother, and all the family, and you will see, bye and bye, how, in some remarkable way, your prayers will be and have been answered.

"Your Christmas card is a lovely one, and I thank you warmly for it. I am sure you selected that particular card because the little picture looked so bright and cheerful and just the thing for Christmas. I shall keep it and your letter always.

"I am sending you, with this letter, as a little Christmas gift from me to you a real photograph of you and me taken on the day of my visit to Kitchener. I had it framed and took it with me to France and Belgium and Holland and England and always had it on my desk on the boat across the ocean both ways as well as in the hotels. I have had this one framed for you in a frame like the one I have. It will help you remember the happy time we had at 'Woodside' and I hope will add to your happiness at this Christmas season and always.

"It brings with it lots of love from me to you. Your very true friend,

W. L. Mackenzie King."

Reading this letter one cannot help but be impressed by the manner in which King has attempted to express himself in language that a small child can understand, without at the same time being guilty of that casual condescension so often exhibited by those unused to children. To King, Marilyn is obviously not just a child, but a person—an individual with a background and a personality all her own. He treats her as such. There is no attempt to "write down" to her, although the imagery expressed is clear and understandable.

It is apparent, too, that King knows just how attentive a child can be in respect to detail. He does not merely say: "I keep your picture with me always." He points out that he takes it along with him to France, to Belgium, to Holland, to England, that he has it with him in his hotel and "on the boat across the ocean both ways." He realizes that the child will see his letter as a series of pictures, and what a magnificent series of varied scenes he paints for her in one single sentence!

After studying this letter one can hazard a guess as to the kind of stories King used to tell to the inmates of the Sick Children's Hospital in Toronto. Bible stories, perhaps; travel stories; stories of adventure. Whatever the subject, they would be told in such a manner as to appeal to the imagination of the very young. There would be no puzzled expressions on their faces when young King had finished his tale.

It is interesting, too, to note King's insistence that the spirit of Marilyn's father will be "watching over" her. It fits in with King's firm belief in the continuation of the human personality.

MR. KING AT HOME

KING LIVES IN two worlds, the present and the past. Perhaps he dreams a little of the future, too, but it is from the present that he snatches his triumphs and his satisfactions. From the past he draws strength and guidance and spiritual and intellectual nourishment.

King has always kept abreast of international affairs. His views on social reform can hardly be described as reactionary or antiquated; but in his own private life he is hopelessly Victorian. There is nothing modern about his preferences in literature, art, or social behaviour. He does not fully comprehend the work of most Canadian painters, and the ultra-modern in architecture and the present vogue of functionalism as opposed to more decorative forms of architecture leave him unmoved. But he can enthuse over the work of the accepted Old Masters, the Gothic beauty of the Parliament Buildings, the slender spires of an old cathedral.

He loves inanimate things which link the present with the past—old buildings, old pieces of furniture, old books and pictures. In a world of social, scientific and political change he is a supreme traditionist.

Perhaps this is one reason why he has always harboured an intense affection for Laurier House. It stands, an old, nondescript, gray-brick building, in Ottawa's once-fashionable Sandy Hill district. Today, a few of the city's first families still linger on in Sandy Hill, socially secure amidst the rococo elegance of big, rambling, draughty-halled mansions built on the profits of lumber, pulp-wood, paper, safety matches, street-cars and public utilities. But, for the most part, the Capital's "four hundred" have moved on to greener and more attractive fields, to the Village of Rockcliffe Park, the Aylmer Road, Island Park Drive.

Another reason why King loves Laurier House is that it reminds him of "Woodside", his boyhood home. An atmosphere of faded gentility clings to it, and its old walls and ivy-covered gables exude an elusive and indefinable emanation of time and of memories of things past and gone.

Laurier House is furnished very much as "Woodside" was, with the exception, perhaps, that everything is on a more elaborate scale.

On the ground floor the rooms are high-ceilinged, with tall French windows. Two large drawing rooms reveal considerable taste in decoration, but there is not a modern note to be found. The predominating theme is stiffly nineteenth century. Chairs and tables are antique pieces which King has picked up here and there from time to time. He has refused to have many of them re-covered or repaired, despite the fact that they are threadbare with use and faded with age.

Tables are loaded down with nick-nacks, keep-sakes, souvenirs and curios of all kinds. Here is a glass cabinet containing the scrolls conferring on King the freedom of London and other cities in the United Kingdom and on the Continent. Here are the keys to those cities. Here repose a few treasured volumes which once belonged to Sir Wilfrid, including Hay's *Life of Lincoln*. Here are rare old family photographs and historical manuscripts, a gold-headed walking stick presented to King in 1920 by the Liberal women of Vancouver, a tie-pin made from Saskatchewan River gold, a gift from the Liberal women of Edmonton.

These sentimental relics hold a strange fascination for

King, and over the years he has steadily added to his collection. He possesses a table which once belonged to Matthew Arnold, a set of beautifully-wrought silver-ware, once the property of William Lyon Mackenzie, and many fine tapestries. Amongst this collection of antiques and objets d'art one comes across such odd items as a faded old poster offering a reward of one thousand pounds for "William Lyon Mackenzie, the Rebel!"

The house literally bulges with interesting odds-and-ends, and, each and every one, they take King back into the distant past, recalling his early political triumphs, his boyhood in Berlin, the adventures and vicissitudes shared by his grandparents when the Mackenzies were in exile.

In one of the large downstairs drawing rooms stands a marble bust of King's mother, and, facing it, is a companion piece, a bust of his father. These are the work of an Italian sculptor, Guiseppe Guastala, who worked from photographs. Scattered throughout the house are signed and framed photographs of scores of world figures—statesmen, philanthropists, philosophers, scientists, political friends.

In the richly-panelled dining room hang portraits of King's parents, of Sir Wilfrid Laurier, William Lyon Mackenzie, and Gladstone. Like his hero, Pasteur, King is for men "who would go to the stake for their principles." Among such men he would include Gladstone, Edward Grey, Lincoln, Franklin Roosevelt.

On the third floor, in King's study, dominating the room, is his favourite painting of his mother. A small light illumines the portrait and gives it an eerie, life-like quality. The portrait was painted during one of his mother's frequent visits to Kingsmere and shows her sitting before the fireplace reading from a book. The firelight plays on her face, throwing into relief her fine, sensitive features.

The light above the portrait is turned on first thing each morning by a servant. King turns it off himself, the last thing at night.

It is in this beautiful oak-panelled study "up underneath the eaves" that King spends most of his time. It was the same when he was Prime Minister, here it was that the business of Canada was finally centralized. Here it was that he wrote most of his speeches, made his important decisions, thought out problems of high government policy.

If the downstairs rooms have a touch of the maiden aunt about them, then this room is typically masculine. Hundreds of books line the walls. Big, over-stuffed chairs and a chesterfield before an open fire invite comfort and relaxation. Before the low windows at the front of the house stands King's working desk. It is a room for study and work, and quiet reflection.

"I like working here," King told a visitor. "It keeps me free from interruption and I can think through what I'm working on. Even if I lock myself up in the East Block office there is always in the back of my mind the thought of the people who may be waiting outside. I do most of my work here."

On another occasion he observed: "The profound things of life are not understood in tumult, but are worked out in quiet and reflection."

In contrast to King's Laurier House study, the East Block office which he occupied for so many years as Prime Minister is an austere, run-down dingy relic of Victorian Gothic. It is anything but magnificent in its appointments and no one would imagine that it belonged to a Prime

Minister. King used it seldom and only as a sort of half-way house between Laurier House and the Privy Council Chamber, or for his occasional press conferences. It contains a full-length portrait of Laurier, a small one of William Lyon Mackenzie, one of Lincoln and an assortment of photographs of various Liberal cabinets. When King sat in his old swivel chair, he used to rest his feet on a faded footstool which, like the rest of the furniture, had been left there by Laurier. King never thought much of his office in the East Block and never attempted to improve its appearance. It has a great stone fireplace which is seldom used, antiquated lighting fixtures, and dark, red hangings at the windows and doors which give it a gloomy and somewhat depressing atmosphere.

In Laurier House, King sleeps in a bedroom on the second floor, the same room in which Laurier died. The furnishings are simple, almost monastic. King keeps a few books on his bedside table, although he rarely reads in bed. The one unusual note which is struck is provided by a little pallet or bed in which King's first dog, Pat I, used to sleep.

Anyone who has been a guest at Laurier House or at Kingsmere will tell you that King is the model host. He never entertains on a lavish scale, and, when he was Prime Minister, New Year's Day was the one occasion throughout the year when he held open house. His entertaining, for the most part, is confined to small, select dinner parties of a dozen or so guests usually selected for their congeniality of spirit. Occasionally even smaller, cosier parties are arranged when two or more couples may make up the guest list.

There was a time when King's list of intimate friends was a lengthy one, but it grows shorter with the advance of time as the friends of his youth, of his college days, of his earlier political years pass on, one by one.

Over the years King made it a practice to quietly entertain not only many of his own cabinet ministers and other supporters in the House, but the leaders of opposition groups. Also, such contrasting personalities as John Dafoe, Lord Beaverbrook, Mary Pickford, Smuts, Greer Garson (his favourite picture star), Sir Harry Lauder, Barbara Ann Scott—a varied and distinguished collection of visitors—found themselves at one time or another at Laurier House enjoying the hospitality of Canada's Prime Minister.

King always sets a good table. Well chosen dishes, the right wines and the proper vintages, and company selected on the basis of community of interests, make a dinner at Laurier House a memorable event.

Actually King loves giving "parties." He fusses over the menu, checks the arrangements, even writes the place cards himself.

He picked up this little habit from Sir Wilfrid Laurier who always went to the trouble of writing out place cards in his own hand. "It gives me an opportunity to make a little intimate gesture towards each of my guests," Sir Wilfrid explained. King thought that it was a thoughtful gesture and from that time on practised it himself.

When entertaining at dinner King keeps up a running fire of conversation. He has a remarkable fund of stories and tells them with an inimitable grace and charm. Indeed, this side of his personality, so seldom in evidence in public, is invariably remarked upon by those who find themselves his guests for the first time. King has been in politics so long, has visited so many parts of the world, has led such an active and full life that he is a very fountain-head of information and experience. He loves to chat of his long associations with Churchill and Roosevelt. He has known most of the outstanding men and women of his time. All this makes for interesting conversation and easy and graceful hospitality.

King is full of stories of his student days and of the adventures that befell him when he cycled through Europe on his travelling fellowship from Harvard. There are nostalgic reminiscences of Paris, Berlin, Rome, which he visited as a student; of India, China and Japan which he first visited while still Deputy Minister of Labour; and of London, and Westminster and Buckingham Palace.

Because King sat in the East Block for so many years a great many Canadians have automatically but mistakenly come to think of him as the fixed object which gathers to itself the lowlier forms of vegetation. Yet as a matter of fact the extent and variety of his perigrinations over the years stand as a complete contradiction to the old proverb that a rolling stone gathers no moss. King started travelling around the world while he was still in his early twenties. He has been everywhere and has seen everything. He is undoubtedly the most-travelled Prime Minister this country has known.

"The Hermit of Kingsmere!" "The Recluse of Laurier House!" How misleading and deceptive such captious descriptions can become. In his early twenties King was doing social service work in Chicago's "Jungle," was delivering lectures on political economy and labour reform in the slums of London. Yet, somehow, over the years he became such a permanent fixture in Ottawa that it seemed he had been always part and parcel of the scene. Perhaps one can make allowances, then, for those who instinctively associate him always with the drab, indefinite background of Laurier House and the silences and solitudes of his mountain retreat.

It is when he is in residence at "Moorside", his summer home on the shore of Kingsmere Lake, in the Laurentian Hills, some dozen miles directly north of the Capital, that King really shakes off the mantle of officialdom and becomes just another summer resident.

This was particularly so when he was Prime Minister. His whole attitude changed when he got away from the East Block and Laurier House. Work was still the order of the day but it was at a more leisurely pace. At Laurier House, King was Prime Minister and man of affairs; at Kingsmere he put on the clothing of the country squire and conducted himself accordingly.

It is only natural that a great many people should have the idea that Kingsmere is named after King himself. Actually it is named after King's Mountain which, in turn, received its name from Dr. William F. King (no relation), first head of the Geological Survey of Canada. Because some of the first settlers in the area came from the English Lake country it was perhaps natural that they should name the lake "Kingsmere" rather than "King's Lake."

King has been going to Kingsmere for the past fifty years. When he became Deputy Minister of Labour he bought a small piece of land at the edge of the lake and here he built a modest cottage. Gradually, over the years, he extended his holdings. Never one to invest in bonds, he decided that the lakeside property might one day have an enhanced value and he invested his savings in it.

About 25 years ago he purchased what has since been his main summer home, a pleasant cottage owned by the late Very Rev. Dr. W. T. Herridge, father of W. D. Herridge, who for years was one of the stormy petrels of the political scene. He still keeps his original cottage by the lakeshore which at times is used by members of his staff.

The property is typical Gatineau Hill country—rugged

hills, a few boulder-strewn meadows in between and a plentitude of trees straggling along the ridges. Much of it was once farmed but the original settlers moved west and abandoned it. King acquired a portion of it when it was sold for taxes. The main part of the property is on a commanding rise which provides a magnificent view to three sides: to the north where the Laurentians rise in a series of soft, rolling hills; to the south, looking towards the Capital; and to the west where, through a natural break in the hills, one can look for miles across the flat, fertile valley of the Ottawa River a thousand feet or more below.

King's ventures in the field of agriculture have been fairly limited. Once he tried raising sheep but he found the cost of keeping them through the winter prohibitive. So he traded the sheep to a neighbouring farmer for another small piece of land which included a little stream and waterfall, which had intrigued his fancy. A small orchard provides him with a few plums and apples. He raises some vegetables, and has a flower garden. In recent years his chief agricultural hobby has been keeping bees. He has had some modest success with his apiary and delights in being able to present a jar of Kingsmere honey to a friend or acquaintance.

In 1946 King's bees were the innocent cause of quite a commotion. One evening in October a large bear (there are deer, bear, beaver and many other wild animals in the Gatineau district) visited King's apiary and, seeking to satisfy his sweet-tooth, upset one of the hives. The damage was not discovered until the following morning when the caretaker happened to visit the hives which are situated about 100 yards from the house. He sent word to Harry Clegg, an apiarist from nearby Chelsea, who had been tending the bees, and Clegg came right up, righted the hive and repaired the damage. The next night, however,

KING'S SYNTHETIC RUINS

"A sentimental attachment to the past."

the bear returned and another hive was upset and robbed. Realizing that it was the work of a bear, Clegg set a bear-trap and sometime early the next morning poor Bruin put his foot in it.

The noise of the bear threshing around aroused one of the staff who telephoned for assistance. Armed with guns, Clegg and a nearby farmer arrived on the scene to find that the animal had dragged the trap off into the deep woods. They came upon the unfortunate beast about a quarter of a mile back in the woods and despatched it.

This was the end of the bear, but the noise and confusion had aroused the Prime Minister who met the men upon their return.

King examined the 125-pound animal and observed: "Well, I hope the bees will be safe now."

And then, although it was only about seven in the morning, King decided he might just as well begin his day's work.

In the early days, King's mother and father used to visit him at Kingsmere, and during the summer months usually spent long periods there. An Ottawa woman tells a charming story that provides a cameo-like portrait of Mrs. King. The narrator, together with other children of her own age, used to wander about the lake and, as children will, allow her fancy full rein. When the wind rustled through the grass the children pretended that the fairies were dancing through the fields. "And then, once in a while, the stage-coach would sweep by," she recalls, "And a beautiful woman would be riding in it, her long white hair streaming out behind her in the wind. It was Mrs. King, and we used to pretend that she was the Queen of the Fairies. She had a strange, ethereal beauty about her that impressed us deeply."

King, himself, recalls those early days with a nostalgic

sigh. He always loved that four-mile trip by stage from the railroad station to the lake, and more often than not he would take the reins from the driver and manage the horses himself.

Visitors to "Moorside" are sometimes astonished at some of the things they find there. King, a born collector, has gathered up a singular assortment of curios. They provide a Salvador Dali-like atmosphere to the place, but each one possesses some particular sentimental connotation, bringing back old memories, reviving forgotten moods and experiences, helping him to recapture the elusive and intangible past.

In one of the pastures to the rear of the house stands a life-size pottery donkey carrying saddle-baskets and painted so realistically that at first one is completely deceived. Presented to King by the late Philippe Roy, former minister to France, the donkey is a reminder of a trip which King and Roy took through Normandy years ago.

Hanging from the beams of the side verandah of the cottage is an ancient bell. It once sounded the watches on an old Nova Scotia sailing vessel. The ship was wrecked and dismantled and the bell disposed of. King came across it in a second-hand shop and thought it would make an excellent dinner bell.

At the main entrance to "Moorside" stand two old oil-lamp standards. Many years ago when King learned that the city of Berlin was abandoning its obsolete coal-oil street lighting system he begged two of the old standards and set them up as a reminder of his childhood days. He equipped them with coal-oil lamps and they serve duty today as they did over half a century ago in Berlin.

"One of my earliest recollections of Berlin," King told

a friend, "is of the lamplighter going around from one light to the other, each night. He would put up his little ladder, climb up to the lamp, open it up and then strike his match and light it. I can remember waiting for him to make his rounds in the evening."

But most amazing of all are King's "synthetic ruins." King has constructed walls and arches and arbours using stones from the old Parliament Buildings which were razed by fire during World War I, and from other structures. Set up here and there about the grounds are broken pieces of sculpture from the Houses of Parliament at Westminster, an old window which King saw being ripped from an Ottawa home, which aroused his admiration, the stone doorway of the old Bank of British North America which stood on Wellington street and was razed to make room for the Confederation Building.

These "ruins", weighing many hundreds of tons, have been gathered up by King and re-erected. Invariably the reconstructed window, arch or series of columns frames some particularly fine view. One group of ruins tops a little hill to the rear of the cottage. In the distance, it might be all that remains of some feudal castle. King erected the first group of stones at this spot because he used to like to sit on the top of the hill and read. But sometimes he found it a trifle windy; so he decided to erect a stone windbreak. One thing led to another, until today the group of ruins looks more like the remains of a castle or, perhaps, a miniature Grecian temple. Through the ruins of a great stone archway one looks across the lonely hills; turning, one faces the remains of a stone fireplace which once graced the chambers of the Speaker of the House of Commons at Westminster; and then one walks through a beautifully proportioned arch to stand on a little stone terrace flanked by a row of columns that might have come from Greece or Sicily.

Most of the carved stones are pieces that were removed from Westminster from time to time because they had been damaged by sulphur fumes. King purchased them and had them shipped to Canada.

Someone has said that if King had not gone into social work or politics he might have made a name for himself as a landscape artist. He agrees with this. Certainly his use of the discarded and neglected remains of a hundred craftsmen's toil and artistry reveals a fine appreciation of form and line.

Yet one cannot help but feel that there is something less superficial about these "synthetic ruins" than a mere appreciation of physical beauty. Here is the highest expression of King's peculiarly sentimental attachment to the past, of his adherence to tradition and custom, of his respect for ancestral effort and accomplishment.

For King, one of the happiest days in the year was that on which the roads were at last clear of heavy snow and he could visit Kingsmere for the first time. As a start, he would go up for the day, probably Saturday or Sunday, but, as the Spring days lengthened and it became warmer, he would stay at Kingsmere over the week-ends. Towards the end of June, he would move out for the summer.

There was usually plenty of work to keep one busy; and daily and sometimes hourly contact by telephone or messenger with the East Block did not permit King to forget for very long that he was Prime Minister of Canada. Occasionally a secretary or stenographer drove up to Kingsmere and King spent the morning or the afternoon dictating. But such periods of work were broken by pleasant interludes of complete relaxation, a cup of tea on the verandah or the terrace, a stroll along one of the shady, sequestered paths.

For King there was time for long rambles in the early morning or in the evening. There was time, too, for some quiet reading. Unlike Roosevelt and some other public figures who liked to laze through a two-bit thriller King wasted no time on purely escapist literature. Instead he enjoyed his favourites: Thomas W. Lamont's *My Boyhood in a Country Parsonage,* and David Grayson's *Under My Elms* or *Adventures in Contentment.* Occasionally King found time, also, for a "visit" with his beloved Tennyson, or with Matthew Arnold.

There was opportunity, as well, for homey chats with the gardener and his wife, with the farmers in the district with whom he had been on intimate terms over the years, with some of the old-timers in the little village of Old Chelsea which nestled against the foot of the mountain a few miles away.

And, of course, there were rambles with "Pat."

It was quite impossible, of course, to cut oneself entirely adrift from the cares of state, but on the little mountain-top, by the shores of the lake, or skirting the cedar-fenced fields there was opportunity for quiet contemplation and spiritual and mental replenishment.

Somtimes he would have a few friends up for the week-end. Once in a while his sister, Mrs. Lay, was able to get down from Barrie for a brief stay.

Most of Canada's Governors General who were in office during King's periods of Prime Ministership were frequent guests at Kingsmere. The Willingdons, Tweedsmuirs, Athlones and the Alexanders all found their way, at one time or another, to King's mountain retreat. Britain's visiting Prime Ministers spent some time there when in Canada, including Baldwin, MacDonald, Neville Chamberlain, Attlee. Roosevelt was another wartime guest. By and large, it served as a sort of Canadian Chequers and provided King with some place where he could entertain visiting dignitaries in a more or less informal manner.

Of all the Governors General who visited Kingsmere, however, perhaps the one who loved it best was Lord Tweedsmuir. Buchan and King had been friends of many years standing when the former was appointed Governor General, and in a great many respects they were kindred souls. Buchan loved tramping the Gatineau Hills which reminded him so much of his native Scotland. Often he would go off for the day hiking through the woods and take great delight in dropping in on some farmer and asking if he might have a bite of lunch. He was always very much at home at "Moorside."

The Athlones liked the place so much that they used to drop out uninvited when King was not there, bringing their own lunch-basket. He loaned the cottage to them for a holiday one summer and they were as pleased as children to get away from the pomp and circumstance of Rideau Hall and rusticate in the country.

The Alexanders are also fond of "Moorside." An artist of considerable ability, the present Governor General appears to find a real source of inspiration for his brush in the mountainous country north of the capital. He has roamed the Gatineau area for miles about seeking suitable subjects for his colourful landscapes.

Malcolm MacDonald, when he was British High Commissioner to Canada, was another frequent visitor. He spoke of his stays at Kingsmere with obvious pleasure. Sometimes he was a week-end guest, again he might drop up during the afternoon and stay for tea.

While it is true that King always enjoyed discussing politics and international affairs with his guests, just as often the conversation was desultory and varied. King usually spent a good deal of his time showing his guests around the grounds, leading them along the many forest trails he has cut through the woods, explaining the significance of his "ruins", pointing out the many beautiful song birds that find sanctuary in the area, explaining to them about his bees, his flowers and his raspberry plants.

In the evening, by the fireside, he usually reminisced a great deal. He enjoyed talking about his associations with Baldwin, Chamberlain, Roosevelt, Smuts and scores of other Commonwealth and world figures. He liked to tell about his visit to Germany before the war, of his talks with Goering and Hess and Hitler, of how he came to make his famous "Five Cent Piece" speech, of his mother, and of his boyhood days. Usually the conversation was light and amusing. Often King charmed his guests with uproarious stories about the great and the near-great, until the fire was low and night had settled down upon the listening hills.

The grounds at "Moorside" are only partially fenced, and, as a result, strangers, out for a ramble in the woods, sometimes find themselves following one of King's many private paths. Sometimes these lead the wanderer right to the door of King's cottage.

Once, Douglas Baker, an Ottawa artist, was doing some sketching near Kingsmere, with his wife and two children. Without realizing it they wandered on to the grounds. They had set up their easels and were busily painting when King wandered up. Smiling, he looked over their sketches, pronounced them very good, and then, bidding them good day, proceeded on his walk.

In the meanwhile all members of the family, somewhat

out of countenance at finding themselves face to face with
Mr. King, had been looking him over carefully. When
King was finally out of earshot Baker turned to his wife
and remarked delightedly.

"Say, did you notice? He had the friendliest looking
pair of shoes I have ever seen!"

The cost of maintaining Laurier House and a summer
home in the country has been considerable. Mr. King has
frequently spoken of the matter, and even as late as the day
he retired he expressed the view that Canada should provide
a suitable official residence for its Prime Minister and that
a sum of money should be provided for maintenance and
entertaining.

"The obligations are very great indeed upon the individual who holds the office of Prime Minister of his
country," King told parliament on one occasion. "The state
should seek to make the leader of its government independent of considerations of the kind, that he may give his
whole time and thought and energy to the discharge of his
public duties in the largest possible way."

King knows that he has been unusually lucky in that
his friends came to his assistance early in his career and
provided him with a home of his own. He feels that some
of his successors may not be so fortunate.

X

AT A CASEMENT WINDOW

KING HAS ALWAYS been a great reader. Someone once referred to him as "the student in politics" and that phrase very aptly describes his passion for study and research.

He never formed a taste for light reading, but occasionally he does read merely for the sake of relaxation. He probably could find relaxation digesting the decision of a board of arbitration or even an old copy of Hansard, but his favourite "light" reading consists, for the most part, of history, biography and philosophy. The latter does not have to be profound, however, as witness King's fondness for David Grayson's homespun philosophic meanderings.

Very occasionally, when seeking to get quite away from the world of politics and statesmanship, King gathers together a miscellaneous assortment of reading—letters, scientific treatises, essays, poetry—and chooses at random. Sometimes, he admits, he has as many as four or five different books going at the same time.

He has one favourite comic strip, *Tillie the Toiler,* which he reads faithfully every day.

The four walls of his third-floor library at Laurier House are lined with hundreds of volumes. History, biography, philosophy, poetry and works on sociology, economics and politics predominate, with here and there a discreet scattering of books on a much wider range of subjects, many of them the writings of friends and acquaintances.

His collection of Canadiana is not impressive, although it does contain many valuable items dealing mostly with the early history and political development of the Dominion.

King does attempt to keep abreast of the work of Canadian authors. Canadian novels of outstanding merit are usually read. Similarly he tries to find the time to read contemporary non-fiction particularly if it is within the range of his personal interests. During the war he made an effort to keep up with the unprecedented spate of books dealing with Canadian participation and with international problems generally. But the author had to be a recognized authority. Selection was important because King could not afford to devote his few spare moments to books which demonstrated loose thinking or unskilled, clumsy treatment.

Most of the volumes which pass through King's hands soon take on the appearance of old friends, for, like Tennyson and some others, he believes that books should be used. As a result, books which genuinely interest him soon contain extensive marginal notes and observations. He finds, when he picks up an old favourite, that, with very little trouble, he can turn to the specific passages or chapters that most interest him.

King has always been a great lover of poetry and he can quote extensively from most of the standard poets and from the works of a good many who today are not particularly popular. Recently he surprised a visitor to Laurier House by reciting the whole of Shelley's *To a Skylark*. He is fond of Burns and of Tennyson. The deep humanity and emotional appeal of the one and the rich imagery and profound philosophy of the other strike responsive chords in his heart and mind.

No phrase-maker himself, King is always ready with an apt quotation, and nine chances out of ten it will be poetical. His speeches in or out of the House were frequently interspersed with passages from the poets.

It was typical of King, for instance, that he should conclude his address to the National Liberal Convention in 1948 with a few lines of poetry, this time from the works of a seventeenth century divine:

Therefore, though few may praise, or help, or heed us,
Let us work on with head, or heart, or hand,
For this we know—the future ages need us,
And we must help our time to take its stand.

If one turns to the official report of the Liberal Convention of 1919, one finds him closing his address of thanks to the delegates by paying tribute to his late chieftain in Tennyson's words. Here was a man, said King:

Who never sold the truth to save the hour,
Nor paltered with Eternal God for power;
Who let the turbid streams of rumour flow
Thro' either babbling world of high or low;
Whose life was work, whose language rife
With rugged maxims hewn from life.

On his return from Britain in 1941 King concluded his address calling for an increased war effort with the following lines:

Rise! for the day is passing,
And you lie dreaming on;
The others have buckled their armour
And forth to the fight have gone.
A place in the ranks await you,
Each man has some part to play;
The Past and the Future are nothing
In the face of the stern Today.

Few of King's speeches fail to contain at least one poetical quotation. Invariably King dredges them up from the slough of memory. They are not picked at random from *Bartlett's Familiar Quotations*. They are lines which King remembers from college days or which he came across in later years and committed to memory.

In this connection, King's feats of memory are truly prodigious. He began training his memory as a young man and although he has never revealed what particular system, if any, he followed, he has a filing-cabinet type of memory which enables him to recall names, dates and other details with uncanny accuracy. Although in recent years he did not depend upon his memory when making long addresses, in his early years he used to memorize all his speeches and deliver them as if they were entirely extemporaneous

On one such occasion King, as usual, had prepared his speech well in advance. It was one of his more ambitious efforts and ran to more than thirty pages. As King began to speak one of his secretaries took up his place behind the platform, a copy of King's speech on his knee. Well over an hour later a member of the platform committee wandered around to the back of the platform. "How far has he got?" he inquired of the secretary, who was carefully checking King's progress. "Believe it or not," said the secretary with a grin of incredulity, "but he's down to the bottom of his thirty-fourth page and he hasn't yet missed a comma."

King seldom quoted William Lyon Mackenzie, but occasionally he would use a passage or two from the works of his rebel grandparent to drive home a point. Perhaps his favourite quotation from Mackenzie is that in which the latter refers to his early recollections of the struggles of his widowed mother, and to the privations suffered by the working men he knew as a youth:

"Well may I love the poor, greatly may I esteem the humble and lowly, for poverty and adversity were my nurses, and in youth were want and misery my familiar friends. Even now it yields a sweet satisfaction to my soul, that I can claim kindred with the obscure cottar, and the humble labourer, of my native, ever-honoured, ever-loved Scotland."

When King delivered this quotation in the House it was an impressive performance.

One of King's prized possessions is Mackenzie's old Bible. It is a small, battered, dog-eared volume with many of its pages cut and mutilated. Mackenzie apparently used it as a book of ready reference in his old newspaper publishing days and from it he used to cut appropriate passages when he was rushed for time. Other passages are heavily underlined in pencil and invariably these are ones condemning the hypocrisy of the "Scribes and Pharisees", the ammunition he needed in his fight against the Family Compact.

"Woe unto you, lawyers! for ye have taken away the key of knowledge: ye entered not into yourselves and them that were entering in ye hindered" . . . "Go to now, ye rich men, weep and howl for your miseries that shall come upon you. Your riches are corrupted and your garments are moth-eaten."

King handles the ancient and tattered book with a reverential air.

When King was in England as a young man he met the late J. M. Barrie, author of the immortal *Peter Pan*. They became fast friends, and a unique souvenir of their friendship is a short, whimsical ghost-story written in Barrie's own hand, especially for King.

The circumstances surrounding the writing of the little tale are interesting. Barrie and King spent a week-end together at Hever Castle, in Kent, the home of Col. the

Hon. J. J. Astor and of Lady Violet Astor. The castle is one of those said to be haunted by the ghost of Anne Boleyn. During their visit there was talk about poor Anne's phantom. One thing led to another, and, finally, to the writing of the ghost-story. In it Barrie tells of Anne's ghost visiting King at Laurier House, in the dead of night. The story, unpublished of course, constitutes a collector's item of rare value. King is very proud of it and has had it beautifully bound in limp leather. It is one of his most prized possessions.

No doubt one of the things which attracted King to Barrie was the latter's whimsical and sympathetic approach to youth. It fitted in with King's lifelong interest in children and his memories of his own happy boyhood.

King is eternally coming up with some little-known quotation to express a subtle shade of meaning.

"Speech is but broken light upon the depths of the unspoken," he said in the House of Commons, on the occasion of his seventy-third birthday, quoting George Eliot.

He was thanking the members for their expressions of regard.

It was a quotation he had used in *The Secret of Heroism* so many years before, to describe his own inadequacy of words in paying tribute to the memory of his friend Harper.

But history is the department of literature which attracts King most of all. He believes that it is not merely a record of past events, to be read as such, but that history stands as a sign-post to the future and should be considered in that light. If King does not actually believe that history provides a precedent for every human action, he certainly does feel that the majority of present day problems can best

354

be approached in the light of what has gone before. He feels that while events do not always find exact parallels in the past, still the principles underlying human action and behaviour remain immutable throughout the ages. Thus a thorough knowledge of history is indispensable to the individual who enters political life, and prerequisite to a full understanding of current problems.

King believes that Canada has been most fortunate in having a man like Francis Parkman to record her history.

"You can read all kinds of books on Canada, but Parkman should be the foundation."

King would like to see Canada have a monument to Parkman, preferably placed on Parliament Hill, near the Parliamentary Library where the great historian did much of his writing.

He believes that one should not stop with Canadian history, however. The study of international relations should be a challenge to Canadians who "stand between the United States and Britain" and play such an important role in contributing to understanding between these two.

While King is convinced that much may be got out of reading, he is also of the opinion that there is so much being written today that one must be most selective, and read only the best. He recalls the "endless time" he spent as a college youth going through labour records and minutes of old meetings to write various theses and wonders if his time might not have been better employed reading the great works and getting the sweep of history.

He believes that young men ought to devote their time to the best in literature and to the thoughts and policies of the world's great men, at least until their own minds take shape and they begin to be able to form their own opinions.

It is better, he says, that they know of the great achievements of others; this way they see themselves in proportion.

Finally, he admits that while there is much good to be gained from books, one must not overdo it and lose the practical experience of everyday life.

Biography which, after all, is merely a division of history, is, perhaps, King's second love in reading. He has read and studied the standard biographies of most of the world's great men and women: Lincoln, Luther, Pasteur, Napoleon, Madame Curie, Florence Nightingale, Marx, Pitt, Gladstone. Much of this literature was required reading during his college days, but he has never ceased to interest himself in the study of great people, of the motivating forces behind their thoughts and actions.

He has known intimately or been associated closely in a political or professional way with many of the outstanding men and women of the past three or four decades. His position in parliament over that long period brought him into intimate contact with all the great British and Commonwealth leaders. He seldom failed to find the opportunity to make the acquaintance of people whom he admired, but sought them out when the opportune moment presented itself. To list the world figures whose friendship he has cultivated throughout the years would be to present a fairly complete roster of the outstanding literary, political, theological and sociological celebrities of his time.

Among the books of modern biography or autobiography to be found on the shelves of King's library are books by or about them inscribed to King by Mussolini, Lloyd George, Winston Churchill, J. S. Spender, Stanley Baldwin, Philip Snowden, Ramsay MacDonald, to mention but a few.

Sometimes when King is entertaining a visitor at Laurier House he goes to one of his bookshelves and from a row of

KING AND ST. LAURENT

"In his seventy-fourth year he was now ready to step aside."

books written by members of his family (he calls it "the treasure of the humble") takes down a file of faded documents and exhibits them with pride. They are the collection of agreements which he was instrumental in effecting between the management and the employees of various key industries in the United States during World War I, and which resulted either in the prevention or settlement of strikes. He is intensely proud of this dog-eared bundle of papers which represent, in capsule form, the practical and concrete results of his labour relations work during the period of the war, and which, he believes, constituted a not inconsiderable contribution to the Allied war effort.

He will exhibit, too, with a certain, thoughtful air of reverence, the two books written by his brother, and his father's famous legal work on the law of defamation.

"My father must have felt that some member of the family might some day be prominent in public life," King observed dryly on once occasion, when referring to this treatise on libel.

There, also, is King's own contribution to the family shelf of literary accomplishment: *Industry and Humanity* (1918); *The Secret of Heroism* (1906); *The Message of the Carillon and other Addresses* (1927); *Canada at Britain's Side* (1941); and *Canada and the Fight for Freedom* (1944).

King's library contains most, if not all, of the works of his friend, John Buchan, all of them autographed by the author.

One, *The Minto Biography*, bears on its flyleaf the inscription: "W. L. Mackenzie King, with the affectionate respect of his friend, John Buchan, Sept. 15, 1924."

"He was staying with me when he got his first copy," King explained when exhibiting the volume to a friend. "We went down to the customs together to get it out."

Incidentally, Tweedsmuir's book, *Augustus,* published during the period of his vice-royalty in Ottawa, was dedicated to King. King's copy bears the simple inscription: "Rex from J. B."

Long before his retirement King expressed his eagerness to get down to the actual work of writing, not only his personal memoirs, but a history of some of the great events of the times in which he had lived.

"From time to time," he told the National Liberal Federation in January, 1947, "I have read in the press that I had already entered upon the task of writing my memoirs. Indeed, I have received from more than one publishing house enquiries as to whether their representative might not discuss with me terms upon which the memoirs might be published. I do not deny that there are a few things which I should like to say, or to leave in written form, which I hope might encourage younger men to take some part in public life, and which I would also hope might be helpful to them in the service of their country.

"I should like to leave, too, some account, were that possible, of some of the great events of our times, as I have watched them develop, and have glimpsed them from behind the scenes. Such a record might be of interest and value to a succeeding generation if not to our own.

"I must tell you, however, that this is not a task which can be performed in a day, nor yet in a year, nor is it a task that could be entered upon so long as one's responsibilities continue to be what mine have been in the past, and what they are at present. I regret to have to say that up to this moment I have not found it possible to write a single line."

Following his retirement as Prime Minister, King found it more difficult to settle down to work than he had anticipated. In the first place his health was none too good, and he was constantly being consulted by officials in the East Block as to what had been done about this or about that. In addition, faced with the certainty of a greatly diminished income, he had to make plans to reduce his standard of living to some extent, and, generally speaking, put his house in order.

In 1946 King had announced that Frederick W. Gibson, M.A., of Kingston, had been temporarily appointed to the staff of the Dominion Archives to catalogue official correspondence from the office of the Prime Minister which King had turned over to the Archives some time previously.

But it was not until the Spring of 1949 that King was able to announce concrete plans for the writing of his memoirs and, perhaps, some additional papers.

The plan had been made possible as a result of a grant of $100,000 from the Rockefeller Foundation of New York to McGill University to be used over a three-year period for the preparation of King's memoirs!

Thus the Rockefeller Foundation, which had made possible the writing of *Industry and Humanity,* King's first major work, was to make possible the preparation and publication of what would be his last important contribution to public life, the story of his own career and of the times in which he had moved.

"The object of the grant," explained King, "is to afford me the assistance necessary for the effective use of the very extensive personal and official files that have accumulated in my long career, and to help me meet the expenses involved.

"It is intended to expedite the writing and early publication of memoirs by myself to be, not entirely but chiefly, a Canadian biography and Canadian history."

Up to the present, he admitted, he had been unable to

make a beginning on anything in the nature of memoirs, his illness having placed distinct limitations on his activities.

Just how King intends to go about the preparation of his memoirs is a question that only he can answer. He has plenty of material. He has the official diary which over the years he dictated each day to his confidential secretary, the official correspondence from his own office, and, in addition, many personal notes he has jotted down in more or less methodical fashion throughout the years.

While the voluminous and detailed official reports may provide the stuff for an historical work covering his years in public life, they will not provide the intimate details of King's career which so many people hope some day to learn. The question is: will King, in writing his memoirs, produce an intimate, human document which will permit the secret recesses of his mind and heart; or will it be merely a serious, analytical and historical study of his own career as a public servant, political leader and Prime Minister? King has promised that it will be both.

There are those who will say that King is emotionally incapable of baring his private life to the world. It has been said of him that he regards public display of personality as akin to the larger indecencies. Will he write about Billy King as well as about W. L. Mackenzie King, the statesman?

King is not capable of writing a "pot-boiler", even if he would. He will want anything he puts his name to to stand the acid test of time.

Thus, it may be some years before King's memoirs are ready for publication.

It is doubtful if Canadians will be able to assess the full measure of the man until King's private correspondence has been collected and published. It is multitudinous in extent, and it is, for the most part, of a distinctly personal nature—letters to his intimate friends, to the members of his family, to his political colleagues and acquaintances.

King has always made a practice of writing these personal letters in longhand, so that even his secretaries have little knowledge of the contents of most of them. But this vast treasure-house of correspondence does exist, and if even a part of it can be gathered and annotated much of the silence and shadow that surrounds the person of Canada's former Prime Minister will be effectually and permanently dispelled.

XI

"THE OLD MAN"

FOR A GOOD many years now they had called him "The Old Man." It was a title susceptible to a multiplicity of interpretations. When it was used by King's friends and associates it invariably carried with it the full measure of their respect and admiration. Not infrequently its use revealed the existence of a warm, personal affection almost filial in its depth and intensity. "The Old Man," they would say, and it was at once an accolade to age and to accomplishment.

But those who did not love King were apt to give the words a different connotation. "THAT old man!" they would snort with impatience, frustration, or just plain dislike, and the term would lose all its benevolence and become an epithet of disdain and disparagement.

It was not that King's detractors would have one visualize a fussy, faltering, fumbling old man, some horrible example of physical and mental decrepitude clinging tenaciously and stubbornly to office. His amazing resilience of physique was too well known, his extraordinary intellectual powers too apparent to permit the successful promulgation of such a canard.

What his critics did seek to imply, however, by an inflection of the voice or a shrug of the shoulder was that King had been around too long for the good of the country and that the people of Canada were weary to death of seeing him in power year after year. They were obsessed by his obstinate refusal to remove himself from

362

their path. The monotonous continuity of his success had strained their patience to the breaking point and the years of their bondage pressed heavily upon them. "That old man, King," they muttered into their beards, and their groans indicated the extent of their suffering and despair under the yoke of this modern political Pharoah.

But no matter where one stood, whether on the heights, in the company of the Prime Minister, or in the Valley of Frustration, where the opposition forces rallied, whether one admired him or despised him, or whether one belonged to that group which had not quite made up its mind, that homely and descriptive phrase seemed to fit King like a well-worn glove.

Mr. King was old. He was old in years and he was old in office. He was the oldest living parliamentarian of any stature who remained to give lustre to the Canadian parliamentary scene. Gone were all the more brilliant and colourful figures of the early decades of the new century who, from both sides of the House, had shone brightly enough to detract from or occasionally eclipse his never-waning luminosity.

Gone were Mr. Lapointe and Sir Robert Borden, Mr. Cahan and Mr. Woodsworth. Gone were Dandurand and Bennett, Meighen and others of a like ilk. Mr. Lapointe had possessed the gift of statesmanship to a degree which had been exceeded by few of his compatriots. He had been a great "show window" of the Liberal party. Sir Robert Borden, slow-thinking, steady, reliable had had his own particular niche. Mr. Cahan, who had exhibited little patience with anyone who did not agree with him, had nevertheless a fine mind, had possessed vision, and great personal charm.

As for Mr. Woodsworth, he had demonstrated qualities

of moral greatness which had won him the respect of
every member of the House. One might quarrel with his
policies, might question his judgment, but one never
doubted the sincerity nor the morality of his actions. When
members rose in their places to pay final tribute to his
memory not a few eyes were bright with tears. The House
had never known a more courageous fighter, a finer gentle-
man, nor one who had been more steadfast to his trust.

Mr. Dandurand unquestionably had held title to most
of those cardinal qualities which lift parliamentary life and
effort above the mere level of party consideration and conflict. Meighen, as partisan a soul as ever sat in Parliament,
used to say of Dandurand, when the latter was Liberal
leader in the Senate, that one could always rely upon his
fairness and political rectitude. Because his word was as
good as his bond Dandurand was able to pilot Liberal
legislation through the Senate at a time when the government was sometimes without an actual majority there.

But if only a tattered remnant of the Old Guard
remained, a new, eager, determined and well-equipped
battalion of younger parliamentarians was coming up to
reinforce the thinning line. The problems they were called
upon to face were many, and of great complexity and
magnitude. Time alone can test their individual capacities
and talents; yet it would seem safe to assume that from their
number will arise leaders and administrators worthy of
taking their place alongside the most eminent of their
predecessors.

Mr. St. Laurent one considers by himself, in the isolation
of his advancing years. In the advocate turned politician,
had he placed his briefs aside thirty or even twenty years
before, one might have witnessed the development of a
truly remarkable and outstanding national figure. But he

arrived late on the scene. Time dogs his footsteps, and his future, though it be illustrious and bright, must of necessity be brief.

The war was over now and King was experiencing a sudden easing of the burden he had carried for so many years. There was a sense of freedom, of escape from doom, the clouds were lifting, and the road ahead looked brighter.

This sense of relief, and of hope for the future soon found expression in King's changed attitude in the House. More and more he delegated important tasks to his colleagues, less and less he took part in involved discussion and hectic debate. The weight of the years began to drag more heavily upon him and to an increasing extent he found himself in the mood to philosophize and reminisce. Perhaps with the end of his parliamentary career in sight, he felt that it was only proper that he should make an attempt to impart to the younger members of the House some of the profound conclusions he had reached over the years.

It was soon apparent that the years the Prime Minister had spent in politics, the bitter battles on the hustings, the asperities and ascerbities of parliamentary debate, the clash of personalities around the council table, the cabinet disagreements and cleavages, the postponements and disappointments—all these had failed to leave any permanent scars of cynicism or bitterness within his heart.

"There is no satisfaction to equal it," he told his friends, referring to the rewards of a public career. "I feel it is the realization of one's highest nature. It is the happiness of working for one's fellow men, and in public life the opportunities are greatest to help one's fellow men.

"Aristotle said every man was born to be a citizen, and

he was right. You don't fulfil your life until you serve your fellows, and public life gives you the best chance.

"You have your depressed moments and your difficult times. But you are carried away by the thought of protecting some unfortunate group of people. It is not only what you are able to do but what you were able to prevent. The public doesn't always know about the latter, but it is important."

A good many of the more seriously inclined young men in the House of Commons began to take Mr. King's philosophical dissertations to heart. Many of them agreed that, in preparing themselves for a political career, they could do much worse than follow King's precept and example.

"We do not need to induce good men to enter public life because most of them are eager to enter it," King observed. "But we do need to make it possible for them to enter public life."

He believed that the financial reward for public service should be at least commensurate with that offered by industry and the professions.

He was convinced that the standard of the average member of parliament had steadily improved over the years.

"In integrity, ability and general soundness, we are away ahead," he asserted.

"Politics," said King, "is a great school. You are learning all the time." King spoke from experience. By heritage and nature a student, he had never ceased to study and observe. That is why, sometimes, he seemed to know more about his opponents' policies than they did themselves.

King is pleased that he has lived to see the steady improvement in the unity of the country.

"People talk of disunity," he once said, "but the troubles

are mostly on the surface. The years of war have revealed a greater expression of Canadian unity than has ever before been shown, and under great stress. It has been tremendously pleasing."

When he was a child, King told his friends, his mother had cautioned him and the other children to keep their differences in the family. She realized that they would have disputes but believed they should not carry them outside of the home or discuss them with outsiders. King thought this was a principle of conduct that was also good for the unity of a political party or a nation.

King is grateful that he has had the opportunity to serve his country during such an eventful period. "I wouldn't have missed a part of the Victorian era for anything," he told a friend, "and to see the development of the greater brotherhood of the world. There will be tremendous difficulties, but conditions are improving. We must get rid of the force of evil. There is nothing more real than the forces of good and evil . . . I am indeed happy to be in office at this time, to have seen the war through to an end and now to be here during the period of reconstruction."

No one, he thinks, has the right to look too much to the future. To do one's duty as one goes along, that is the important thing. "I have always found the present sufficiently interesting to occupy most of my thought," he explained. "Do the best one can and the future will shape out itself. . . . The very things that sometimes seem to block our paths in one direction turn out to be the best for us in the long run . . . If one has faith, then life is full of interest . . . Faith is the one thing to cling to above everything else . . ."

Members of Parliament on both sides of the House had learned to watch King closely. To some extent they had learned to read his mind. Despite the fact that his bland and inscrutable expression was difficult to penetrate, and usually defied analysis, King sometimes gave himself away by little characteristic mannerisms. Sometimes he would indicate his displeasure by an impatient shrug of the shoulders and a nervous twitching of the mouth. Another favourite outlet for his feelings was to tap his desk slowly with the stub of the pencil which he always carried in his vest pocket. Occasionally he would flush to the very top of his sparsely-thatched head. But when he rose to reply to some attack or other his words were always measured, and if sometimes they had a searing effect on his opponents they could never properly be referred to as "outbursts" of temper. He was slow to anger, and he was quick to forget differences which arose in the heat of debate. Usually by the time he reached the government lobby on his way out of the House he had thrown off any ill-feeling and was ready to chuckle over the exchanges that had occurred.

But if he sometimes tolerated abuse and heckling, it was only up to a certain point. Once that he made up his mind that an opposition member was overstepping the bounds of reason and propriety he was quick to retaliate, and he could strike with all the deadly speed and accuracy of a cobra.

One opposition member who for some time led his party in the House used to say that he had to go easy with King. "I know that because I am young, Mr. King allows me a certain amount of latitude," he confessed, "but unless I really am prepared to slug it out hand-to-hand with the Old Man I take care to pull my punches." Because of this member's healthy respect for King's ability as a rough-and-tumble fighter he didn't often over-step the mark, and as for King he made no attempt to capitalize on his opponent's inexperience.

In the old days there were those who were not afraid to slug it out with King, including Meighen and Bennett. Meighen had a rapier-like thrust in debate, and as often as not his blade was tipped with a venom of words that was fatal in its effect. Bennett, whose lung-power was equalled only by his capacity for selecting the bitter, biting, ego-puncturing phrase, often succeeded in getting under King's skin; but on the other hand King's habit of keeping a rein on his temper and his refusal, sometimes, to accept the challenge when it was hurled at him infuriated Bennett to the point of exasperation and despair.

Not, however, that King always turned the other cheek. When his back was to the wall he could fight like a tiger and like a tiger he was dangerous when cornered.

One recalled the occasion, during the war, when the late R. B. Hanson, then House Leader for the Progressive Conservatives, had been attacking King all one evening. Patiently and without outward sign of embarrassment or concern King had sat there in his seat calmly listening to Mr. Hanson's seemingly endless diatribe. At last, however, King began to tap his desk nervously with his pencil, the blood rose to his face, at first faintly then suffusing it completely. Suddenly his eyes grew cold and hard and a moment later he was on his feet shaking a threatening finger at Mr. Hanson.

"I warn you . . ." the Prime Minister shouted angrily. "I warn you!"

The warning was sufficient. Mr. Hanson's attack quickly ebbed and died. To save face he continued on for a few minutes but he chose his words more carefully. It was easier to change tack and run before the impending storm than attempt to face into it.

King had never been given to the habit of attempting

humorous sallies in the House. One often wondered why he placed this obvious hobble on his talent for drollery and repartee. But occasionally he would unbend in the House and then he would surprise everyone, sometimes even himself.

Once the beloved late W. K. "Billy" Esling, the Conservative member for Kootenay West, was holding forth with great earnestness on the vexing Doukhobor question. "What would the Prime Minister do, I should like to know," he asked the House seriously, "if one evening he discovered three Doukhobor women in his garden?"

Like a flash King was on his feet.

"I should send for the leaders of the Opposition," he shot back, amidst laughter. (The "leaders of the Opposition" at that time were R. B. Bennett, and Robert Gardiner of the U.F.A., both of them bachelors).

So far as his friendships with other parliamentarians went, King had never drawn the "colour" line. If he had enemies in the ranks of the Opposition he had friends there too. He always included the membership of the House in his coterie of friends and if one of the members was celebrating a birthday or an anniversary or some other happy occasion King usually heard about it and sent a message of congratulation or took notice of the event in some other personal way. He liked to think that political differences could be confined to the House and he saw no reason why men who were divided in their political views should not share other interests and sympathies.

The tremendous respect and admiration which he held for Sir Robert Borden was a case in point. Despite the fact that they were widely separated in many of their political ideologies they were nevertheless very close personal friends. Again and again, King's House friendships eradicated political chalk-lines and ignored the petty bickerings and narrow prejudices of party strife. King had always respected the true democracy of ideas. He would stand up for his own; you were entitled to yours. The circumstance that invariably attracted him, however, was that one should have ideas and be ready to fight for them.

This belief that one could maintain a warm, personal regard for another, quite apart from differences of policy and party, grew and strengthened with King the longer he remained in public life. Increasingly he recognized the intellectual and spiritual value of friendship and during his last years in the House he liked to think that he was leaving behind him many friends and few, if any, enemies.

Nothing pleased him more than to be remembered by some member of the opposition. On one occasion when he had been confined to his home through illness, Gordon Graydon had called Laurier House a number of times to inquire as to his condition. The day King returned to the House, after the Orders of the Day had been dealt with, he crossed the floor and thanked Mr. Graydon.

"It's something that not many members bother to do," was his significant comment.

As King's reign drew to a close he was satisfied that he had been true to his own self, that he had been loyal to the ideals he cherished in his youth. Thus, sweet and reassuring to King must have been the words used by *The Times* on on the occasion of his receiving the Order of Merit, when it said: "He has been loyal to Canada, loyal to the Commonwealth, and loyal also to the larger vision of the brotherhood of humanity."

King was the last to maintain that he had been without fault. He had been called vain and opinionated. Vanity is one of the most common of all the human frailties and perhaps King had his moments of appreciative self-appraisal. By the same process of reasoning, however, the fact that he was capable of being impressed, at times, with a sense of his own importance, provides an effective answer to another charge that is frequently made: that he is not normal from an emotional standpoint.

Self-confidence and a belief in one's own powers and abilities—in one's own destiny—is generally accepted as a prerequisite to greatness; and the dividing line between self-confidence, self-assurance, self-esteem—call it what one will—and vanity, is a very thin and sometimes indiscernable one. If King is vain, then in this respect he follows the pattern set by most political leaders of his time. Roosevelt, despite his many great qualities, was an avid spotlight seeker. He wooed publicity with all the ardour and enthusiasm of a matinee idol. And who would venture to state, categorically, that Churchill, with his inevitable "stage" cigar and his "V for Victory" sign (bestowed upon the populace like a benediction) was not himself a bit of an egotist?

If King is vain then his vanity is based upon his intellectual accomplishments, his satisfaction over the fact that he has been privileged to live a full and active life, upon the belief that he has been able to make a worthwhile contribution to the life of his country.

Despite the fact that King always commanded attention and respect as a result of the sheer intellectual power of his personality, he is not impressive physically, nor does he possess that extroverted type of personality that sometimes commands immediate if only passing attention. Five feet six-and-a-half inches in his stockinged feet, he apparently inherited his lack of height from his Grandfather

Mackenzie who was half an inch shorter than King. But whereas Mackenzie was, to use his own description, "a diminutive little creature," all nerves and sinews, as lean and hard as a whip-handle, King, with his 182 pounds, has always had to wage an unceasing battle against increasing weight and a tendency towards softness. Mackenzie's enemies used to refer to him as a "whippersnapper." No one ever applied such a disparaging term to King, perhaps on account of his weight. At the age of 50, however, King could not do what his grandfather had been able to do at the same age—jump over a cane which had been laid across the backs of two chairs!

As the end of the road drew nearer, King began to display an almost boyish enthusiasm at the statistical records of statesmanship which he was about to equal or exceed. Even in 1946 it was apparent that he was out to break Sir Robert Walpole's record of 7,620 days as a Prime Minister.

But first, as a sort of "preliminary", King equalled, on June 7, 1946, the record of 6,937 days of service as Prime Minister established by Sir John A. Macdonald. On September 5, 1942 he had equalled Sir Wilfrid Laurier's record of 5,564 days, and on May 12, 1946 he had equalled the record set by William Pitt.

On April 20, 1948 he reached the final milestone, equalling Walpole's impressive record.

It was, of course, an occasion for speech-making in the House, but what pleased King most of all was the fact that two of those who rose to extend their congratulations had been close personal friends of his parents. Both parliamentarians, as it happened, were members of the Progressive Conservative Party: John R. MacNicol, the member for Toronto-Davenport, and ubiquitous "Tommy" Church, the member for Toronto-Broadview.

King had a little speech written out for the occasion. His attainment of the record, he said, made it abundantly clear that to gain and retain power in a free country, to help shape the policies of its government, it was not necessary that the head of a political party or of an administration should be either a superman or a dictator. It signified the opportunities which a democracy afforded to a man of "average industry, intelligence and integrity" who was prepared to give his time to public service. They were humble words and King intended them as such, and they were also in the way of an encouraging word to ambitious and politically and socially-minded young Canadians to seek honour and success in the public service of their country.

In many ways it was a great day for the Prime Minister, but the attainment of the record had received so much advance publicity and had been heralded and anticipated so persistently and obviously that when at length it was achieved, from the news standpoint at least, it lacked the interest-stirring elements of spontaneity and surprise. Newspapermen cast about in vain for some new angle upon which to base a newsworthy story, but it seemed as if they had already completely exhausted its possibilities.

At last, however, Dick Sanburn, of the Ottawa Bureau of the Southam News Services, had a flash of inspiration. The sixth-floor corridor of the House of Commons, leading to the Parliamentary restaurant, is lined with the portraits of Empire parliamentary figures, past and present. Over the first picture, that of Walpole, Sanburn hung a sheet of very black carbon paper. It barely covered Walpole's face and its jet black colour suggested mourning. On the lower part of the glass he pasted an envelope with one word printed in inch-high letters—"SCRATCHED!"

Then he walked down to the Press Gallery to write a story about it.

In 1947 when King was in London attending the marriage of H.R.H. Princess Elizabeth, he was invested by His Majesty the King with the Order of Merit, a decoration limited to twenty-four living members. He had been the first Canadian to receive this signal honour.

Over the years honours of one kind or another had come with rather monotonous if gratifying regularity. They had come from the leading universities in Canada, Britain and the United States, from academic and professional societies, from foreign countries, from cities and villages. Nor had they come too late. King was still able to enjoy them, to wring the last drop of satisfaction and happiness from these tangible evidences of the esteem and affection in which he was held. Like the scholarships which he had won as a youth in college they were an eloquent recognition of effort and achievement, a well-deserved word of praise and approval at the end of a long and busy day.

XII

EPILOGUE

KING BECAME LEADER of the Liberal party in 1919. He took over at a time when the fortunes of the party were at a low ebb.

Twenty-nine years later, to the day, he stood before the National Liberal Convention in Ottawa and gave a final accounting of his stewardship.

It was, arithmetically at least, an impressive story. For over twenty-one of those twenty-nine years the party had been in power. During King's period of leadership the Liberals had contested seven general elections, and had won six!

During his long and eventful career as Liberal leader—a period which towards the end was often jocularly referred to as "The Reign of Mackenzie King"—he had had his ups and downs.

He had been in power in times of piping prosperity and in times not quite so good. When depression struck, fate took a hand and relegated him and his party to the side-lines where they were free of administrative responsibilities.

But it fell to his lot to lead the government during the most important and trying period in Canada's history: the days of World War II. Never, since the days of Confederation, had a Prime Minister and a government been faced with such colossal tasks, such grave and potentially-disastrous situations.

He had carried on successfully throughout the war, had retained power, and had thus remained in a position to

376

deal with the country's immediate post-war problems.

He had fought through the manpower crisis and had preserved national unity.

He had played a unique and effective role in acting as a liaison between Great Britain and the United States, and it was largely because of his belief that the Commonwealth should be regarded as part of a larger community of free peoples, of which the United States must assuredly be an integral component, that Canada had emerged as one of the leading advocates of Atlantic Union.

He had played an equally effective role in extending Canada's status as a free and independent nation, while at the same time preserving a spirit of wholehearted co-operation under the crown.

He had seen steps initiated which were to result in the addition to the Canadian family of a tenth province.

He had made mistakes. The record was not an unblemished one, but it had its golden pages.

In his seventyfourth year he was now ready to step aside. But before he made this one last gesture of renunciation there was one final task to do.

It was to place the mantle of Liberal leadership upon the shoulders of the man whom he had chosen to succeed him.

A few months now, and he would relinquish his post as Prime Minister, and then, in due course, his last tangible tie with parliament, his position as the elected member for Glengarry.

Then, perhaps, would come the opportunity for afternoons of quiet study in his library up underneath the eaves of Laurier House. There would be visits with his friends; uncrowded hours for reflection and self-examination—for memories!

Perhaps, now, he would be able to write his memoirs!

Following his retirement King experienced a sudden lifting of the tremendous burden he had been carrying so long. He found it easier to detach himself from state affairs than he had believed possible. He was now able to stand on the sidelines and view things in new perspective, more objectively, without the ever-present feeling of personal responsibility that had weighed so heavily before. Looking back over his long period in power he was more than ever convinced that he had taken the right road, that his judgment had been sound. He felt that all the policies he had shaped and all the decisions he had reached throughout the years were of minor importance when compared to the major achievement of his career—the preservation of national unity. He believed his wartime policies had been completely vindicated. He felt that his work in this respect might some day be recognized as the vital span which had bridged the most dangerous period of metamorphosis in French-Canadian thought.

King has been called so many names, good and bad, over the years that one could fill a small volume with them. Today he is content to go upon his way very little, if at all, perturbed by the swirling confluence of opinion that eddies about his head.

"They say? What say they? Let them say!"

That is his answer. For King has fought his battles and has celebrated his victories. The "glory and the grandeur" lie behind, and there is little now left in the way of achievement or intellectual satisfaction to pique his fancy.

The best of life lies behind him and he is too much of the philosopher and realist not to realize that his greatest satisfactions in the future will be those that he can salvage from the past.

A friend, dropping in at Laurier House on the occasion of a recent birthday, gathered that King had long since arrived at this conclusion.

They were alone, and King was in a reminiscing mood. Already, one could see, he was looking back upon the past with a wistful eye, counting up his successes, weighing his rewards, balancing up his books—and always with a wary eye on the dwindling sands in the hour-glass.

Habits of a lifetime—habits of work, of study, of leadership—still drove him relentlessly to meet the challenge of the present, and of the future, too, for that matter; but more and more the desire was for a little more time to himself, for some degree of release from the constant pressure of statecraft, for more frequent opportunity for social intercourse and the cultivation of personal friendships.

But on that occasion he was ready enough to justify the busy years, to sweep away with one single gesture any regrets he may have entertained, from time to time, as to the joys and pleasures he may have missed.

Going to his bookshelf he took down a slim volume. It was *The Happy Profession* written by Ellery Sedgwick, a former editor of the *Atlantic Monthly,* and one of King's oldest friends.

With a little smile of satisfaction King thumbed through the volume until he came to the passage he was seeking. "You might take this down," he said. "I think it just about expresses how I feel about things in the twilight of my life."

" 'Boys in their third generation have nothing on me,' " he read. " 'My past is secure, which is more than their future is. I have my memories, rich ones, I think. I have had the fun I have had!' "

There it was! With 21 years as Prime Minister behind

him, with the record of having led his party since 1919, and with the added distinction of having served his country in an official capacity, either as civil servant or parliamentarian, under no less than five sovereigns, King was ready to sit back and rest upon his laurels, and let the future take care of itself.

INDEX

ABBOTT, DOUGLAS, 302, 307
Aberhart, William, 151
Acland, F. A., 278
Acland, Peregrine, 277-8
Ade, George, 56
Addams, Jane, 34
Air Bases Agreement, 169
Air force, Canadian: *see* Armed
  forces
Aird, Sir John, 131
Aitken, Sir Max: *see* Beaverbrook
Alberta coal strike, 45
Alexander, Field Marshal the Vis-
  count, 345-6
Annexation, 61
Armed forces, Canadian: *see also*
  War, *also* Conscription
  autonomy of, 172-3
  casualties, 212, 219, 237
  compulsory military training,
    189-90
  desertions from, 262-3
  Dieppe, 212, 262, 269, 273
  disposition etc. of:
    1st Division, 188, 212, 215
    2nd Division, 189, 219, 269
    3rd Division, 219
    4th Division, 219
    1st Armoured Brigade, 215
    13th Infantry Brigade, 263
    1st Canadian Corps, 215
    Eighth Army, 215-16
    Royal Rifles, 260
    Toronto Scottish, 213-14
    Winnipeg Grenadiers, 260
  enlistment quotas, 204-5
  growth of, 188, 190, 205, 212

Armed forces, Canadian: *(cont'd.)*
  Italy, 215
  Kiska, 263
  mobilization of, 188-90
  NRMA army, 201, 209-10,
    220-4, 229, 239-40, 257-8,
    262-3
  Normandy, 219, 269, 273
  Pacific war, 257-8
  permanent, 188
  postponements, 201, 205-6
  preparedness of, 172-3, 186
  recruiting (policy), 179;
    (methods used), 210
  reinforcements, 221, 224, 230
  repatriation of, 77-8
  reserve forces, 188
  RCAF, 179, 180, 220
  RCN, 179, 219
  Sicily, 215-16
Arnold, Matthew, 48, 334
Astor, Col. the Hon. J. J., 354
Astor, Lady Violet, 354
Athlone, Earl of, 345-6
Atlantic convoy, 219
Atlantic union, 268-9, 377
Atomic bomb, 258, 266
Attlee, Clement, 267, 346
Australia, 127, 182
Autonomy, national, 104-6, 121
Aylesworth, Sir Allen, 94

BAHAMAS, 169
Baker, Douglas, 347
Baldwin, Stanley, 346
Balfour, Arthur James, 160-1
Balfour Declaration, 128
Bank of Montreal, 76

INDEX

INDEX

INDEX